Retouch, Lettering and Design - Kitty Media

LEVEL-C Book II: Original Japanese version
©1994 Futaba Aoi/Mitsuba Kurenai.
Originally published in Japan in 1994
by BIBLOS Co., Ltd. English version in U.S.A.
and CANADA published by Kitty Media
under the license granted by BIBLOS Co., Ltd.

Second printing

Kitty Press
Office of publication 519 8th Avenue, 14th floor
New York, NY 10018.

ISBN: 1-58655-635-5

Printed in Canada.

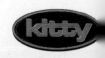

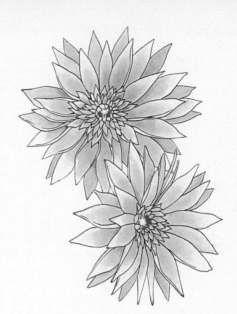

INDEX

WE WERE COMPLETE STRANGERS...
EVERYTHING IS NEW...
LET'S CREATE THE LOVE WE SHARE, STARTING NOW...

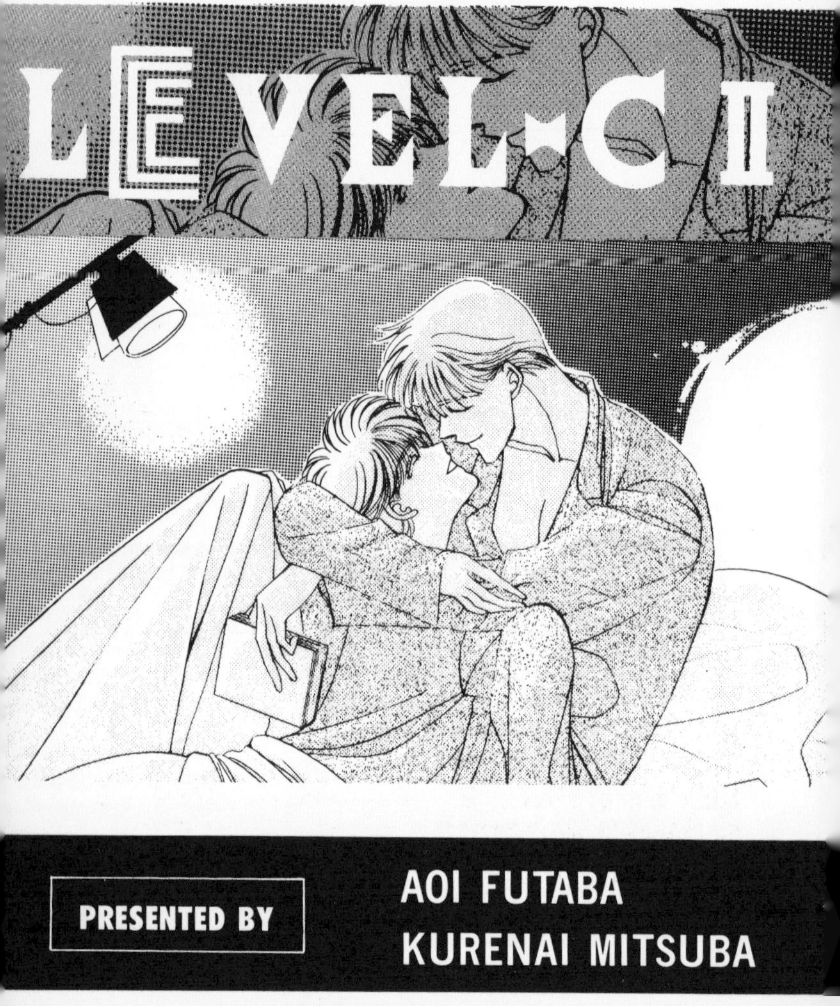
LEVEL-C II

PRESENTED BY

AOI FUTABA
KURENAI MITSUBA

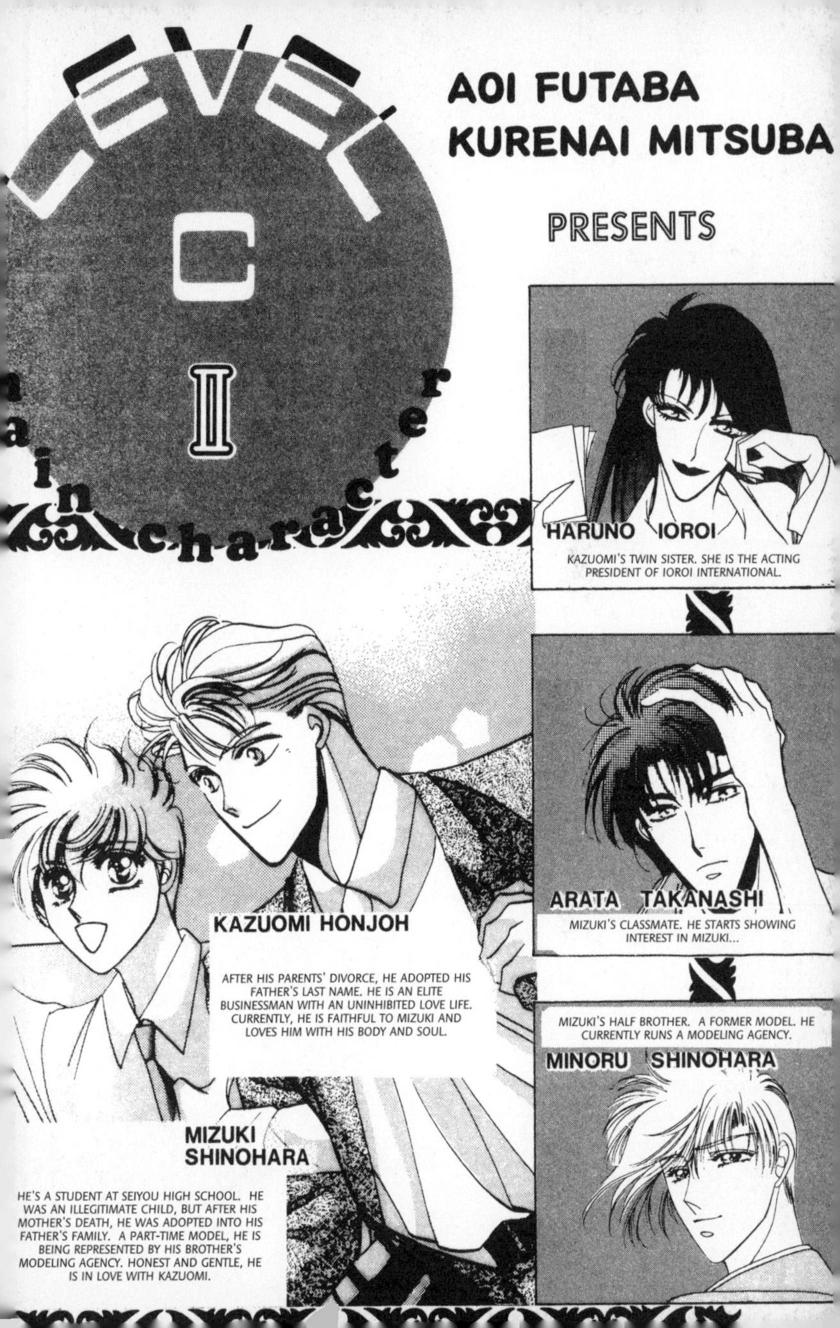

LEVEL C II
main character
AOI FUTABA
KURENAI MITSUBA
PRESENTS
HARUNO IOROI
KAZUOMI'S TWIN SISTER. SHE IS THE ACTING PRESIDENT OF IOROI INTERNATIONAL.
ARATA TAKANASHI
MIZUKI'S CLASSMATE. HE STARTS SHOWING INTEREST IN MIZUKI...
KAZUOMI HONJOH
AFTER HIS PARENTS' DIVORCE, HE ADOPTED HIS FATHER'S LAST NAME. HE IS AN ELITE BUSINESSMAN WITH AN UNINHIBITED LOVE LIFE. CURRENTLY, HE IS FAITHFUL TO MIZUKI AND LOVES HIM WITH HIS BODY AND SOUL.
MIZUKI'S HALF BROTHER. A FORMER MODEL. HE CURRENTLY RUNS A MODELING AGENCY.
MINORU SHINOHARA
MIZUKI SHINOHARA
HE'S A STUDENT AT SEIYOU HIGH SCHOOL. HE WAS AN ILLEGITIMATE CHILD, BUT AFTER HIS MOTHER'S DEATH, HE WAS ADOPTED INTO HIS FATHER'S FAMILY. A PART-TIME MODEL, HE IS BEING REPRESENTED BY HIS BROTHER'S MODELING AGENCY. HONEST AND GENTLE, HE IS IN LOVE WITH KAZUOMI.

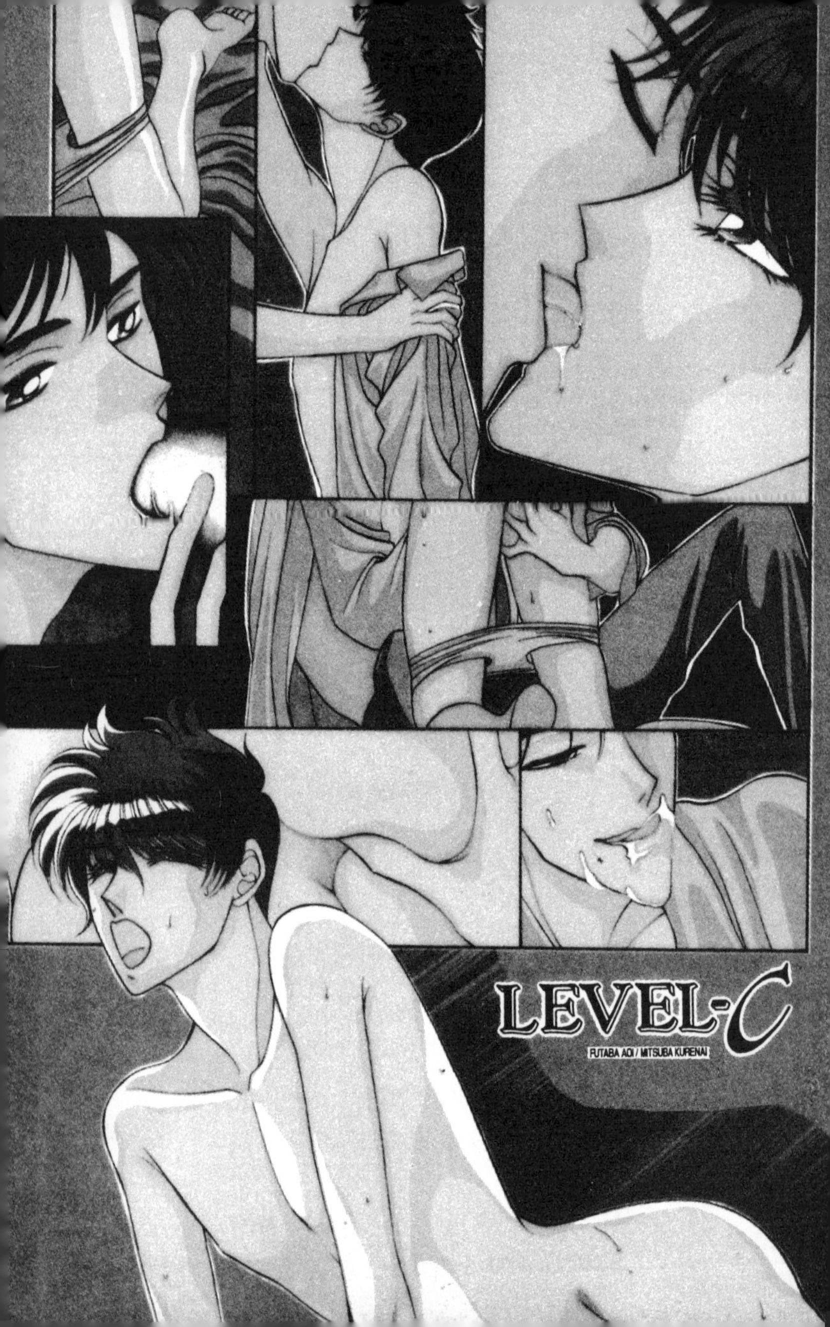
LEVEL-C
FUTABA AOI / MITSUBA KURENAI

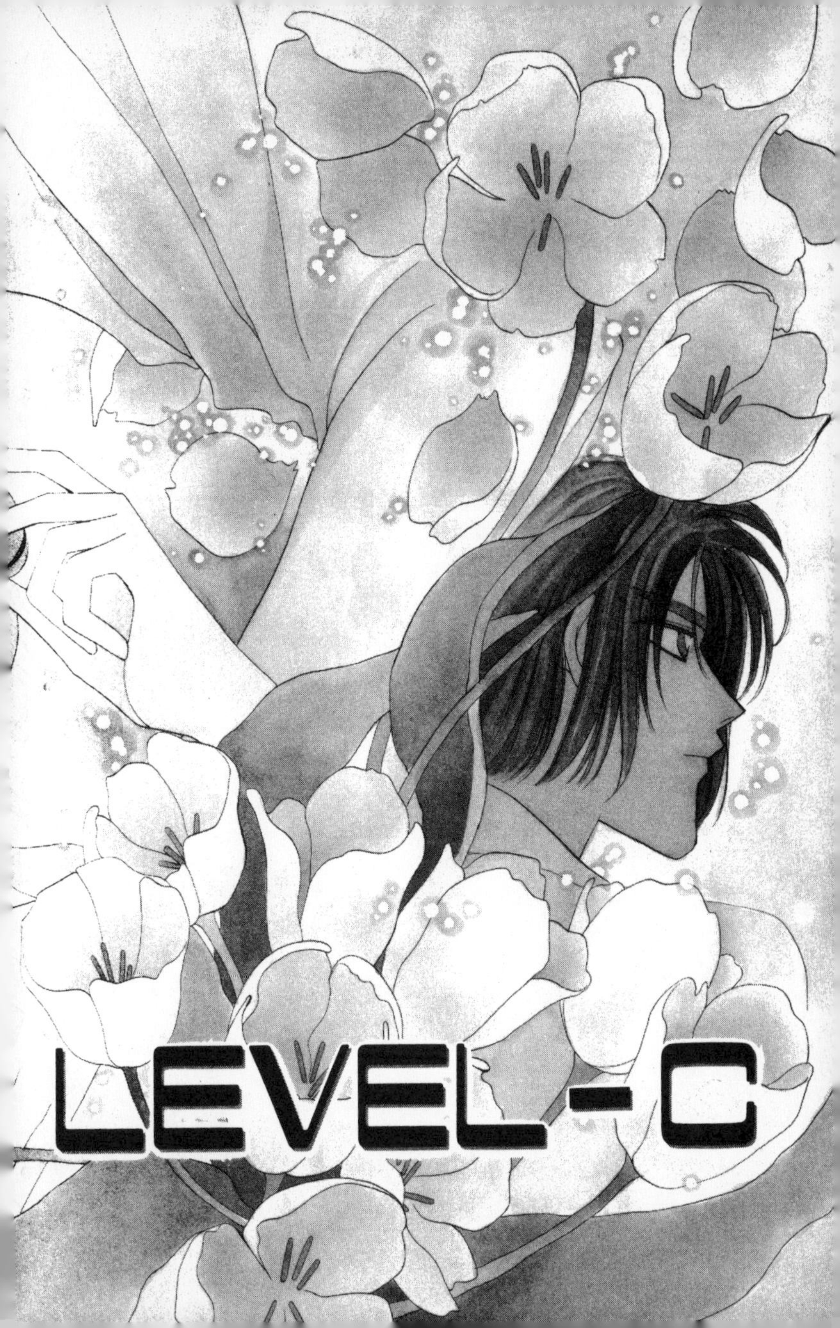
LEVEL-C

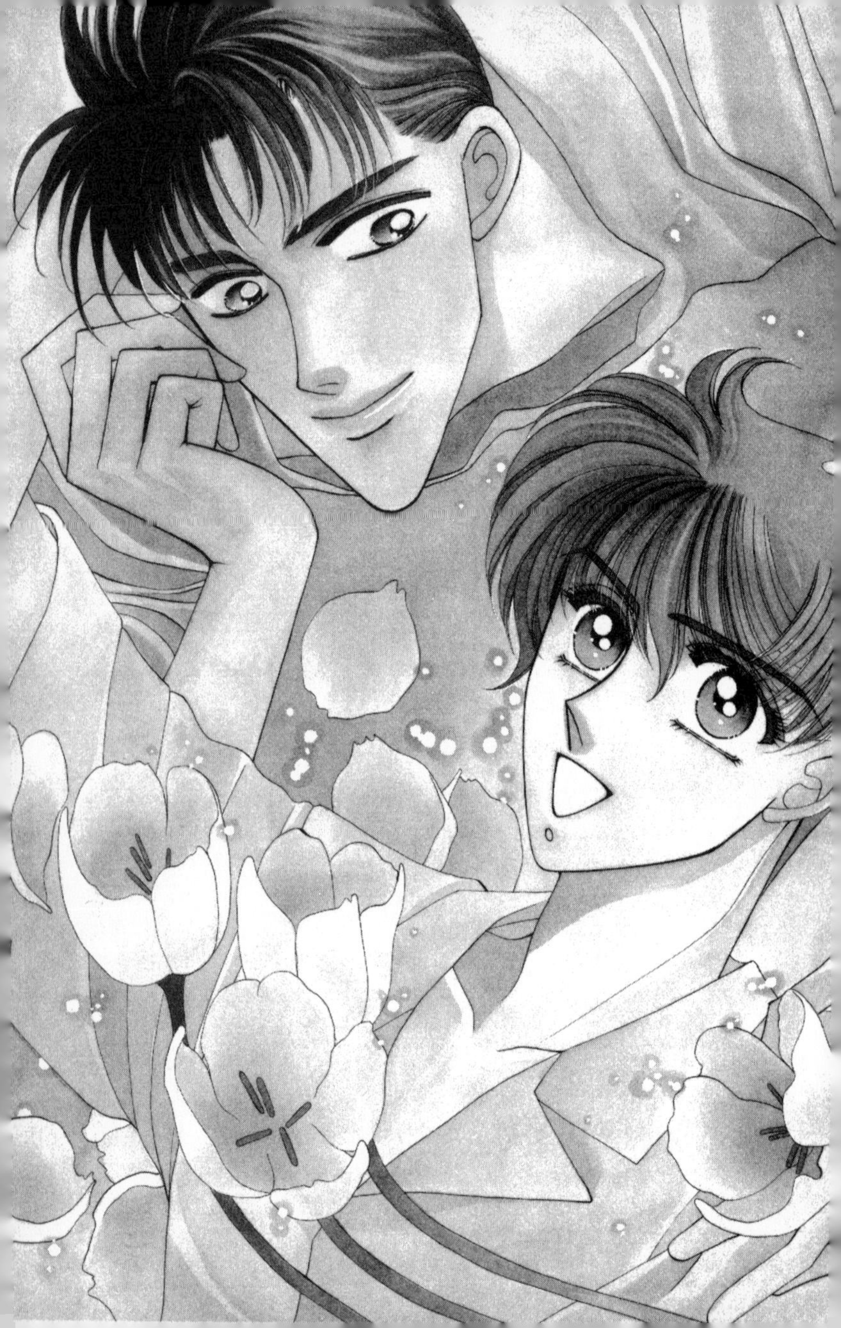

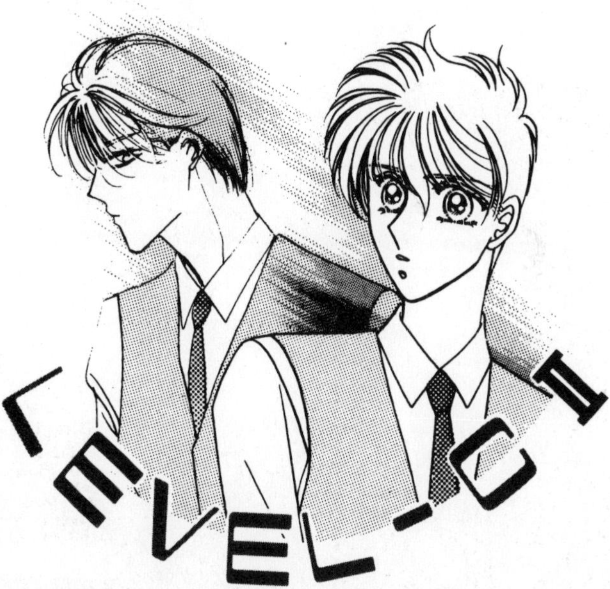
LEVEL-C II

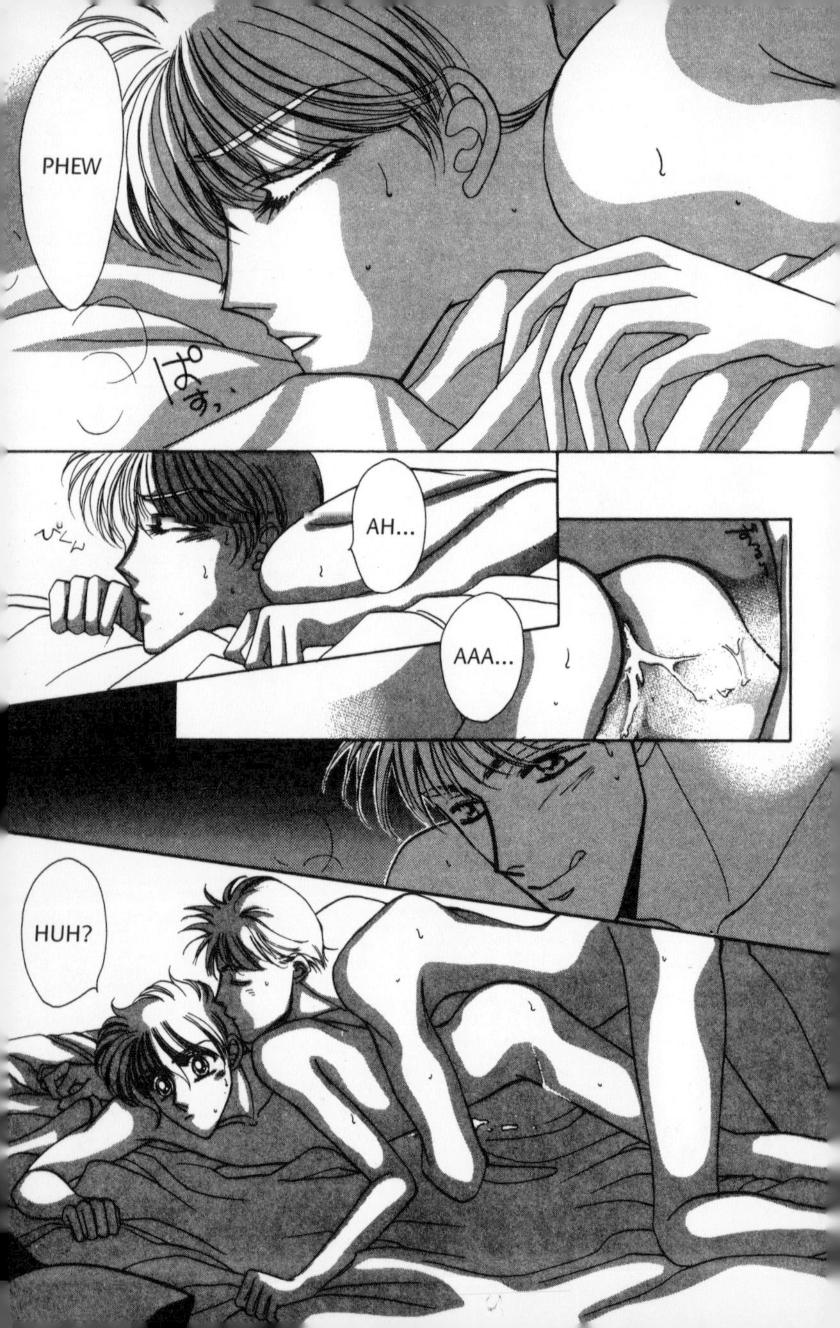
PHEW
ぱすっ
ぴくん
AH...
AAA...
HUH?

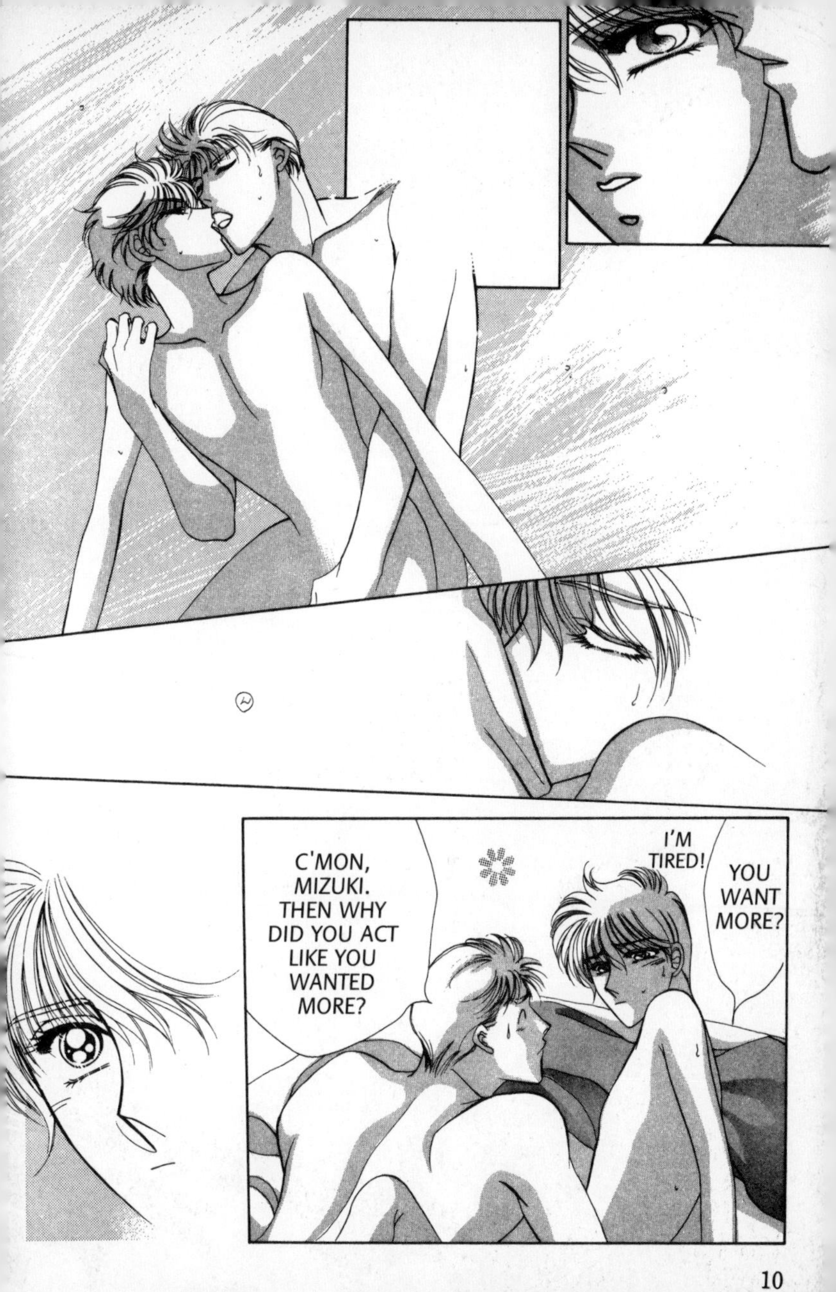
YOU WANT MORE?
I'M TIRED!
C'MON, MIZUKI. THEN WHY DID YOU ACT LIKE YOU WANTED MORE?

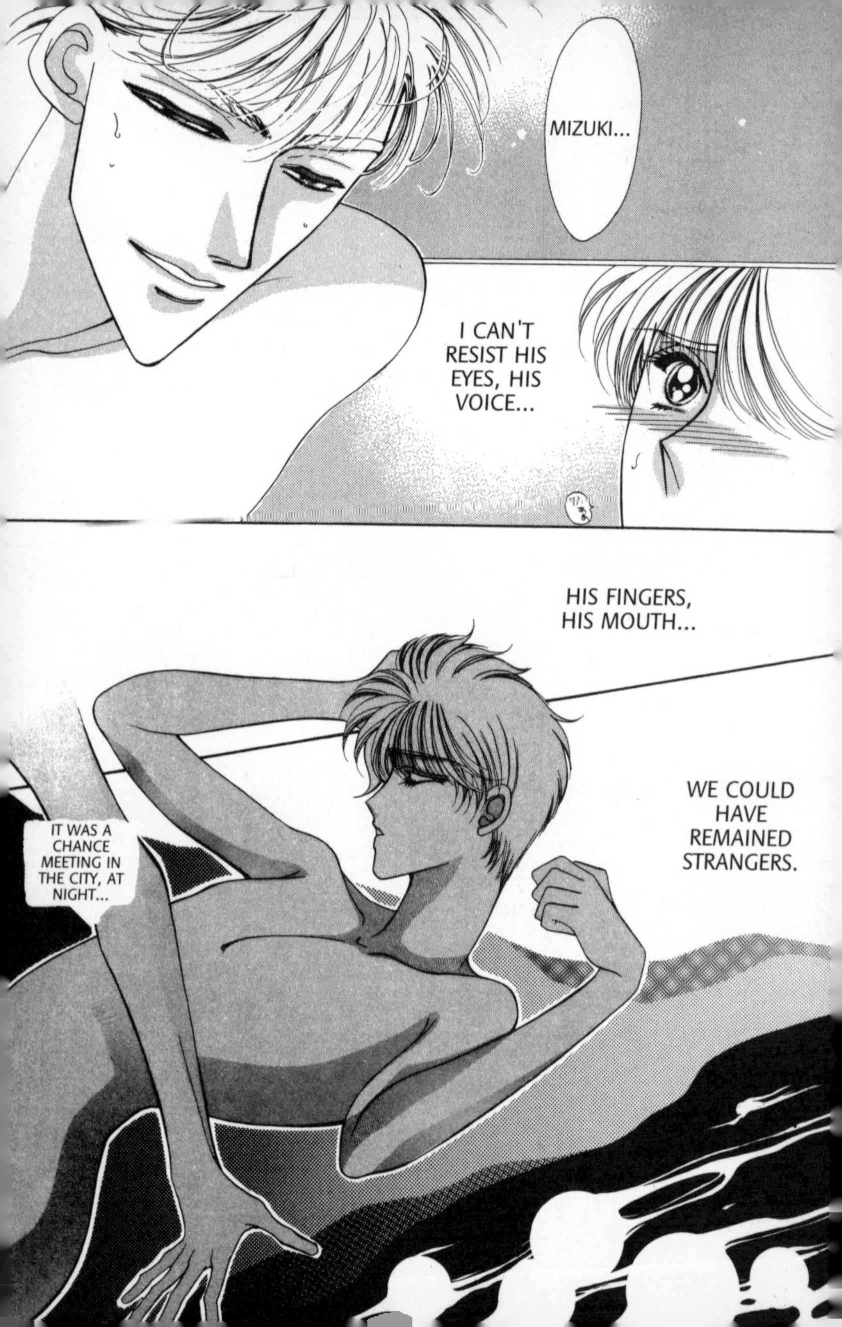
MIZUKI...
I CAN'T RESIST HIS EYES, HIS VOICE...
HIS FINGERS, HIS MOUTH...
WE COULD HAVE REMAINED STRANGERS.
IT WAS A CHANCE MEETING IN THE CITY, AT NIGHT...

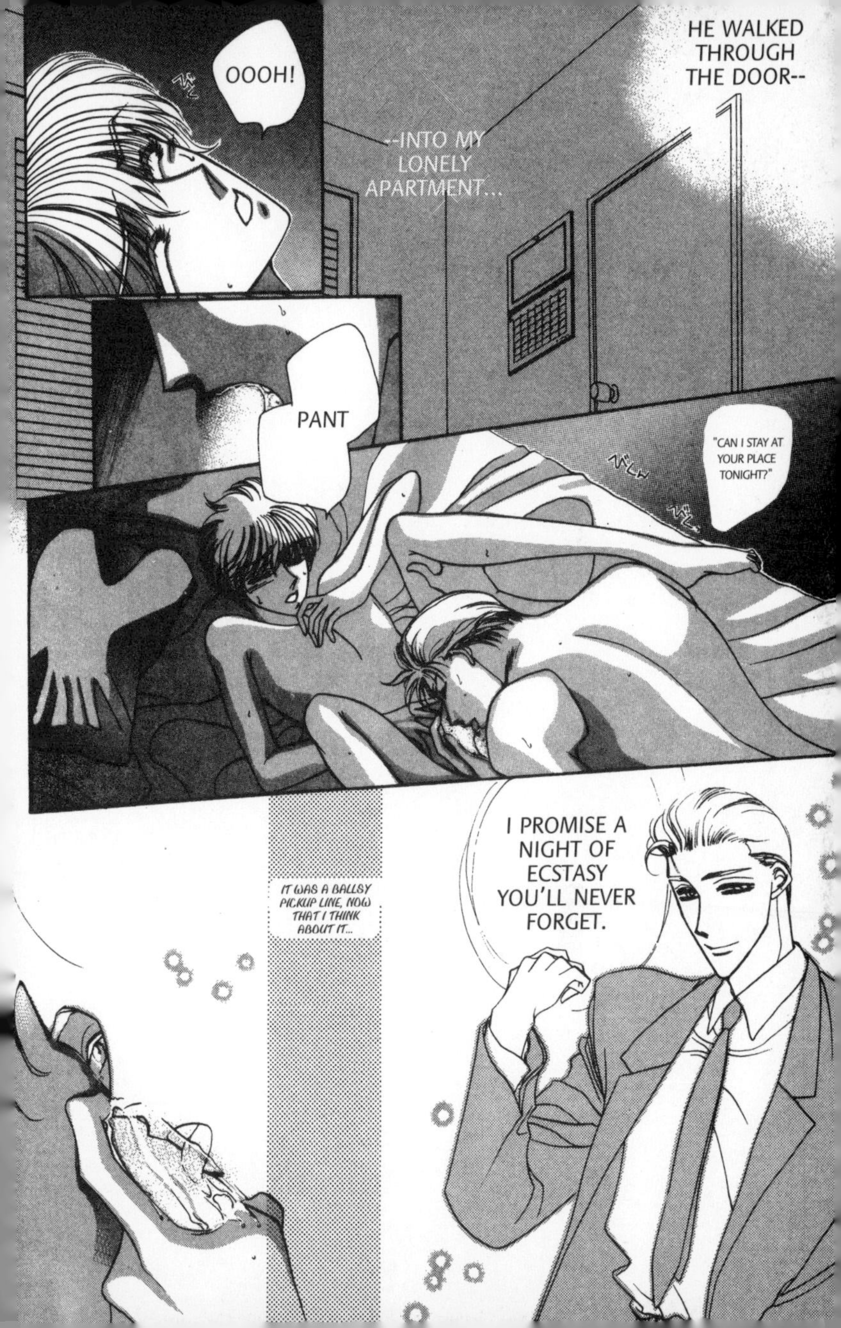
HE WALKED THROUGH THE DOOR--
--INTO MY LONELY APARTMENT...
OOOH!
PANT
"CAN I STAY AT YOUR PLACE TONIGHT?"
I PROMISE A NIGHT OF ECSTASY YOU'LL NEVER FORGET.
IT WAS A BALLSY PICKUP LINE, NOW THAT I THINK ABOUT IT...

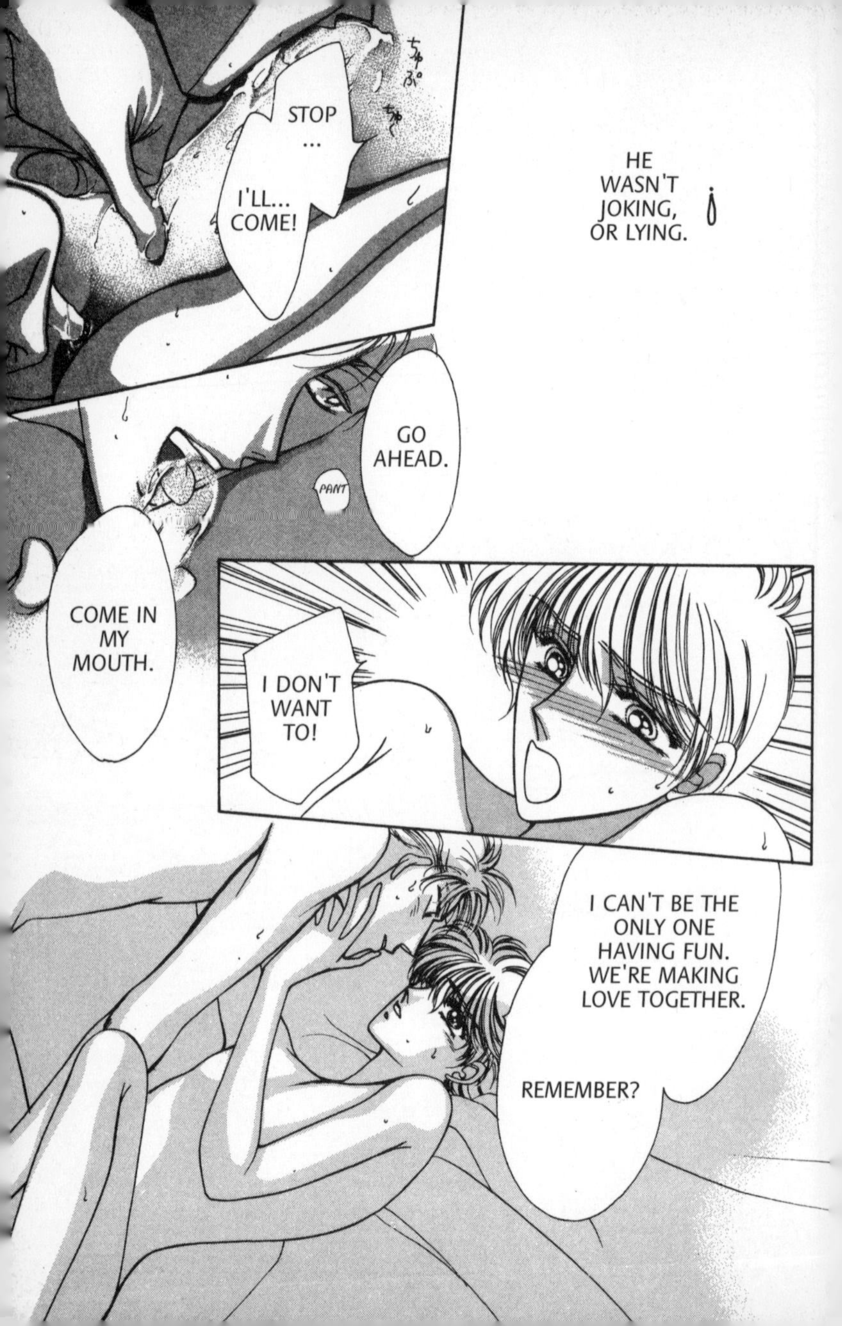
HE WASN'T JOKING, OR LYING.
ちゅぷ
ちゅ
STOP ... I'LL... COME!
GO AHEAD.
PANT
COME IN MY MOUTH.
I DON'T WANT TO!
I CAN'T BE THE ONLY ONE HAVING FUN. WE'RE MAKING LOVE TOGETHER.
REMEMBER?

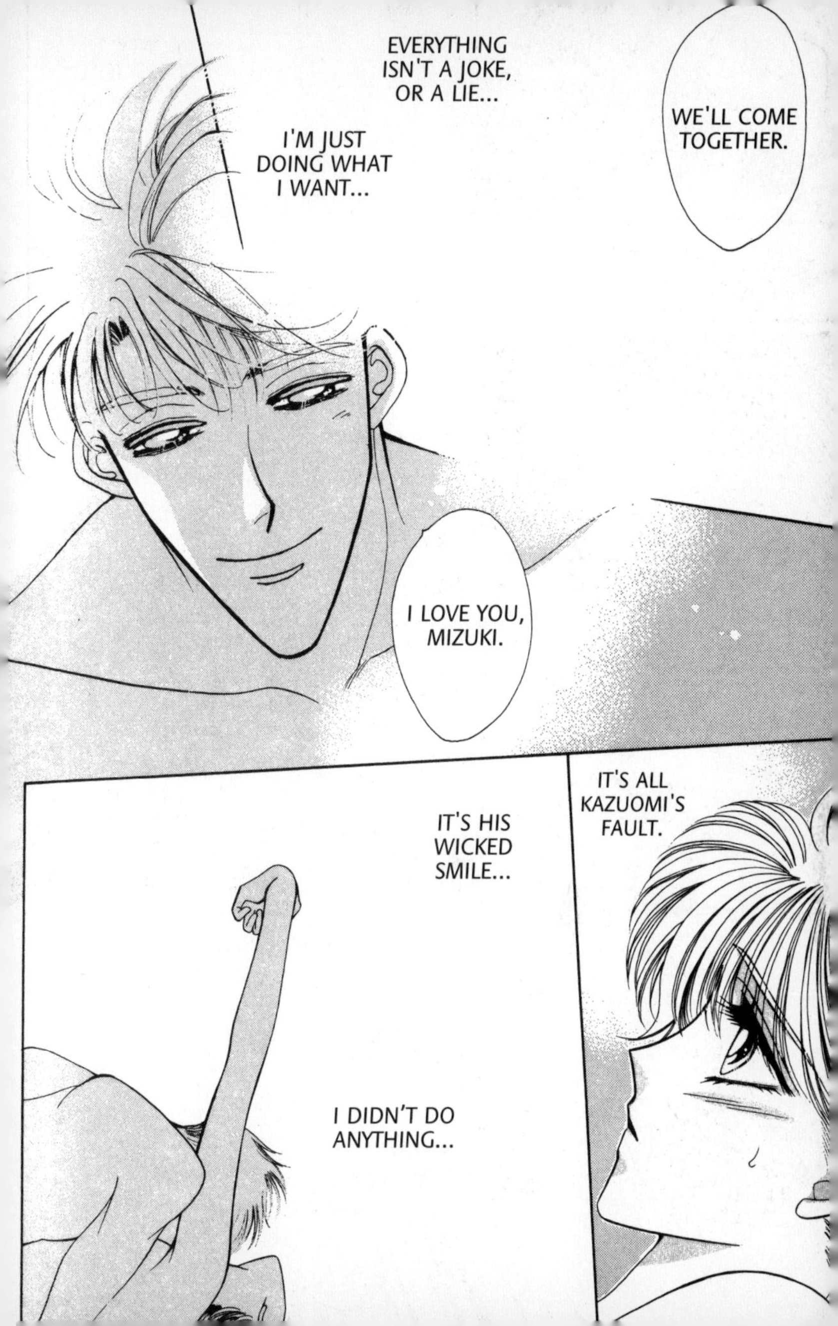
WE'LL COME TOGETHER.
EVERYTHING ISN'T A JOKE, OR A LIE...
I'M JUST DOING WHAT I WANT...
I LOVE YOU, MIZUKI.
IT'S ALL KAZUOMI'S FAULT.
IT'S HIS WICKED SMILE...
I DIDN'T DO ANYTHING...

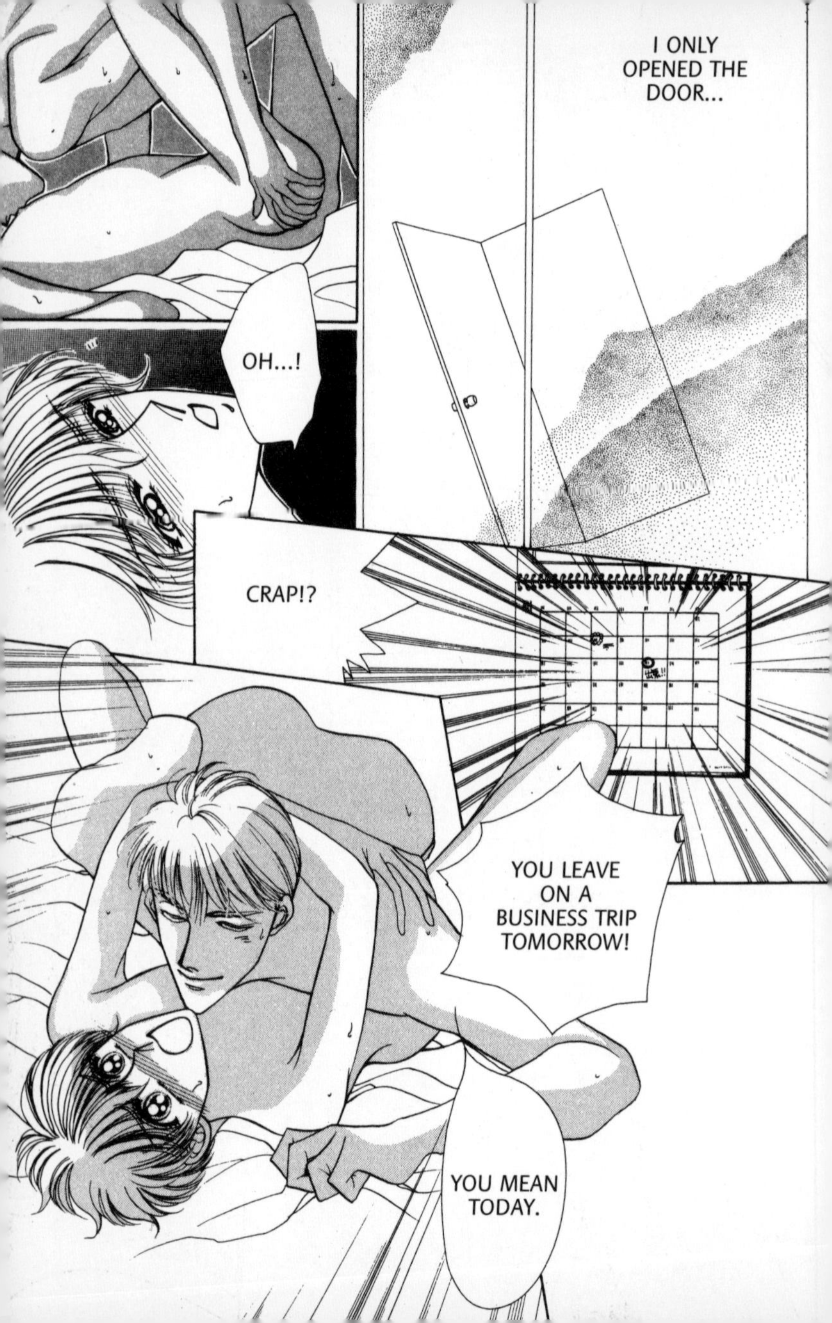
I ONLY OPENED THE DOOR...
OH...!
CRAP!?
YOU LEAVE ON A BUSINESS TRIP TOMORROW!
YOU MEAN TODAY.

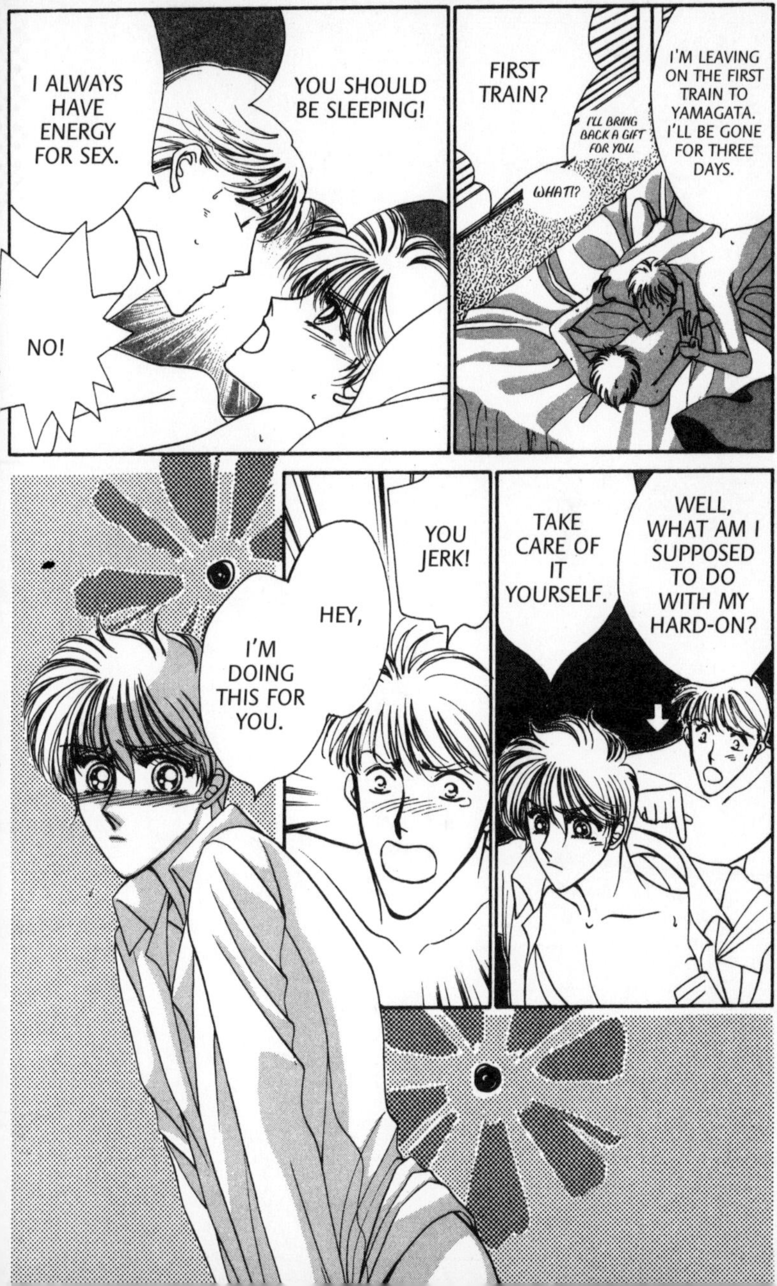
I'M LEAVING ON THE FIRST TRAIN TO YAMAGATA. I'LL BE GONE FOR THREE DAYS.
FIRST TRAIN?
I'LL BRING BACK A GIFT FOR YOU.
WHAT!?
YOU SHOULD BE SLEEPING!
I ALWAYS HAVE ENERGY FOR SEX.
NO!
WELL, WHAT AM I SUPPOSED TO DO WITH MY HARD-ON?
TAKE CARE OF IT YOURSELF.
YOU JERK!
HEY, I'M DOING THIS FOR YOU.

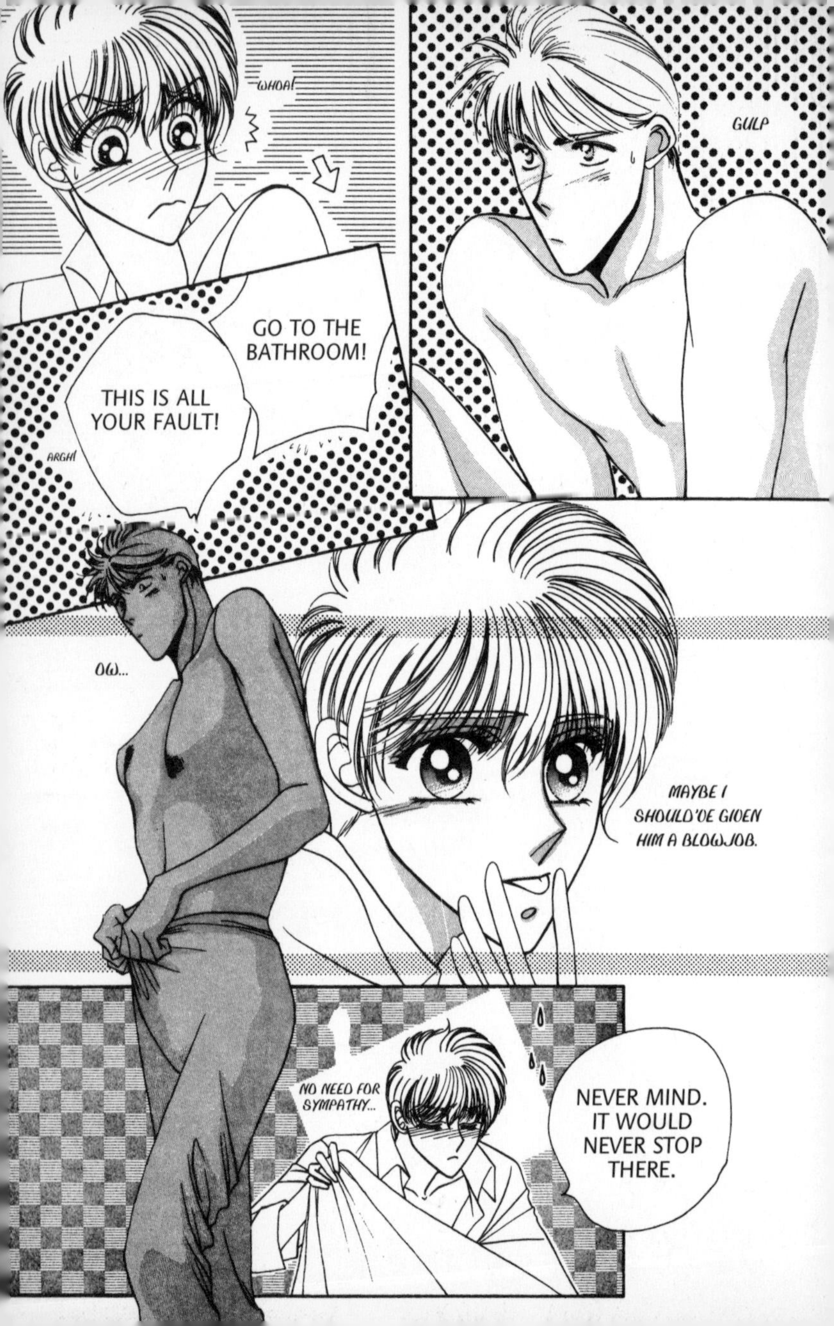
GULP
WHOA!
GO TO THE BATHROOM!
THIS IS ALL YOUR FAULT!
ARGH!
MAYBE I SHOULD'VE GIVEN HIM A BLOWJOB.
OW...
NEVER MIND. IT WOULD NEVER STOP THERE.
NO NEED FOR SYMPATHY...

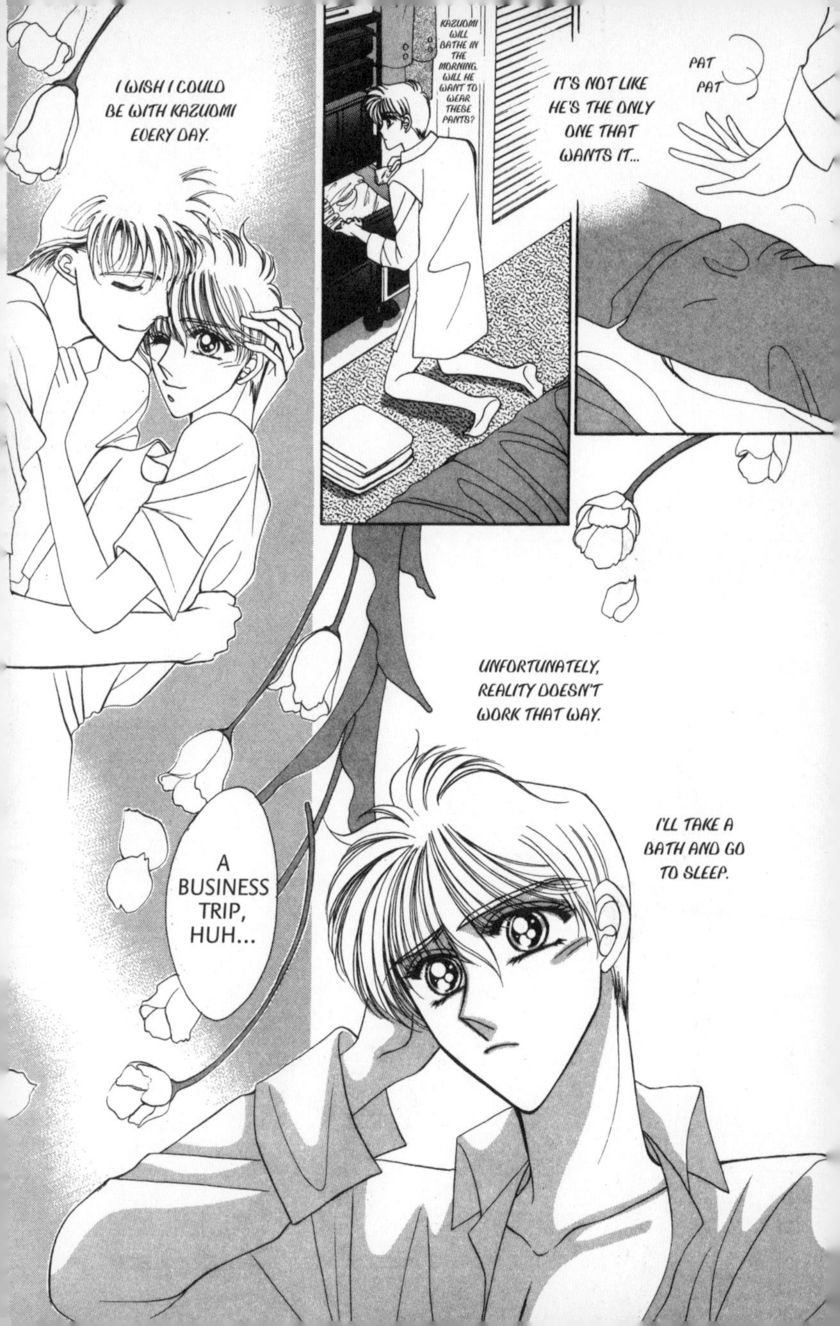
PAT
PAT
IT'S NOT LIKE HE'S THE ONLY ONE THAT WANTS IT...
KAZUOMI WILL BATHE IN THE MORNING. WILL HE WANT TO WEAR THESE PANTS?
I WISH I COULD BE WITH KAZUOMI EVERY DAY.
UNFORTUNATELY, REALITY DOESN'T WORK THAT WAY.
I'LL TAKE A BATH AND GO TO SLEEP.
A BUSINESS TRIP, HUH...

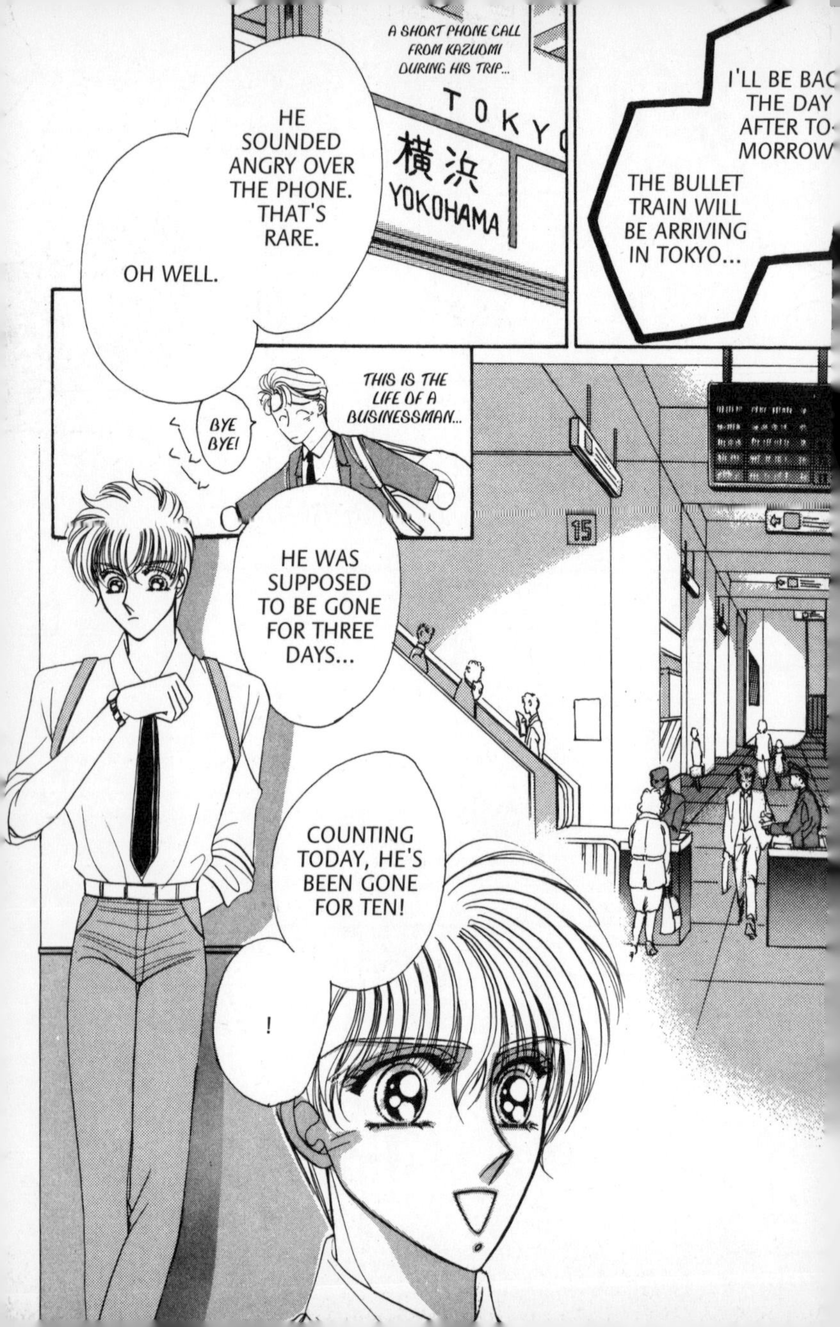
I'LL BE BAC THE DAY AFTER TO- MORROW
THE BULLET TRAIN WILL BE ARRIVING IN TOKYO...
A SHORT PHONE CALL FROM KAZUOMI DURING HIS TRIP...
TOKYO
横浜
YOKOHAMA
HE SOUNDED ANGRY OVER THE PHONE. THAT'S RARE.
OH WELL.
THIS IS THE LIFE OF A BUSINESSMAN...
BYE BYE!
15
HE WAS SUPPOSED TO BE GONE FOR THREE DAYS...
COUNTING TODAY, HE'S BEEN GONE FOR TEN!
!

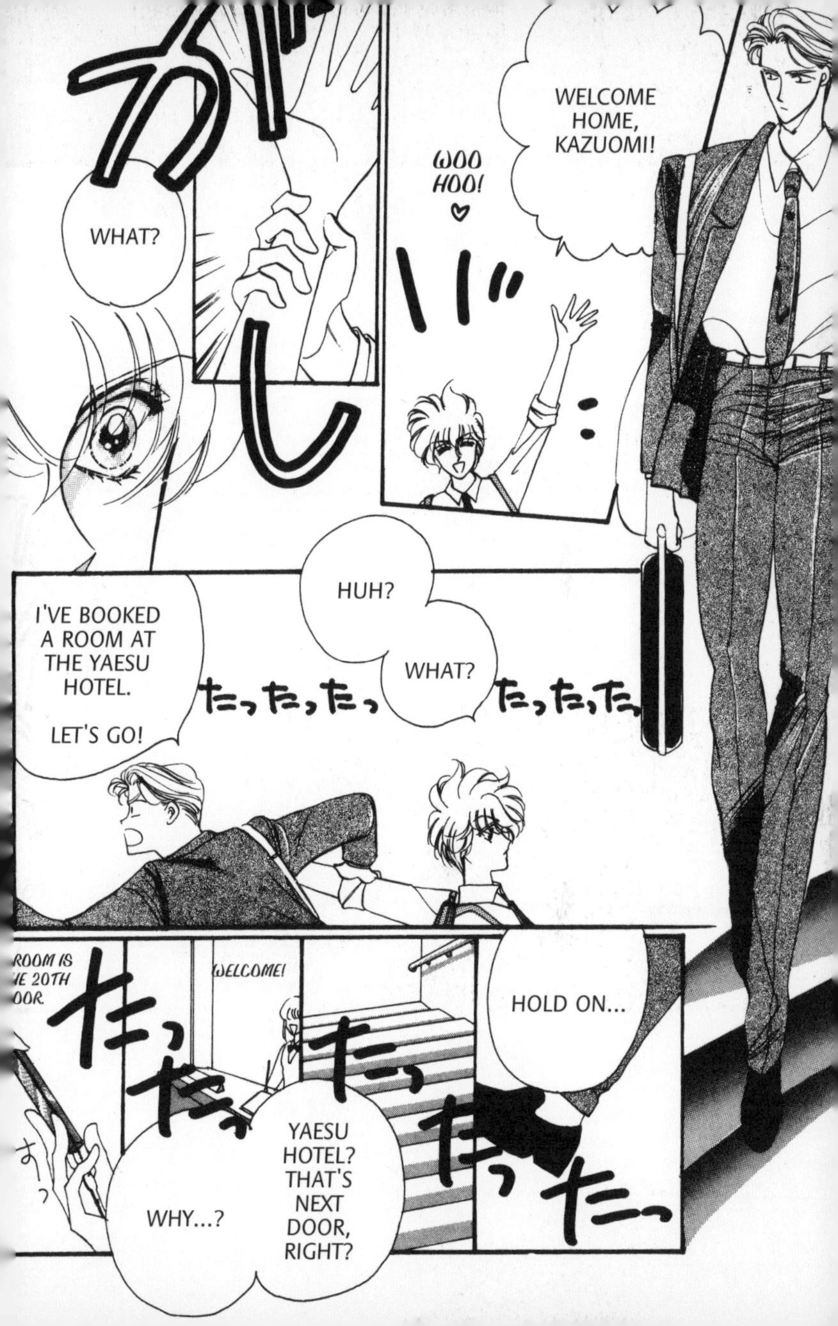
WELCOME HOME, KAZUOMI!
WOO HOO! ♥
バ
がし
WHAT?
HUH?
WHAT?
I'VE BOOKED A ROOM AT THE YAESU HOTEL.
LET'S GO!
たったったっ
たったったっ
HOLD ON...
たったっ
たっ
たっ
たっ
たっ
YAESU HOTEL? THAT'S NEXT DOOR, RIGHT?
WHY...?
WELCOME!
ROOM IS
E 20TH
OOR.
おっ

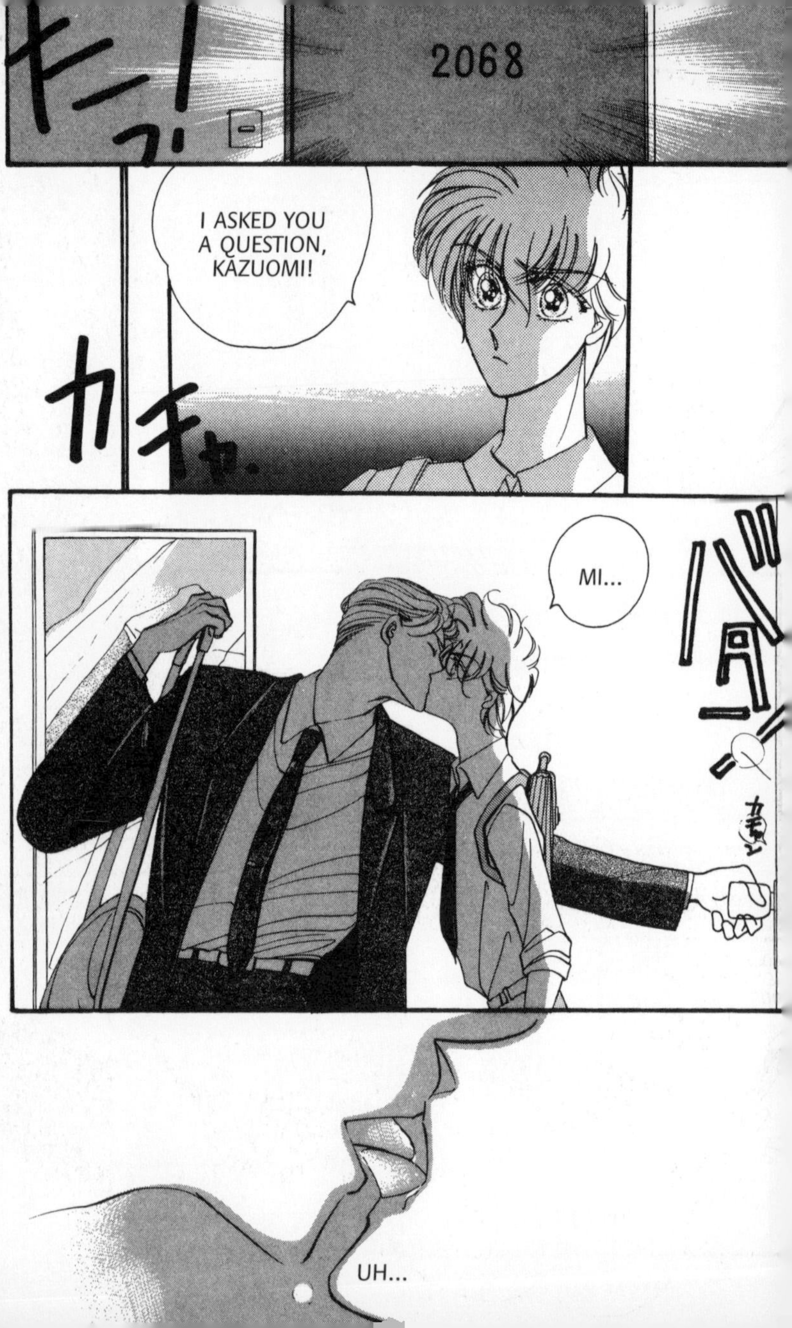

キーッ!
2068
I ASKED YOU A QUESTION, KAZUOMI!
バタン
MI...
UH...

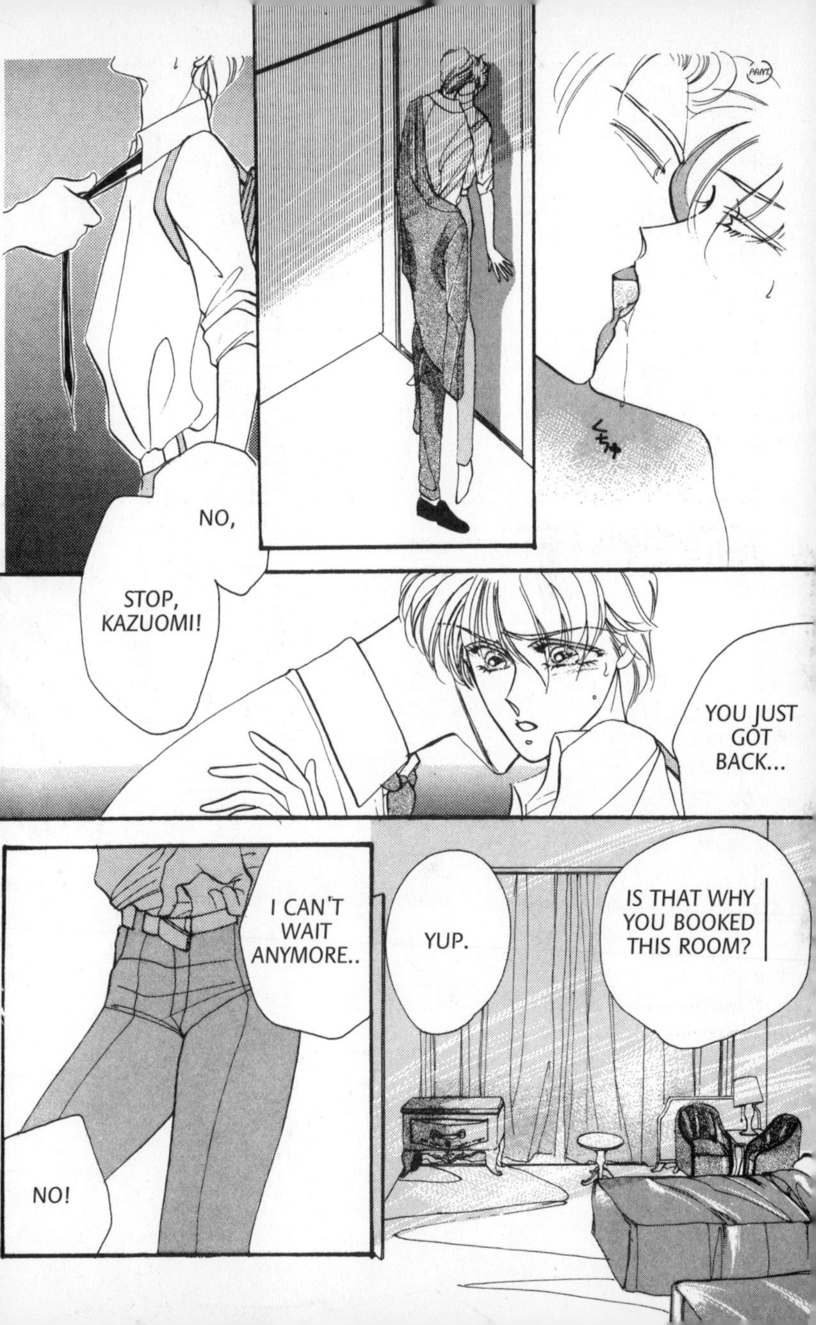
PANT
NO, STOP, KAZUOMI!
YOU JUST GOT BACK...
IS THAT WHY YOU BOOKED THIS ROOM?
YUP.
I CAN'T WAIT ANYMORE..
NO!

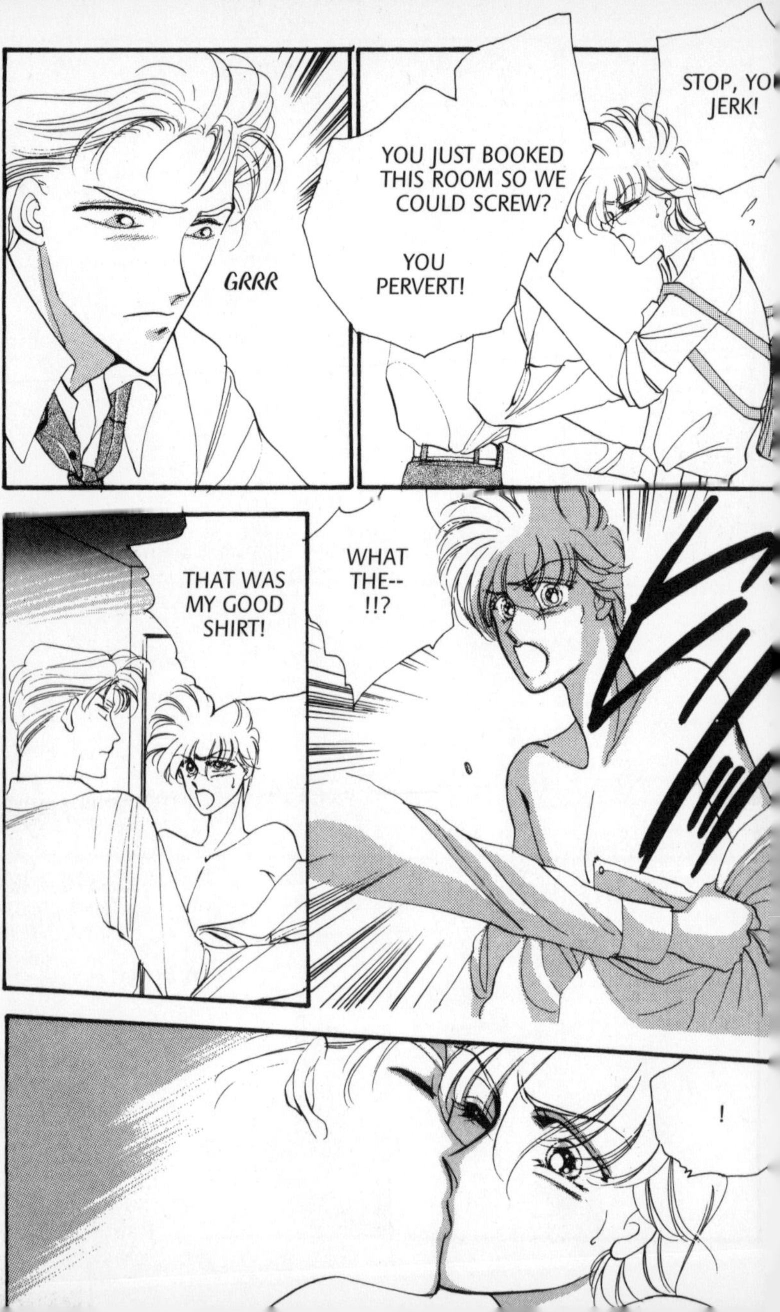
STOP, YO
JERK!
YOU JUST BOOKED THIS ROOM SO WE COULD SCREW?
YOU PERVERT!
GRRR
WHAT THE-- !!?
THAT WAS MY GOOD SHIRT!
!

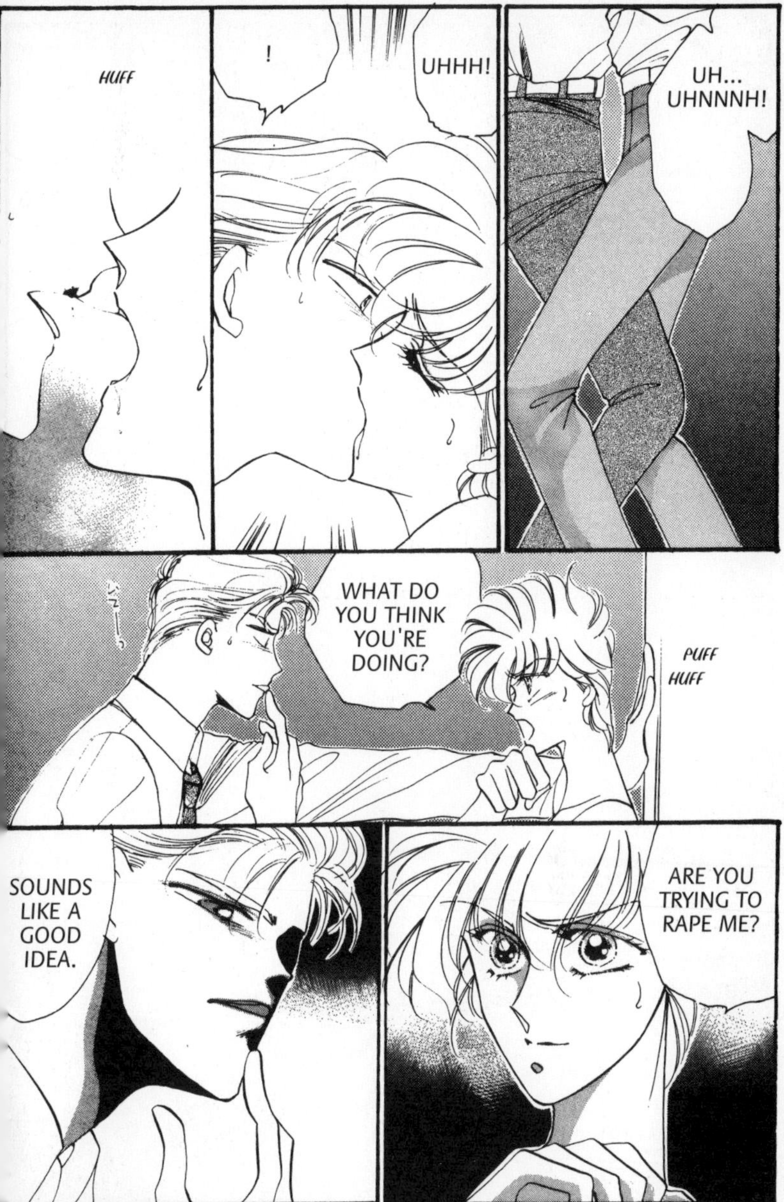
UH... UHNNNH!
UHHH!
!
HUFF
PUFF HUFF
WHAT DO YOU THINK YOU'RE DOING?
ARE YOU TRYING TO RAPE ME?
SOUNDS LIKE A GOOD IDEA.

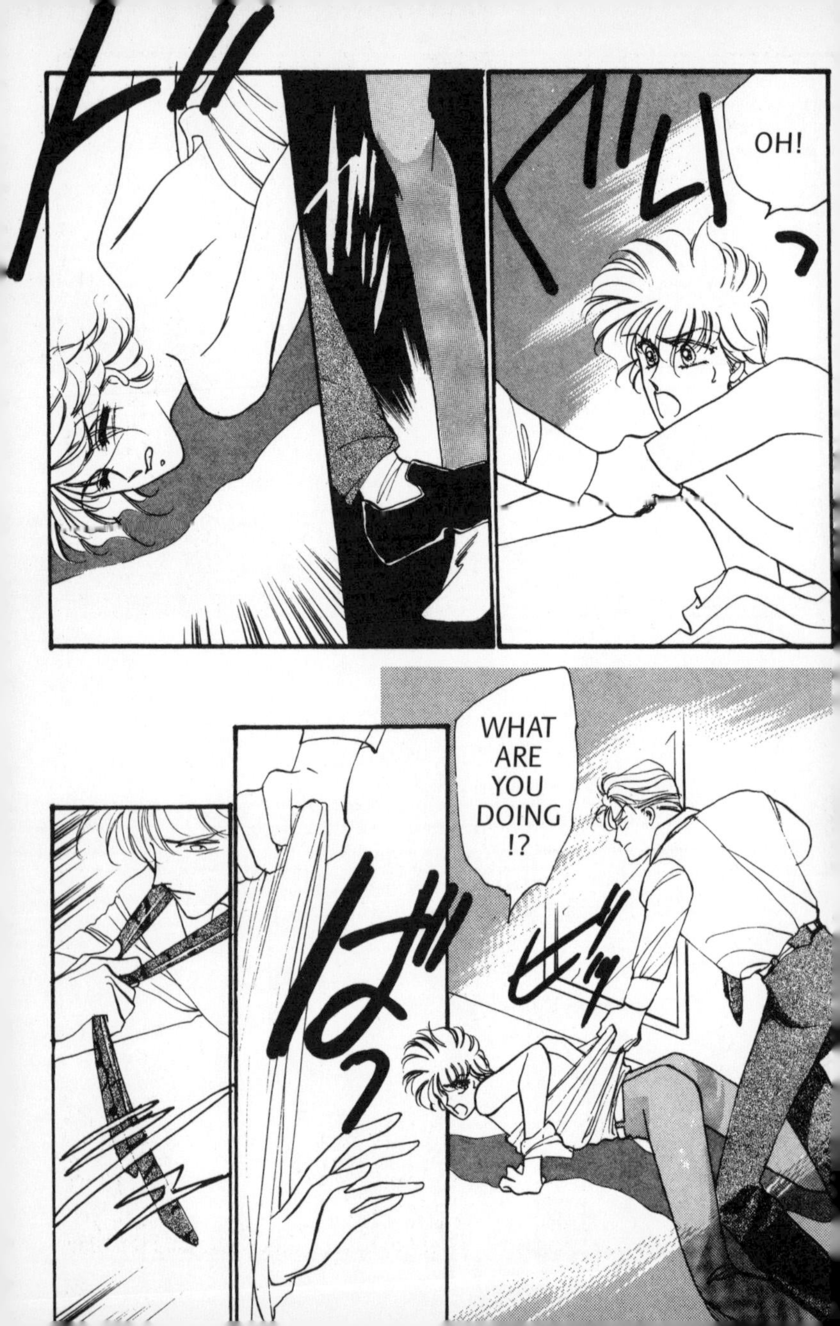
OH!
WHAT ARE YOU DOING !?

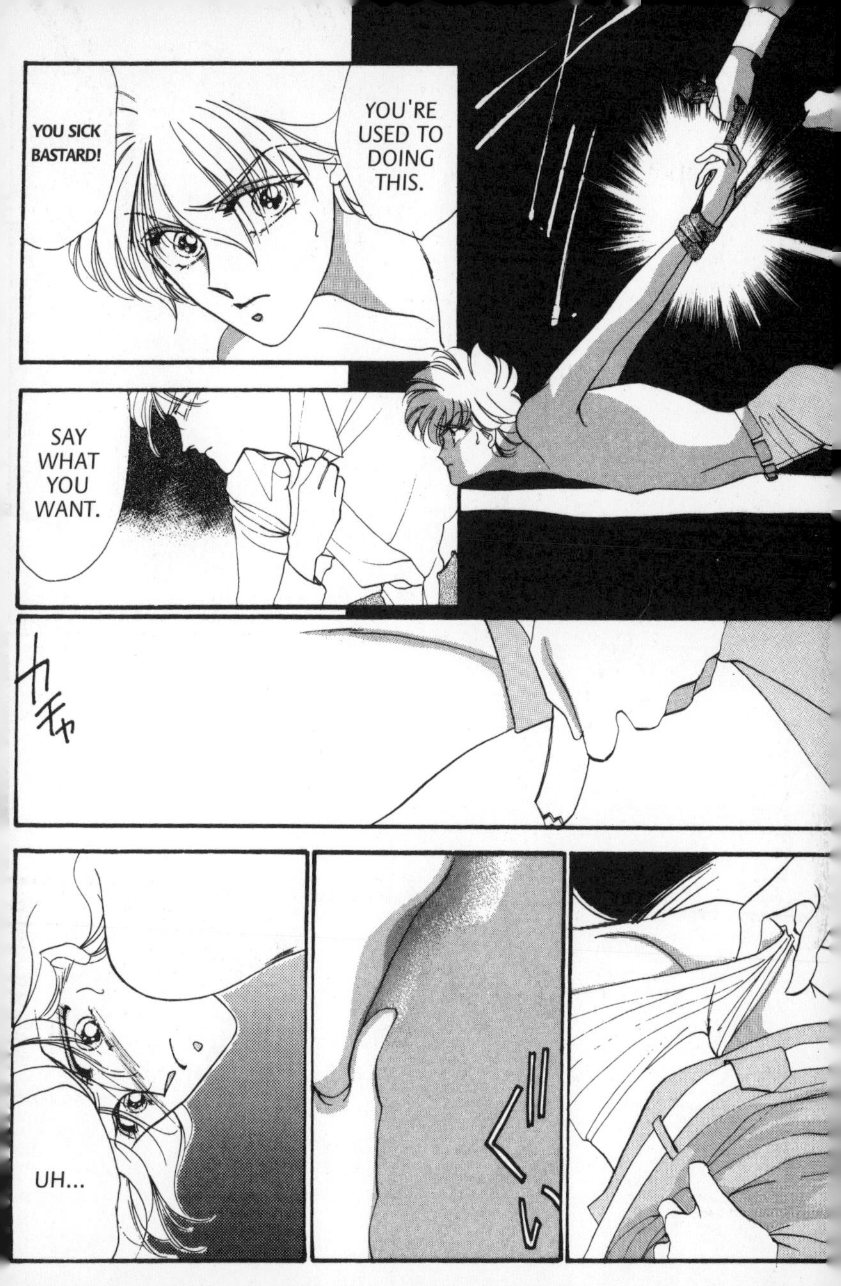
YOU'RE USED TO DOING THIS.
YOU SICK BASTARD!
SAY WHAT YOU WANT.
カチャ
ぐい
UH...

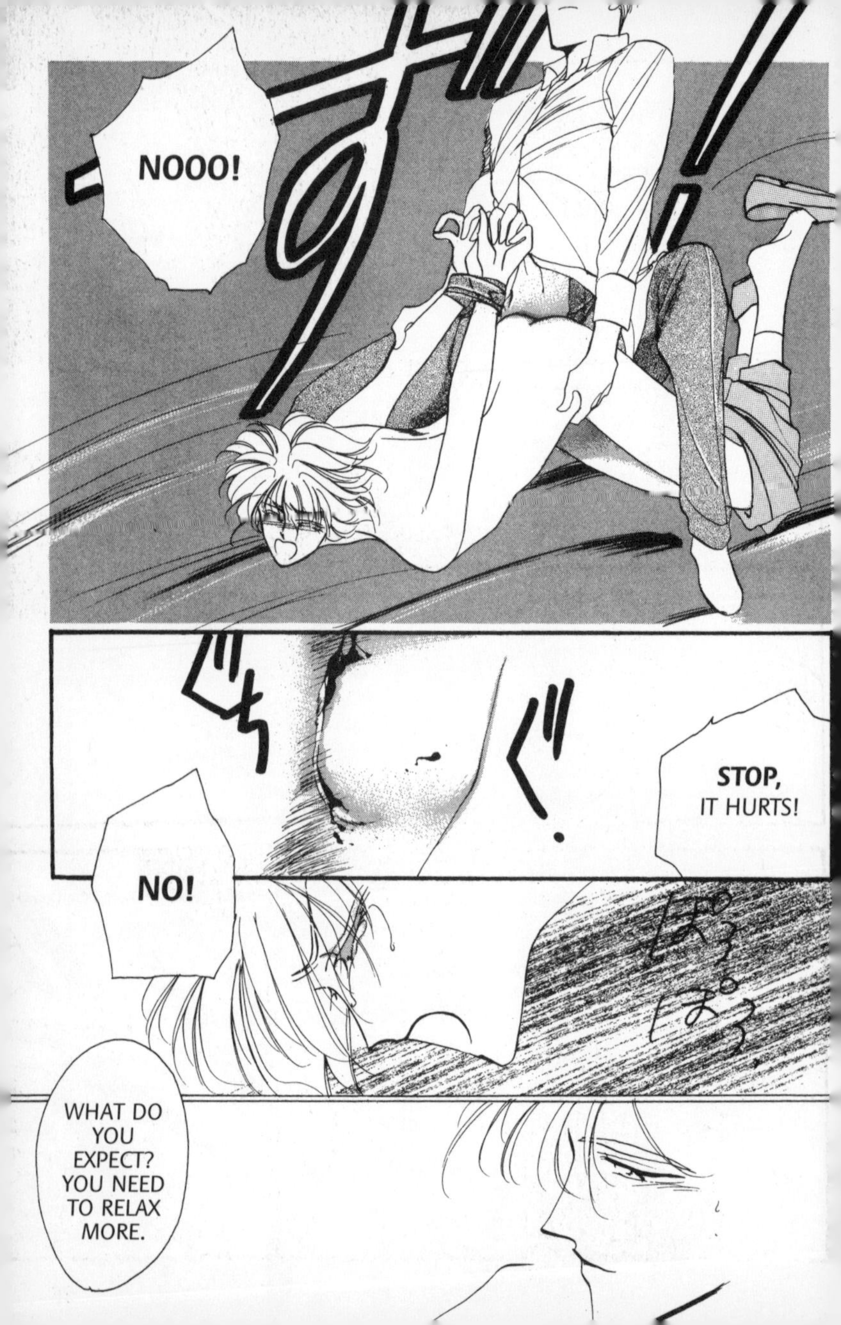
NOOO!
STOP, IT HURTS!
NO!
WHAT DO YOU EXPECT? YOU NEED TO RELAX MORE.

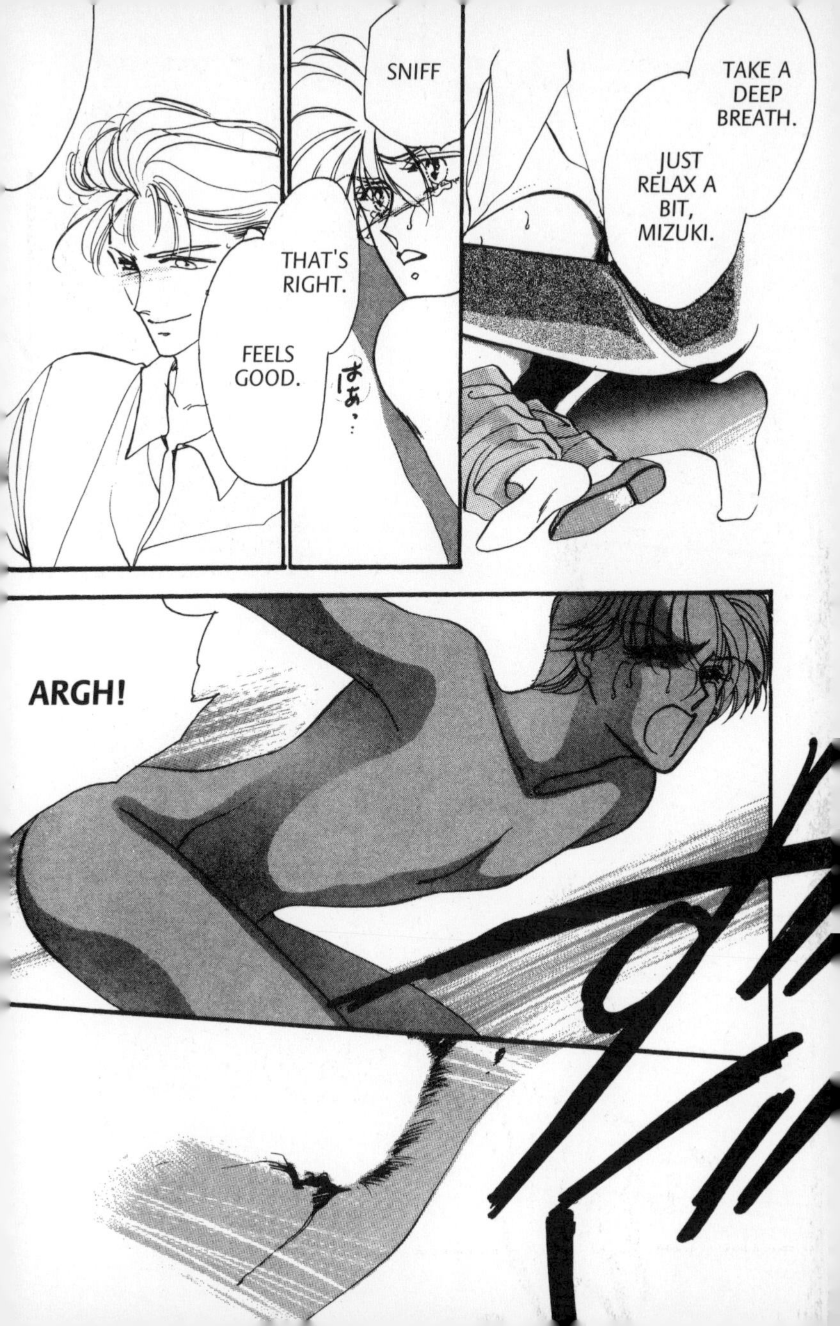
TAKE A DEEP BREATH.
JUST RELAX A BIT, MIZUKI.
SNIFF
はあっ…
THAT'S RIGHT.
FEELS GOOD.
ARGH!

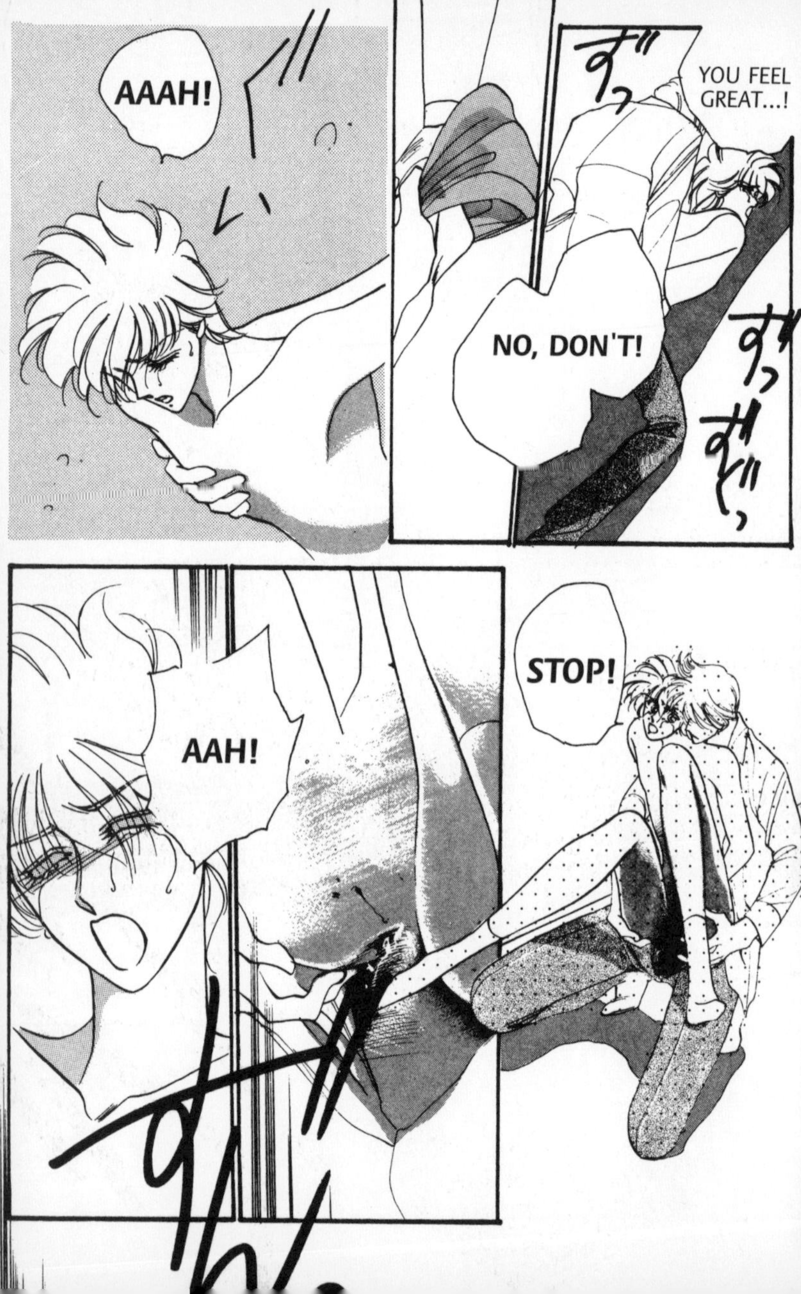
ずっ
YOU FEEL GREAT...!
ずっ ずっ
NO, DON'T!
AAAH!
STOP!
AAH!

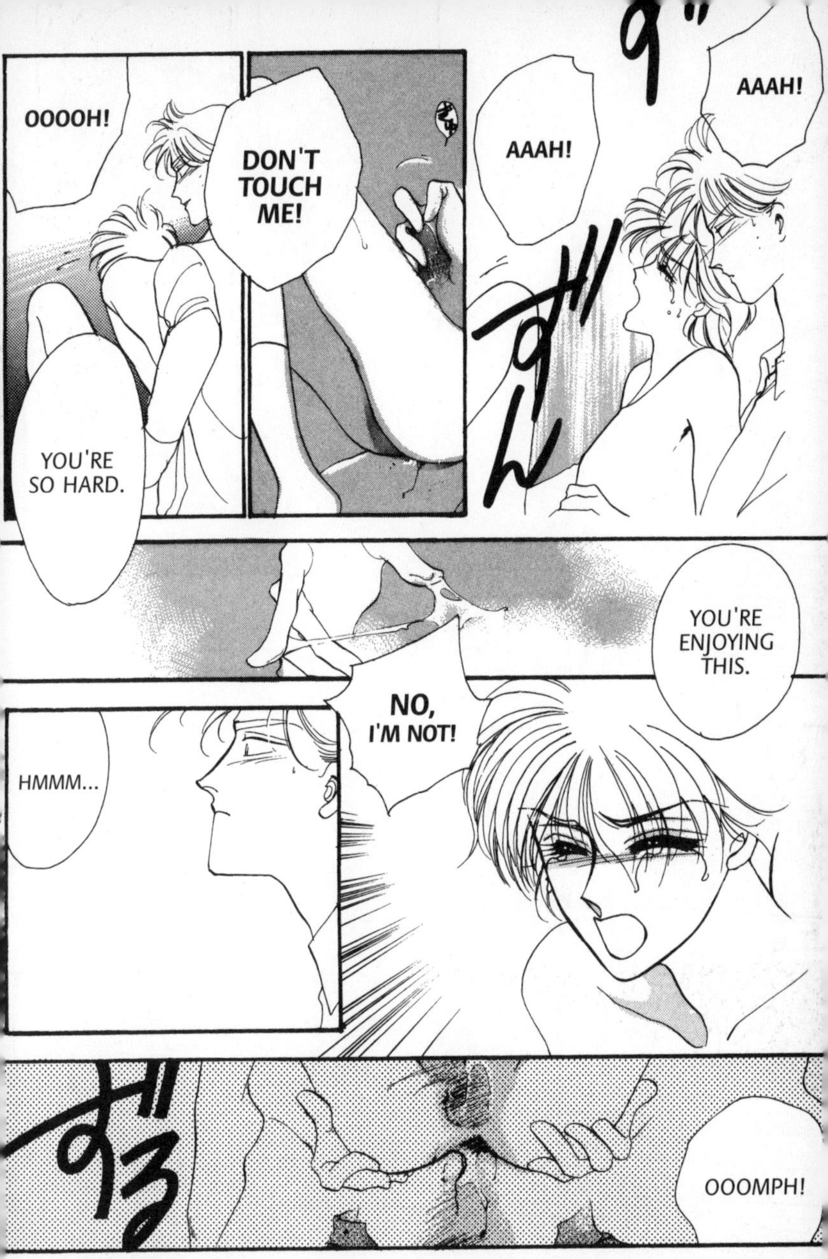
AAAH!
AAAH!
ずん
DON'T TOUCH ME!
OOOOH!
YOU'RE SO HARD.
YOU'RE ENJOYING THIS.
NO, I'M NOT!
HMMM...
OOOMPH!
ずる

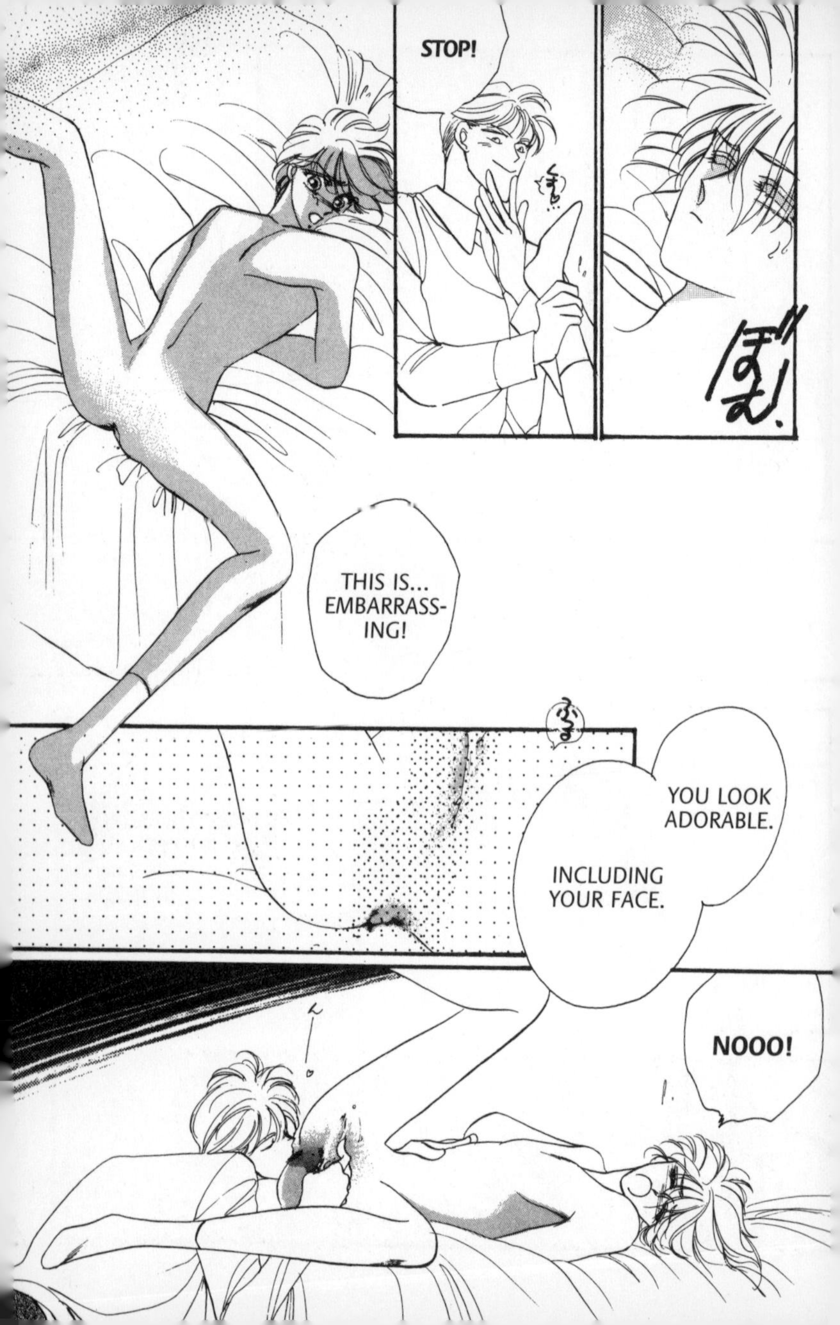
STOP!
THIS IS... EMBARRASS-ING!
YOU LOOK ADORABLE.
INCLUDING YOUR FACE.
NOOO!

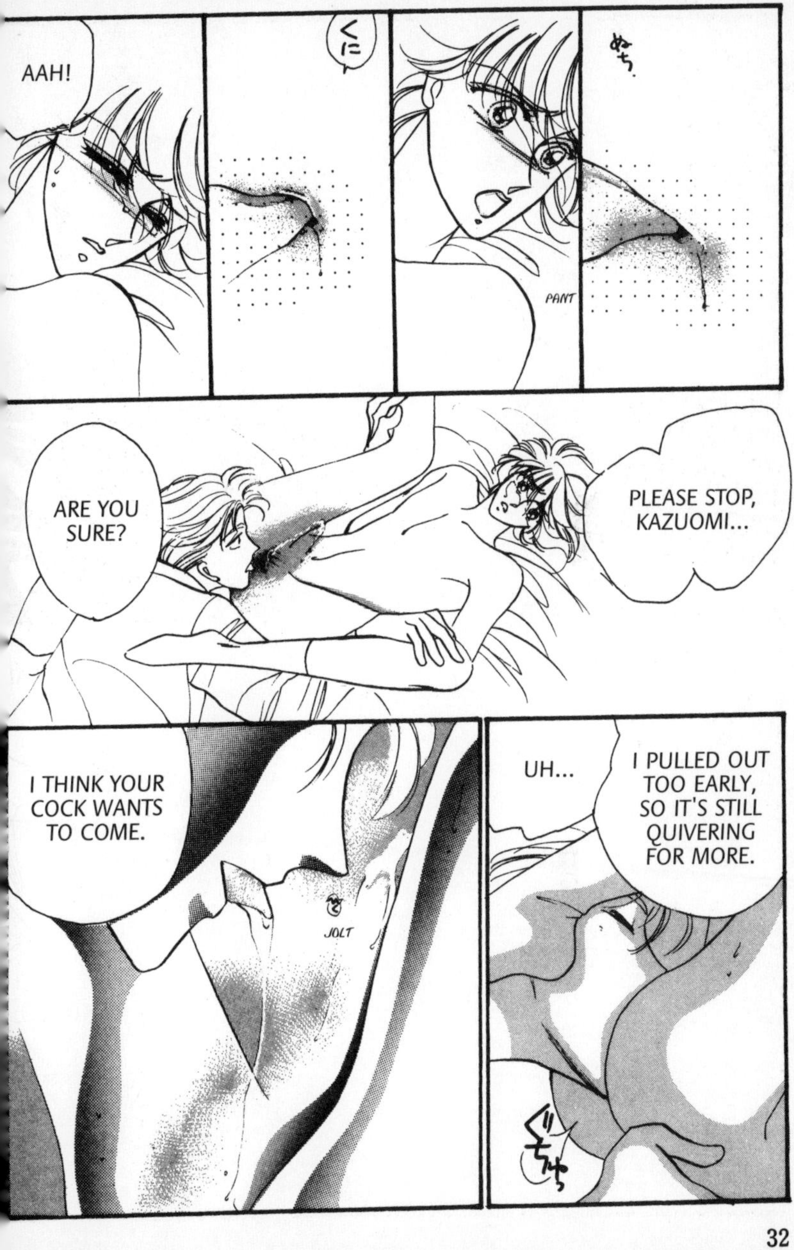

ぬち
PANT
くに
AAH!
PLEASE STOP, KAZUOMI...
ARE YOU SURE?
I PULLED OUT TOO EARLY, SO IT'S STILL QUIVERING FOR MORE.
UH...
I THINK YOUR COCK WANTS TO COME.
JOLT

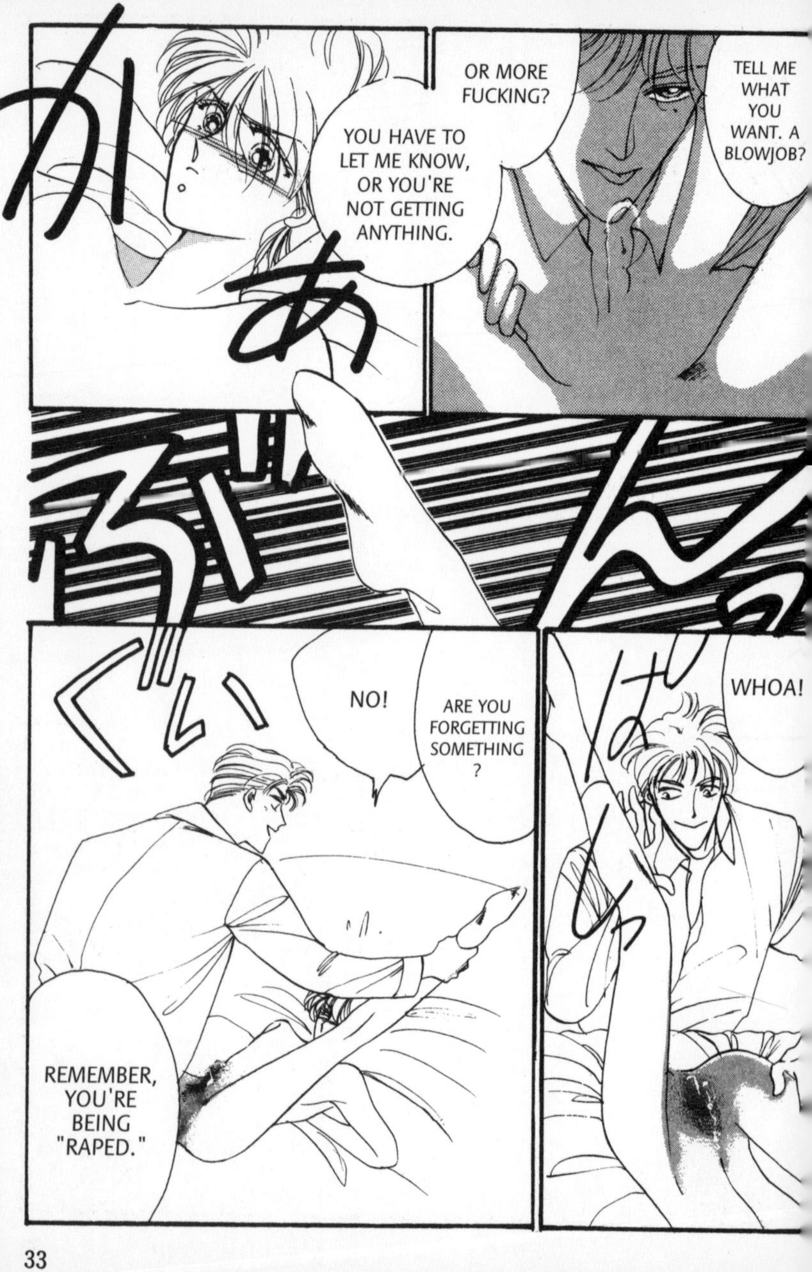
TELL ME WHAT YOU WANT. A BLOWJOB?
OR MORE FUCKING?
YOU HAVE TO LET ME KNOW, OR YOU'RE NOT GETTING ANYTHING.
かあ
WHOA!
ARE YOU FORGETTING SOMETHING?
NO!
REMEMBER, YOU'RE BEING "RAPED."

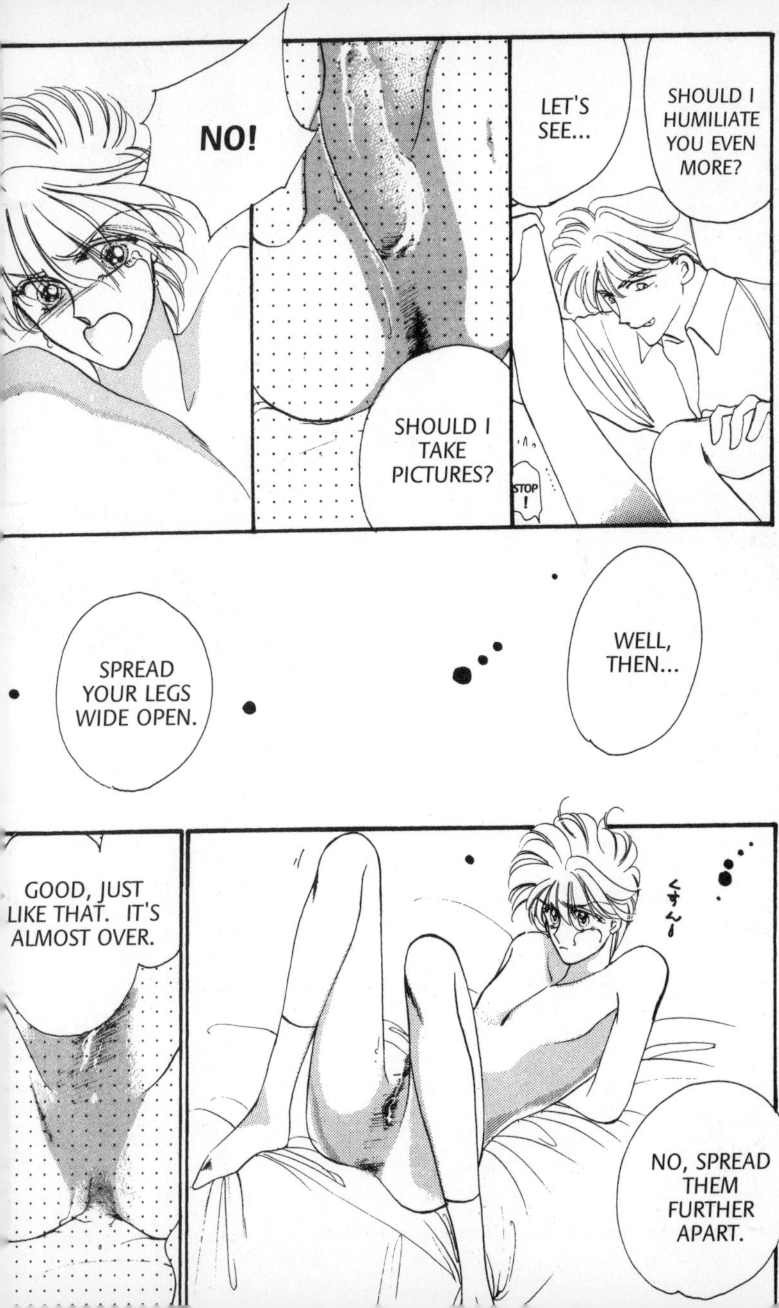
SHOULD I HUMILIATE YOU EVEN MORE?
LET'S SEE...
STOP !
SHOULD I TAKE PICTURES?
NO!
WELL, THEN...
SPREAD YOUR LEGS WIDE OPEN.
くすん
NO, SPREAD THEM FURTHER APART.
GOOD, JUST LIKE THAT. IT'S ALMOST OVER.

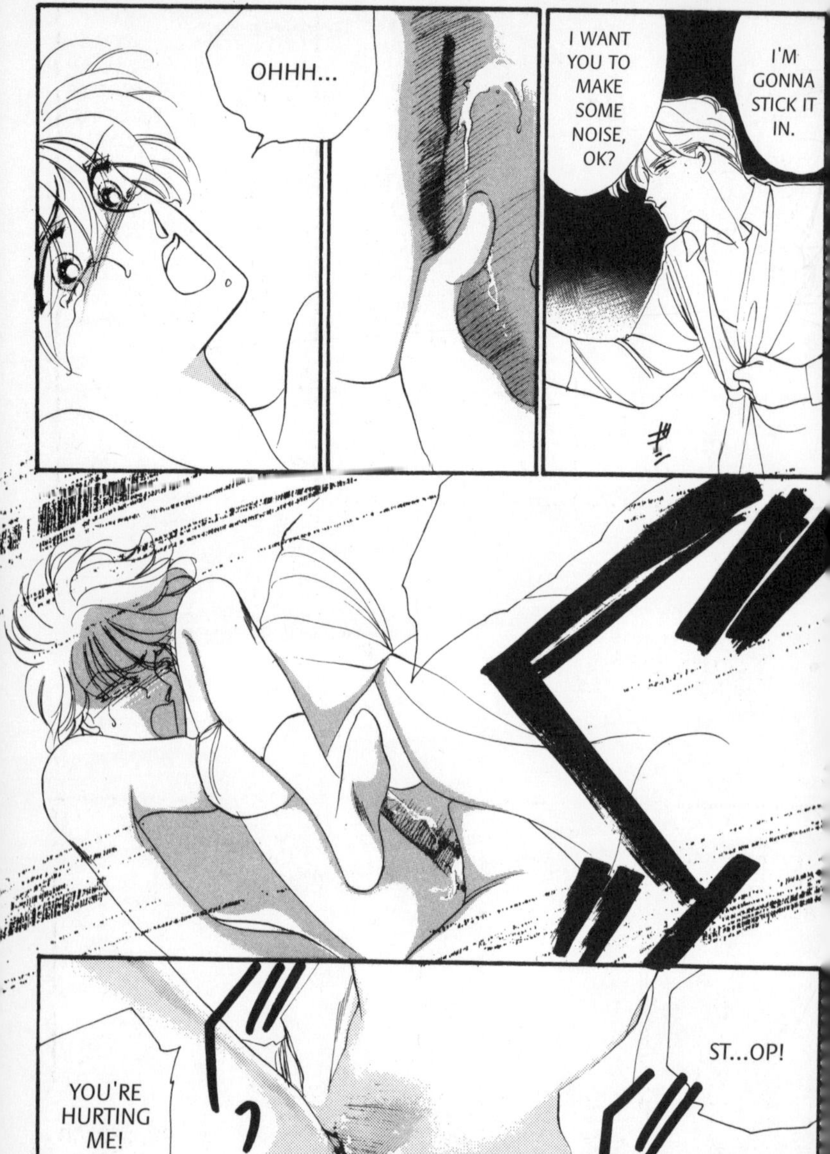
I'M GONNA STICK IT IN.
I WANT YOU TO MAKE SOME NOISE, OK?
OHHH...
ST...OP!
YOU'RE HURTING ME!

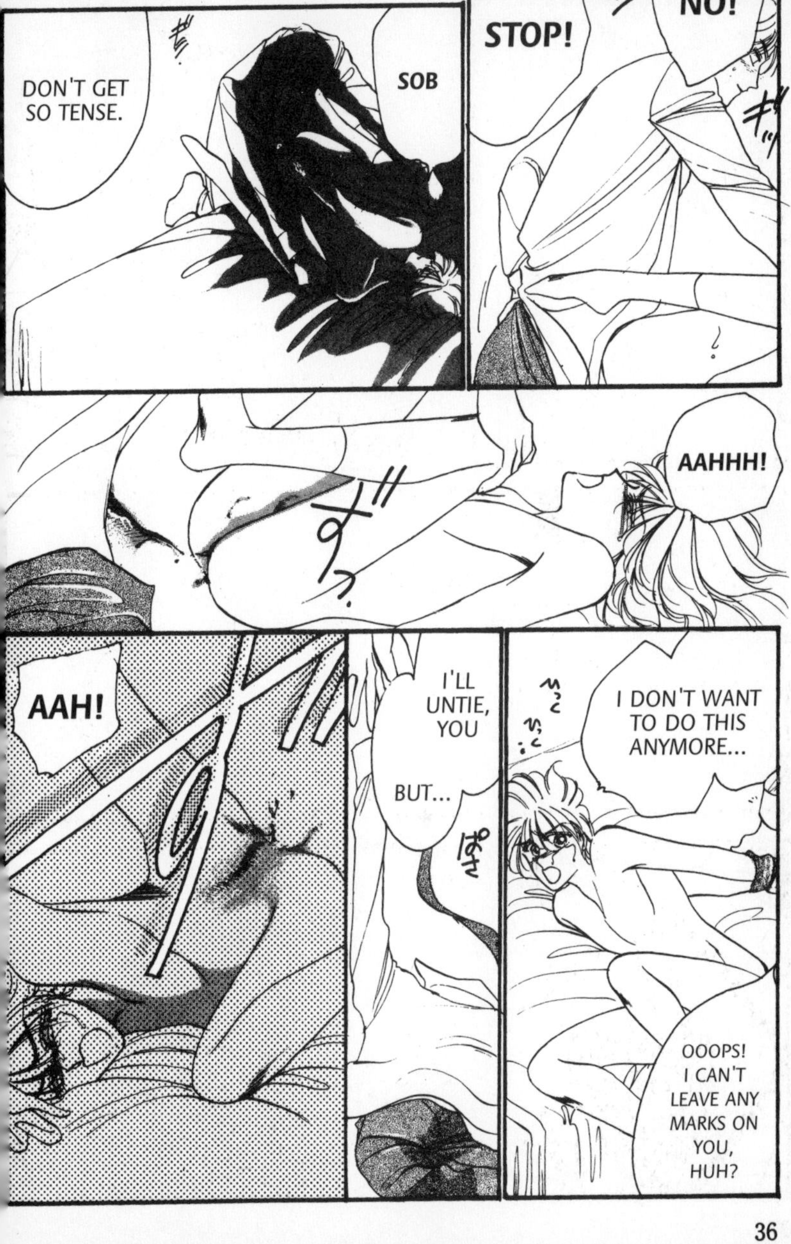
NO!
STOP!
SOB
DON'T GET SO TENSE.
AAHHH!
I DON'T WANT TO DO THIS ANYMORE...
OOOPS! I CAN'T LEAVE ANY MARKS ON YOU, HUH?
I'LL UNTIE, YOU
BUT...
AAH!

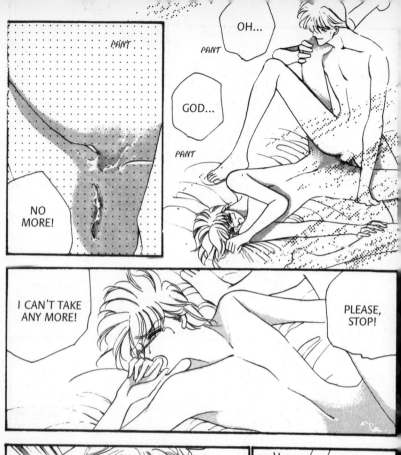

OH...

PANT

PANT

GOD...

PANT

NO MORE!

I CAN'T TAKE ANY MORE!

PLEASE, STOP!

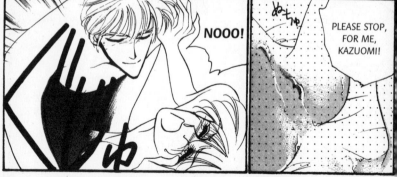

NOOO!

PLEASE STOP, FOR ME, KAZUOMI!

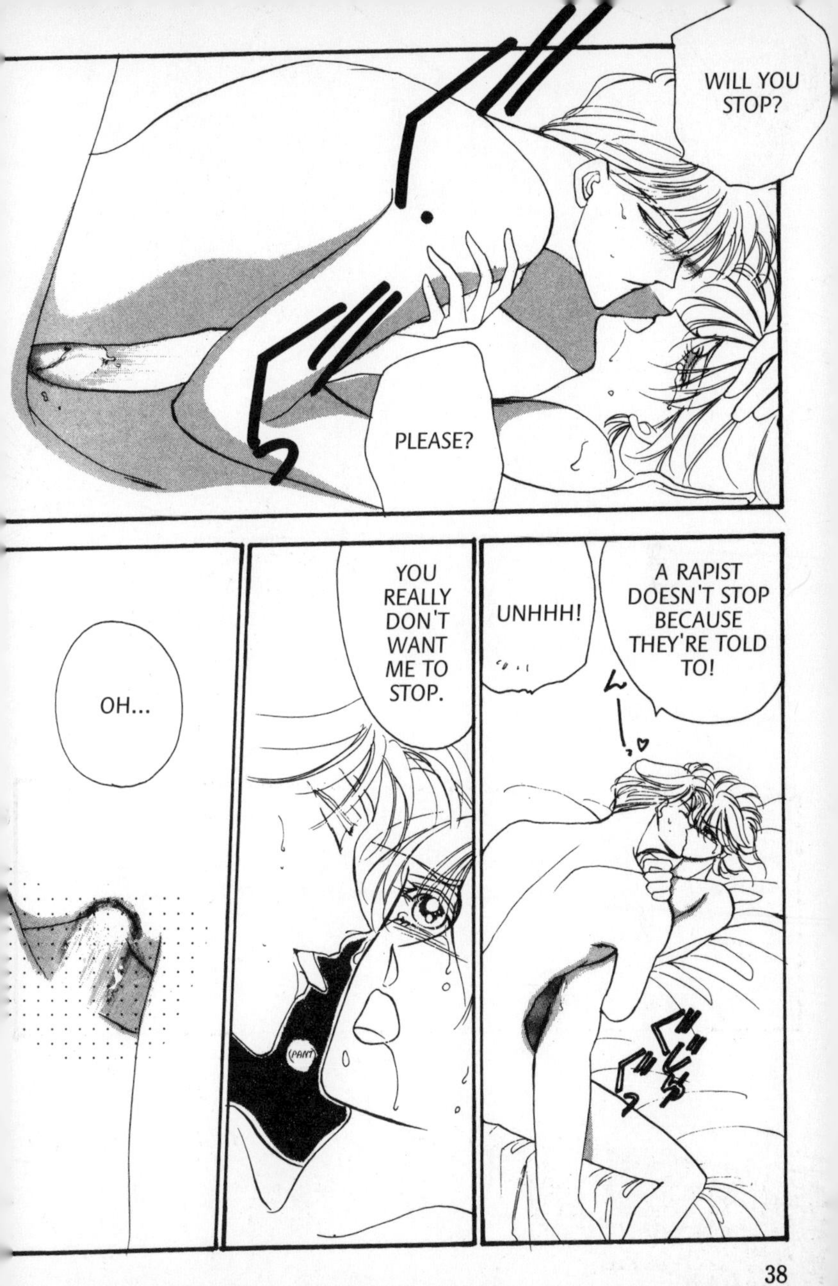
WILL YOU STOP?
PLEASE?
A RAPIST DOESN'T STOP BECAUSE THEY'RE TOLD TO!
UNHHH!
YOU REALLY DON'T WANT ME TO STOP.
PANT
OH...

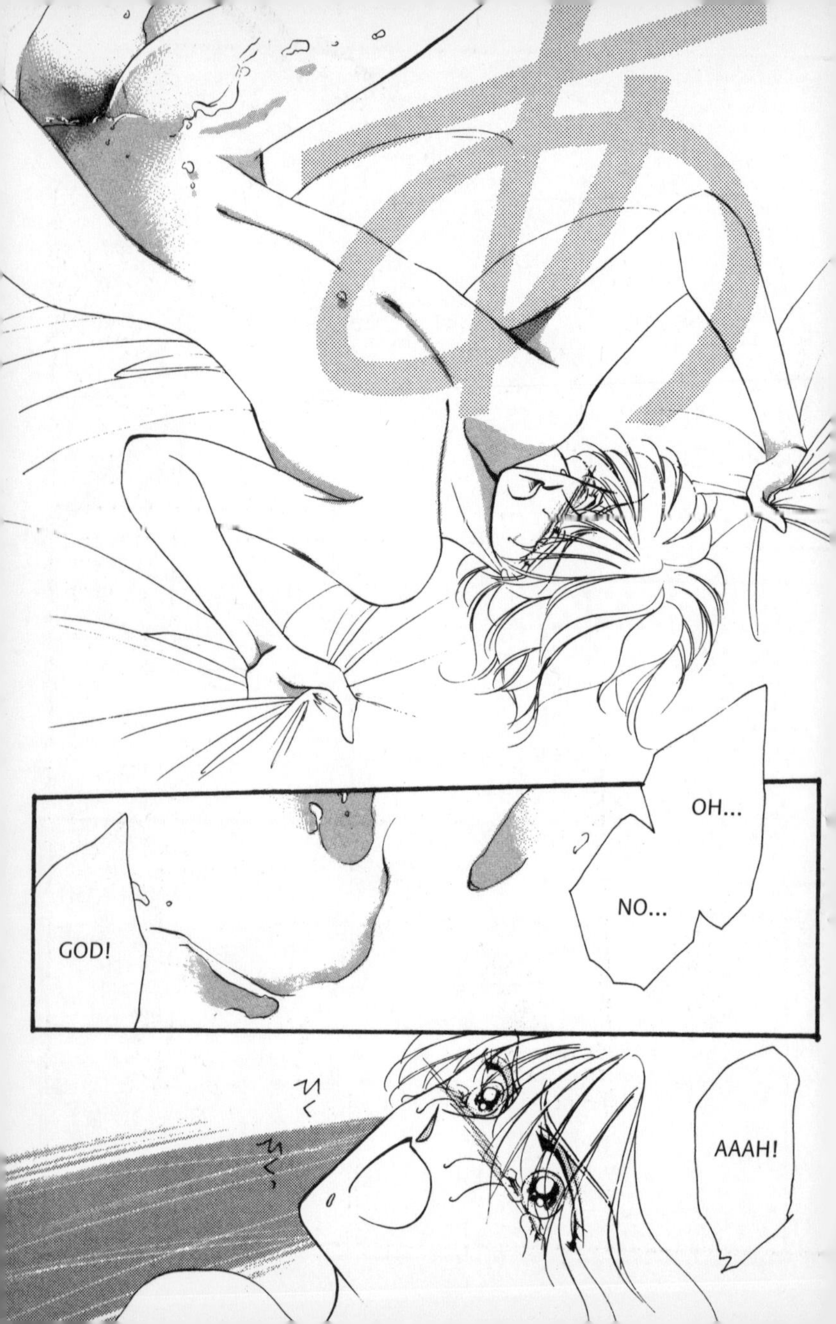
OH...
NO...
GOD!
AAAH!

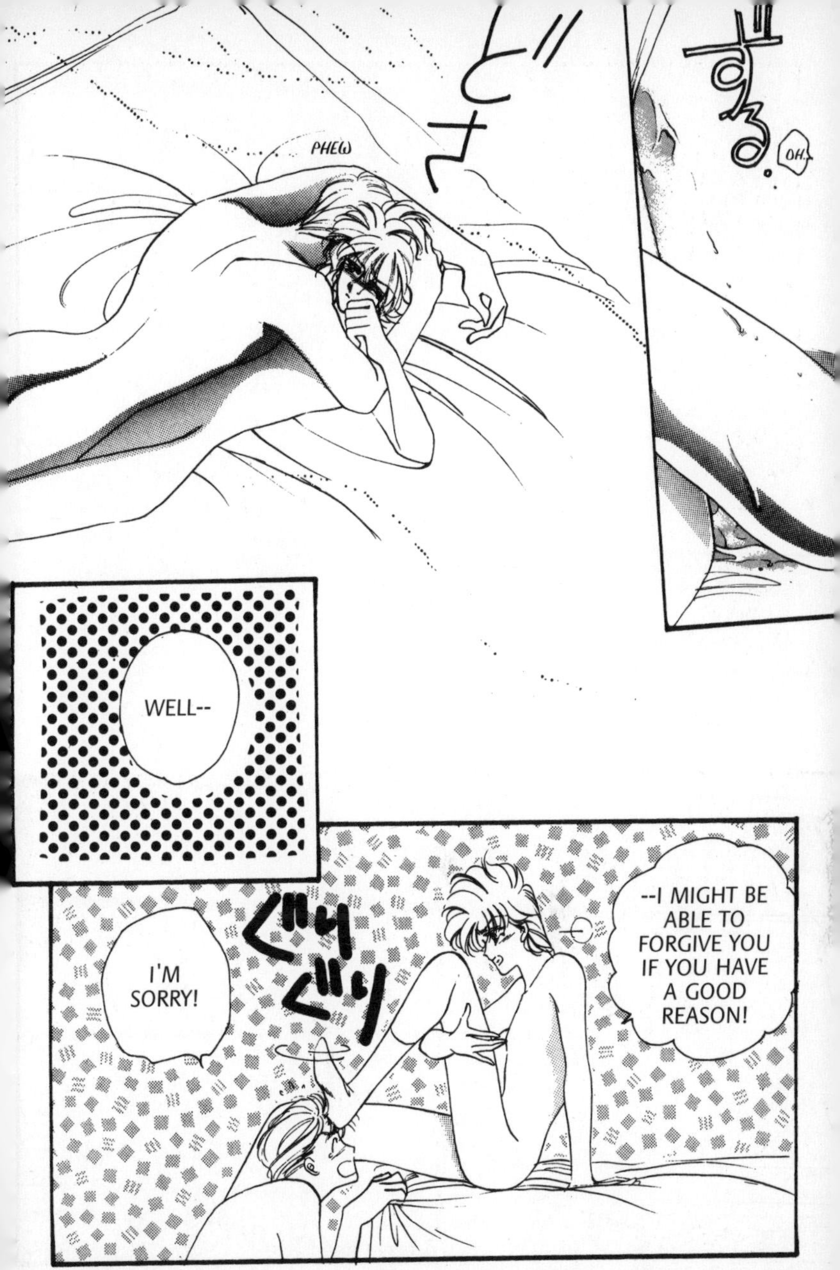
ずる。
OH..
どさ
PHEW
WELL--
--I MIGHT BE ABLE TO FORGIVE YOU IF YOU HAVE A GOOD REASON!
ぐりぐり
I'M SORRY!

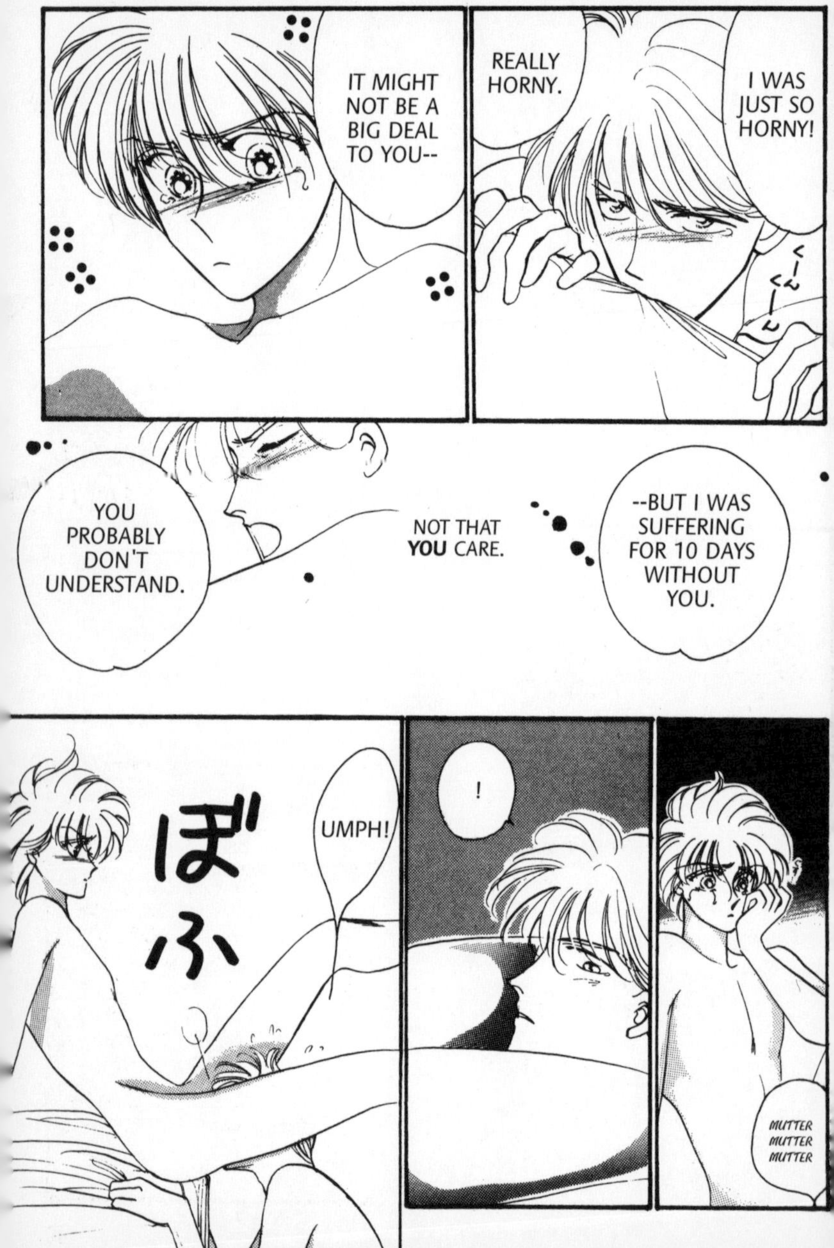

I WAS JUST SO HORNY!
REALLY HORNY.
IT MIGHT NOT BE A BIG DEAL TO YOU--
--BUT I WAS SUFFERING FOR 10 DAYS WITHOUT YOU.
NOT THAT **YOU** CARE.
YOU PROBABLY DON'T UNDERSTAND.
MUTTER MUTTER MUTTER
!
UMPH!
ぼふ

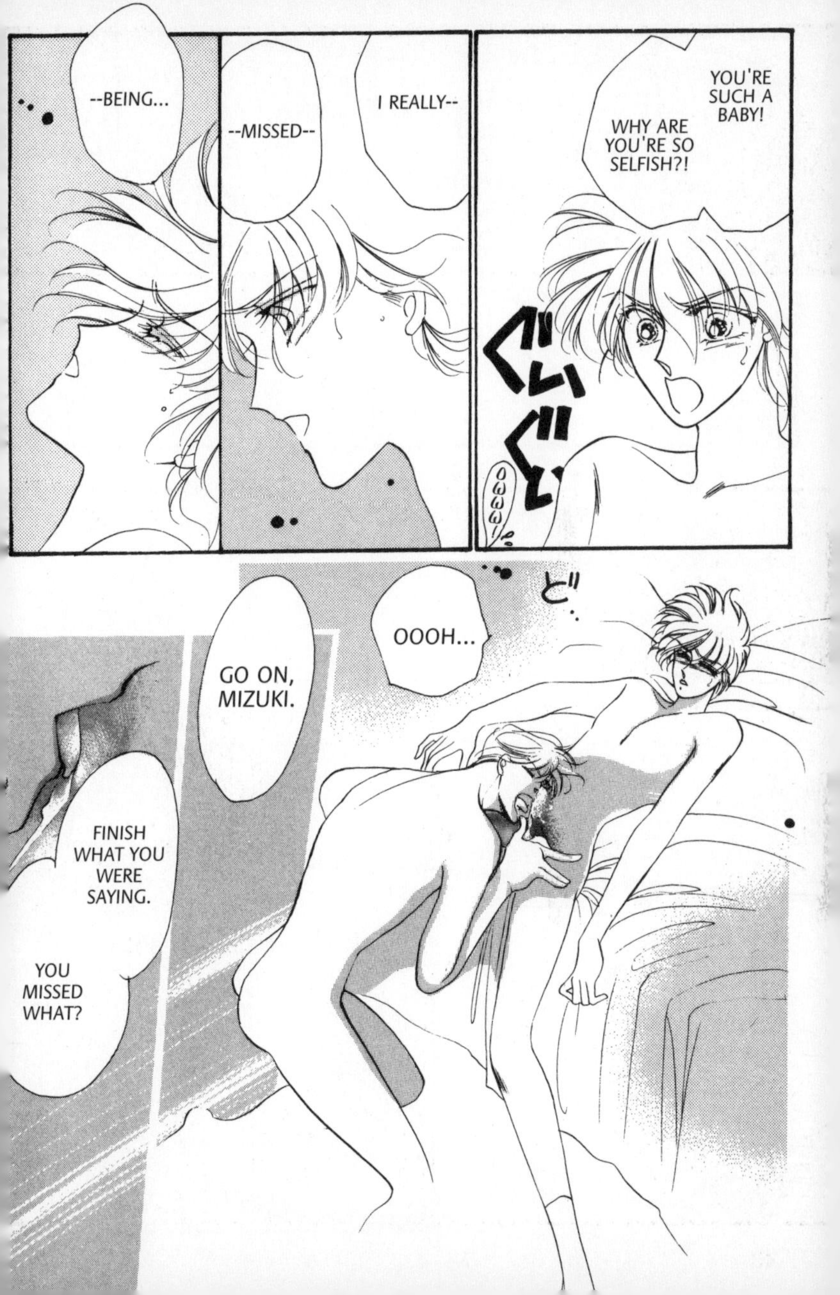
YOU'RE SUCH A BABY!
WHY ARE YOU'RE SO SELFISH?!
ぐいぐい
OWWW!
I REALLY--
--MISSED--
--BEING...
OOOH...
GO ON, MIZUKI.
FINISH WHAT YOU WERE SAYING.
YOU MISSED WHAT?

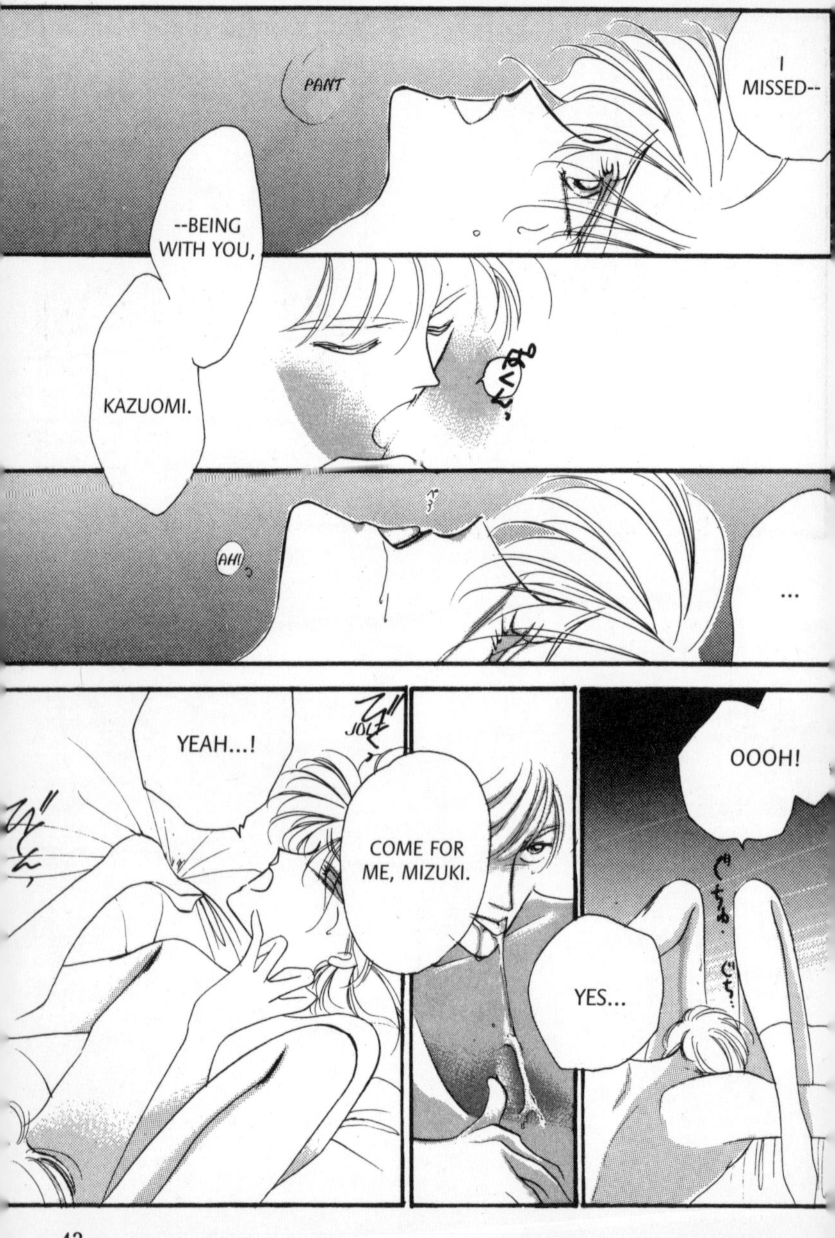
I MISSED--
PANT
--BEING WITH YOU,
KAZUOMI.
...
AH!
OOOH!
YES...
COME FOR ME, MIZUKI.
JOLT
YEAH...!

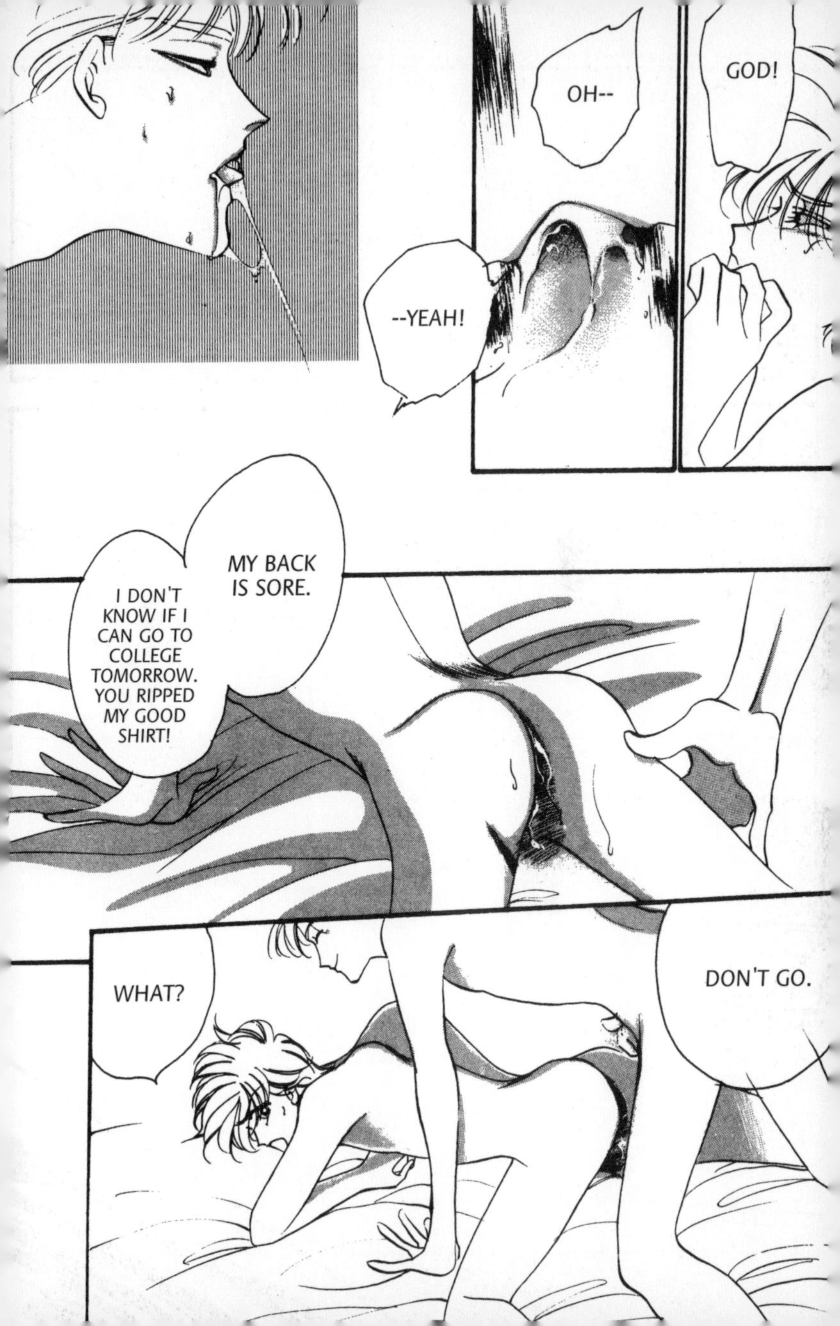
GOD!
OH--
--YEAH!
MY BACK IS SORE.
I DON'T KNOW IF I CAN GO TO COLLEGE TOMORROW. YOU RIPPED MY GOOD SHIRT!
DON'T GO.
WHAT?

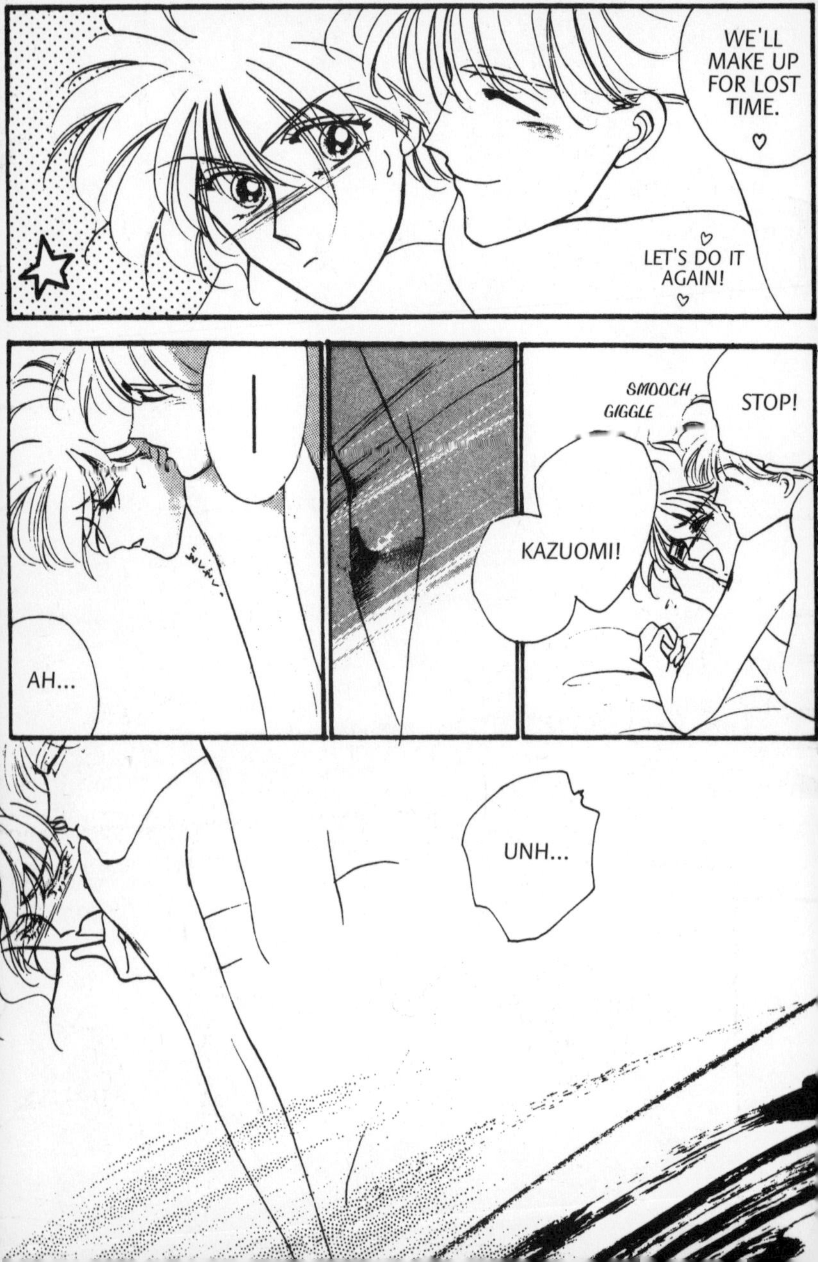
WE'LL MAKE UP FOR LOST TIME.
LET'S DO IT AGAIN!
STOP!
SMOOCH
GIGGLE
KAZUOMI!
AH...
UNH...

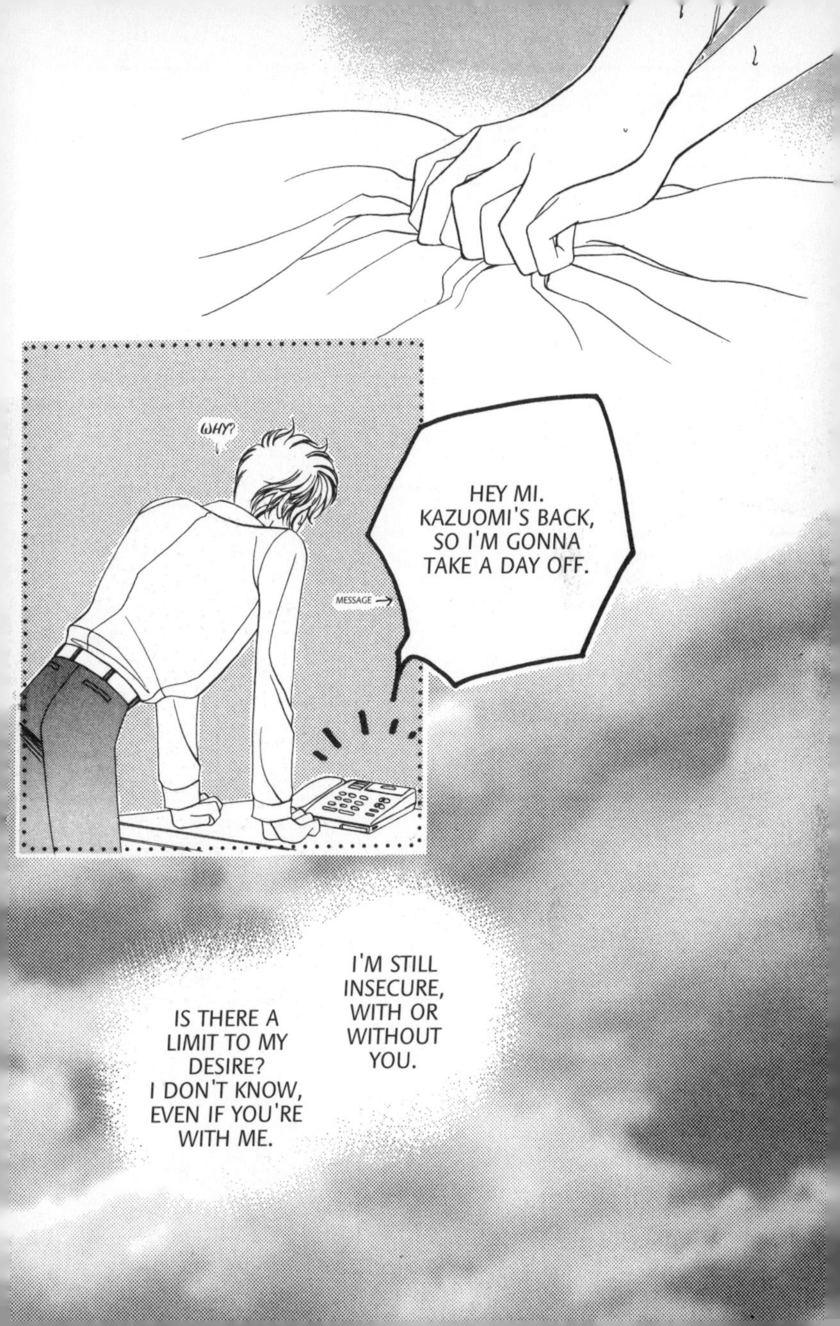
HEY MI. KAZUOMI'S BACK, SO I'M GONNA TAKE A DAY OFF.
MESSAGE
WHY?
I'M STILL INSECURE, WITH OR WITHOUT YOU.
IS THERE A LIMIT TO MY DESIRE? I DON'T KNOW, EVEN IF YOU'RE WITH ME.

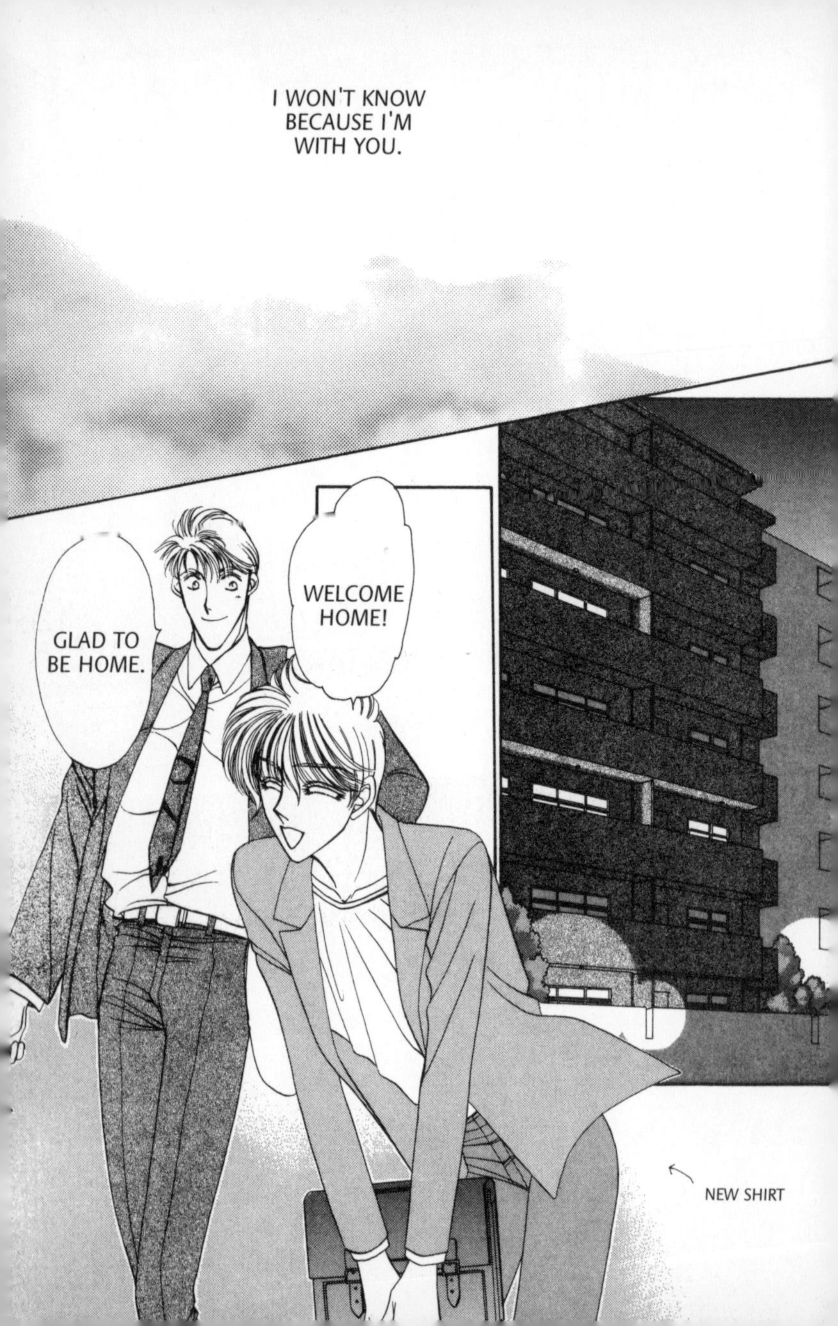
I WON'T KNOW BECAUSE I'M WITH YOU.
WELCOME HOME!
GLAD TO BE HOME.
NEW SHIRT

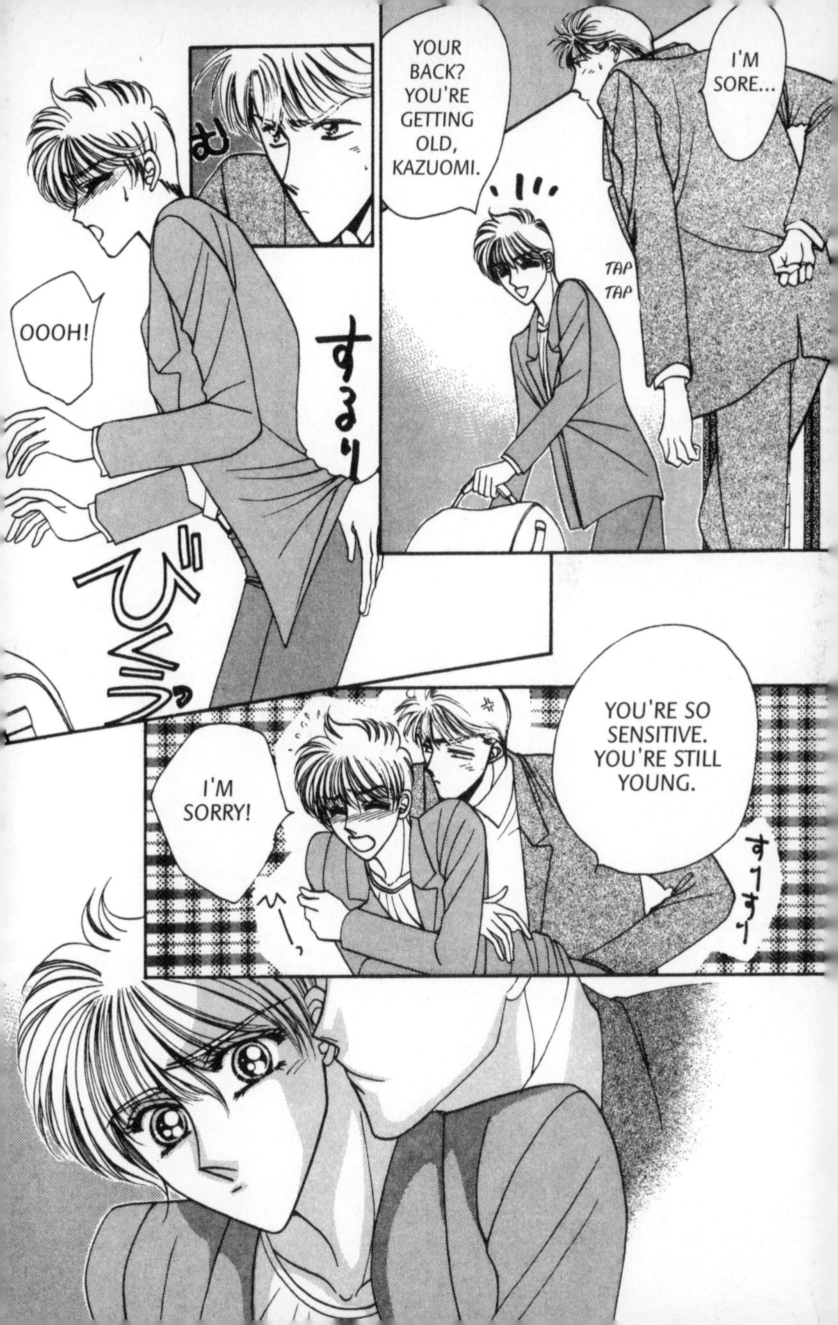
I'M SORE...
YOUR BACK? YOU'RE GETTING OLD, KAZUOMI.
TAP TAP
む
するり
OOOH!
びくっ
YOU'RE SO SENSITIVE. YOU'RE STILL YOUNG.
すりすり
I'M SORRY!

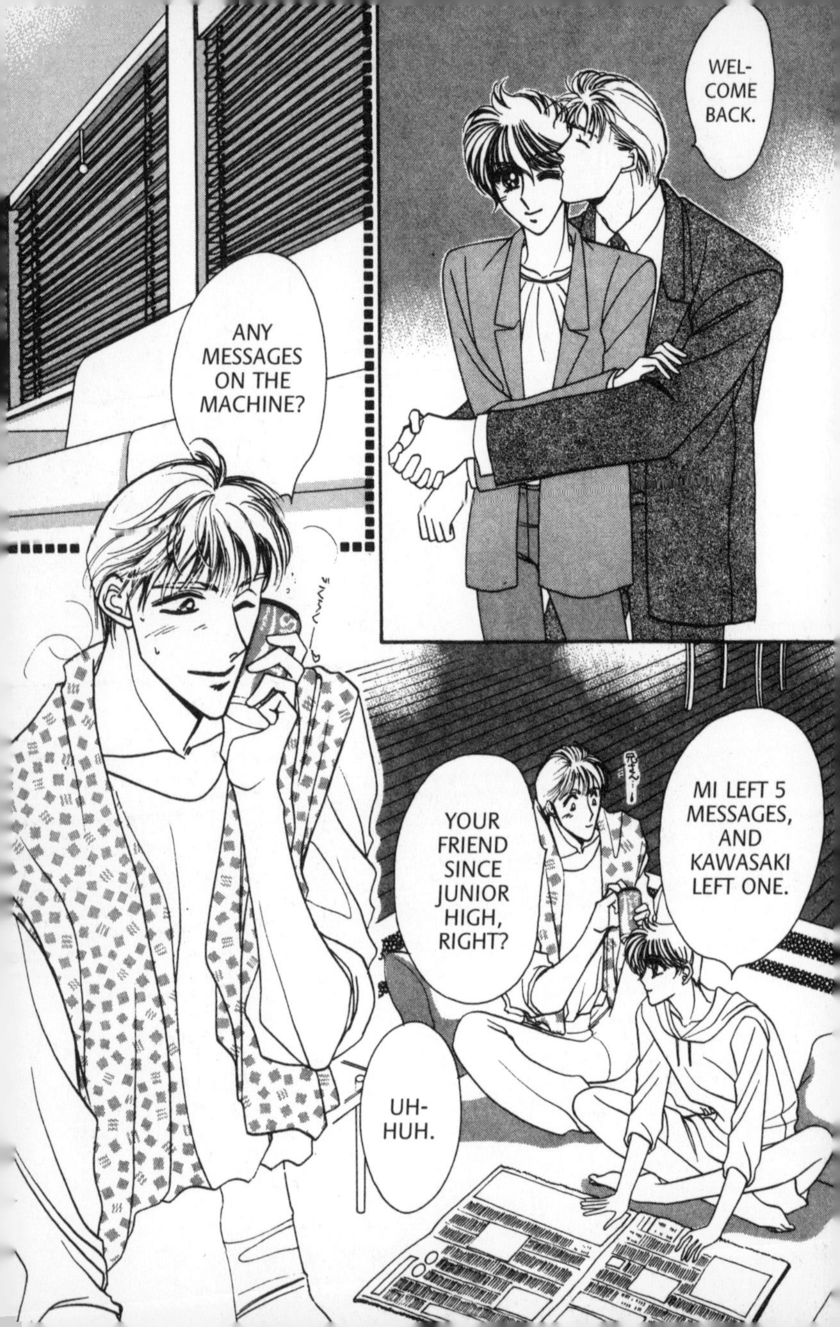
WEL-COME BACK.
ANY MESSAGES ON THE MACHINE?
MI LEFT 5 MESSAGES, AND KAWASAKI LEFT ONE.
YOUR FRIEND SINCE JUNIOR HIGH, RIGHT?
UH-HUH.

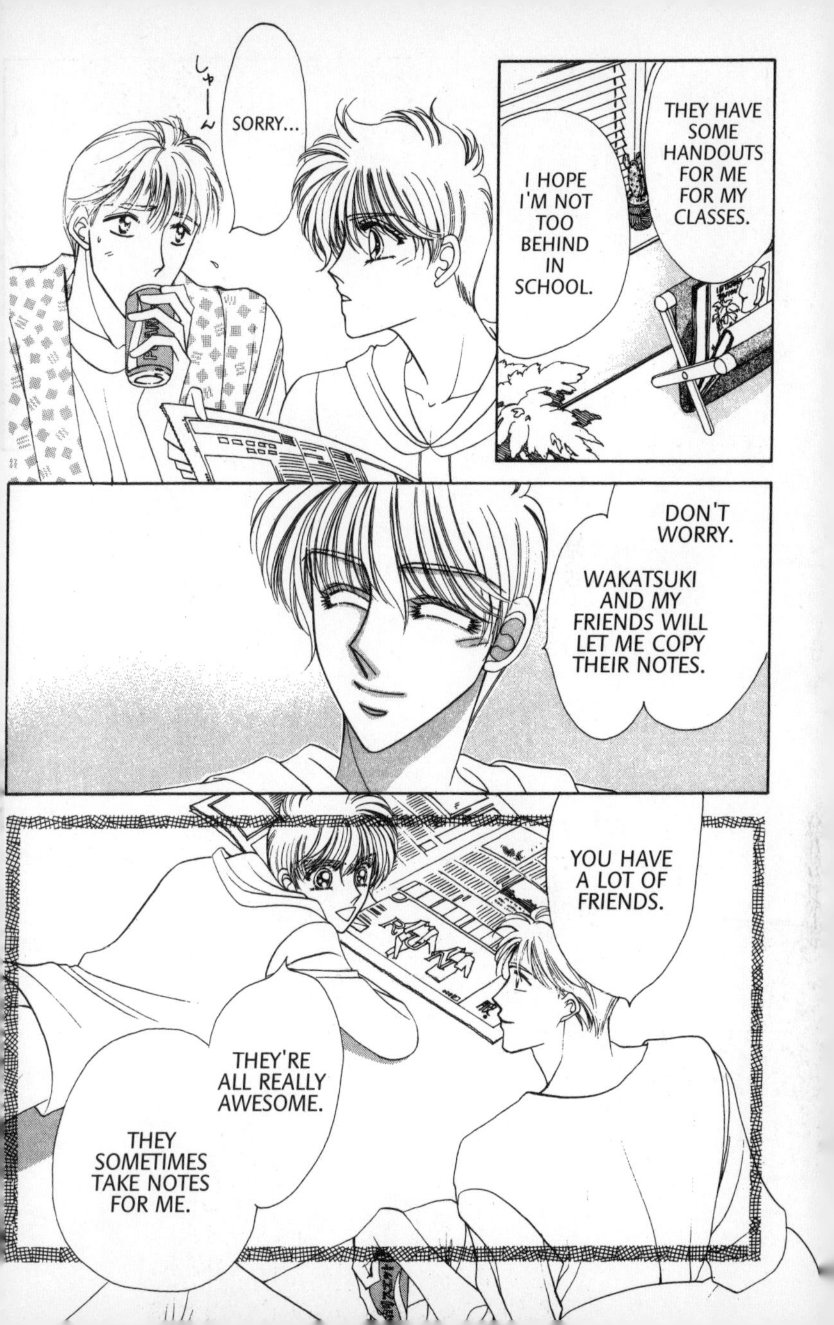
THEY HAVE SOME HANDOUTS FOR ME FOR MY CLASSES.
I HOPE I'M NOT TOO BEHIND IN SCHOOL.
しゃーん
SORRY...
DON'T WORRY.
WAKATSUKI AND MY FRIENDS WILL LET ME COPY THEIR NOTES.
YOU HAVE A LOT OF FRIENDS.
THEY'RE ALL REALLY AWESOME.
THEY SOMETIMES TAKE NOTES FOR ME.

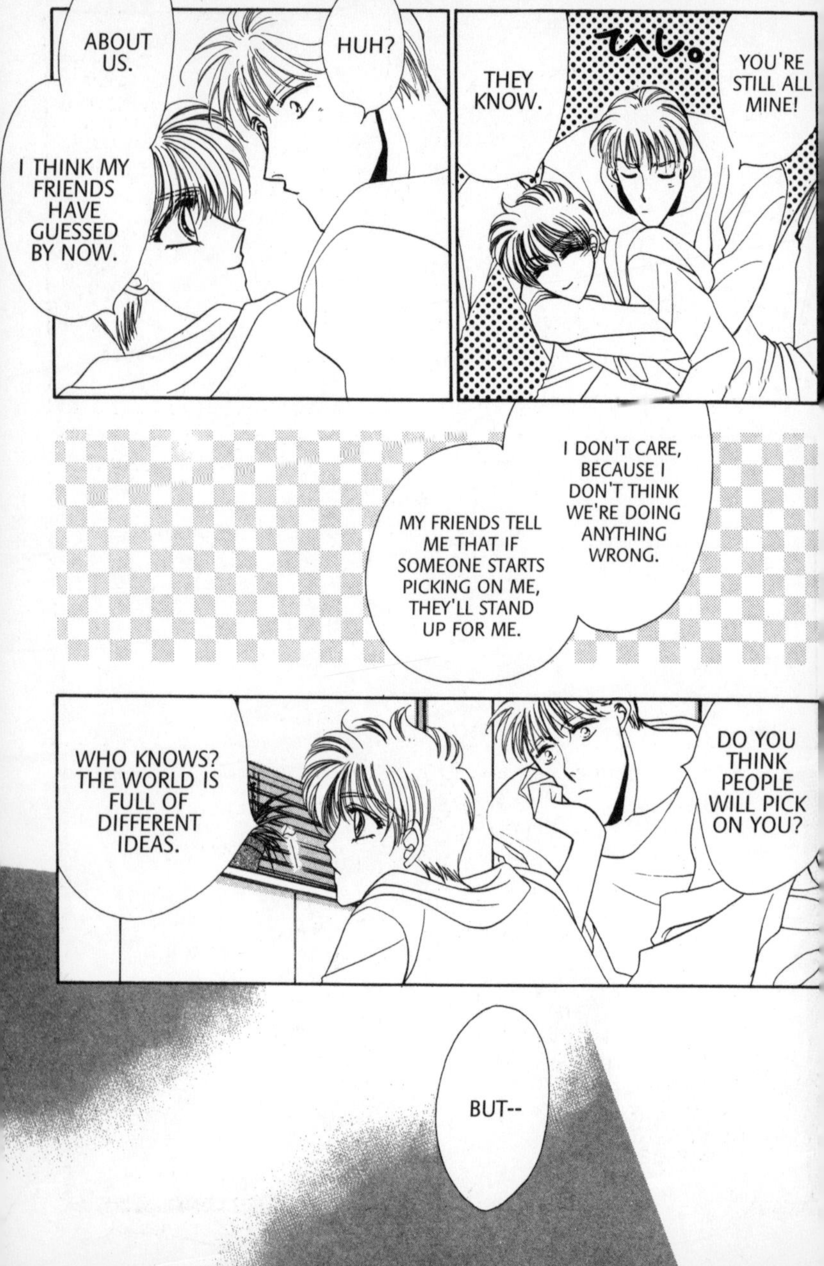
YOU'RE STILL ALL MINE!
ひし。
THEY KNOW.
HUH?
ABOUT US.
I THINK MY FRIENDS HAVE GUESSED BY NOW.
I DON'T CARE, BECAUSE I DON'T THINK WE'RE DOING ANYTHING WRONG.
MY FRIENDS TELL ME THAT IF SOMEONE STARTS PICKING ON ME, THEY'LL STAND UP FOR ME.
DO YOU THINK PEOPLE WILL PICK ON YOU?
WHO KNOWS? THE WORLD IS FULL OF DIFFERENT IDEAS.
BUT--

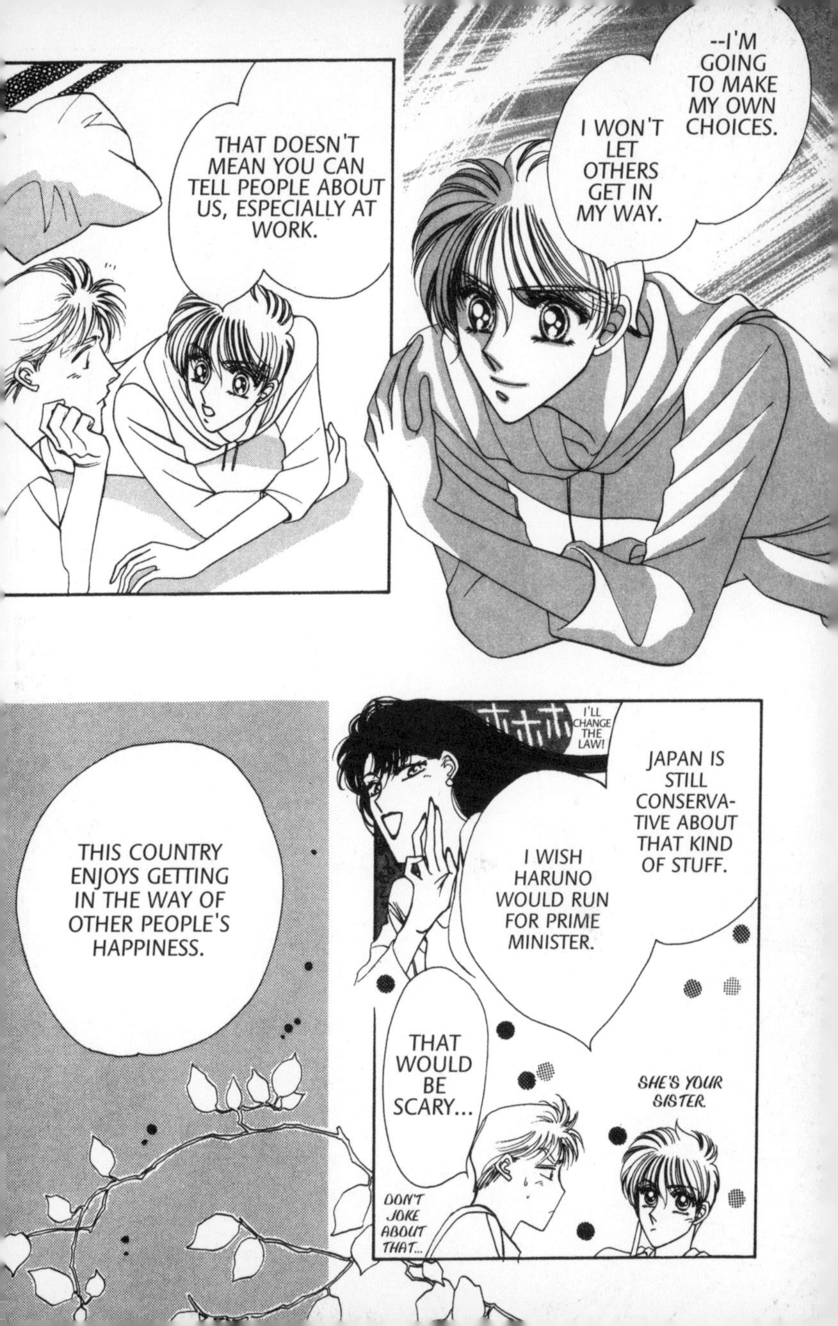
--I'M GOING TO MAKE MY OWN CHOICES.
I WON'T LET OTHERS GET IN MY WAY.
THAT DOESN'T MEAN YOU CAN TELL PEOPLE ABOUT US, ESPECIALLY AT WORK.
I'LL CHANGE THE LAW!
JAPAN IS STILL CONSERVA-TIVE ABOUT THAT KIND OF STUFF.
I WISH HARUNO WOULD RUN FOR PRIME MINISTER.
SHE'S YOUR SISTER.
THAT WOULD BE SCARY...
DON'T JOKE ABOUT THAT...
THIS COUNTRY ENJOYS GETTING IN THE WAY OF OTHER PEOPLE'S HAPPINESS.

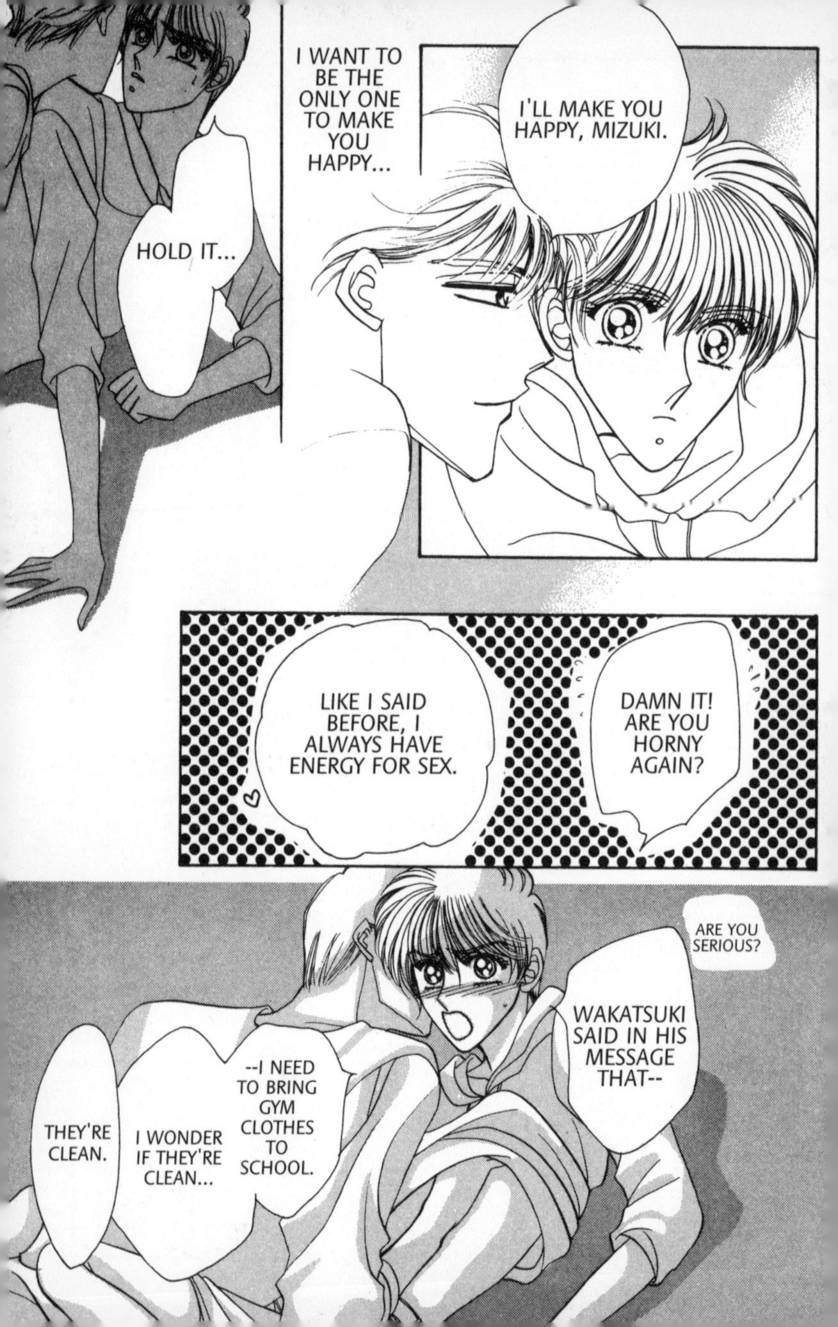
I'LL MAKE YOU HAPPY, MIZUKI.
I WANT TO BE THE ONLY ONE TO MAKE YOU HAPPY...
HOLD IT...
DAMN IT! ARE YOU HORNY AGAIN?
LIKE I SAID BEFORE, I ALWAYS HAVE ENERGY FOR SEX.
ARE YOU SERIOUS?
WAKATSUKI SAID IN HIS MESSAGE THAT--
--I NEED TO BRING GYM CLOTHES TO SCHOOL.
I WONDER IF THEY'RE CLEAN...
THEY'RE CLEAN.

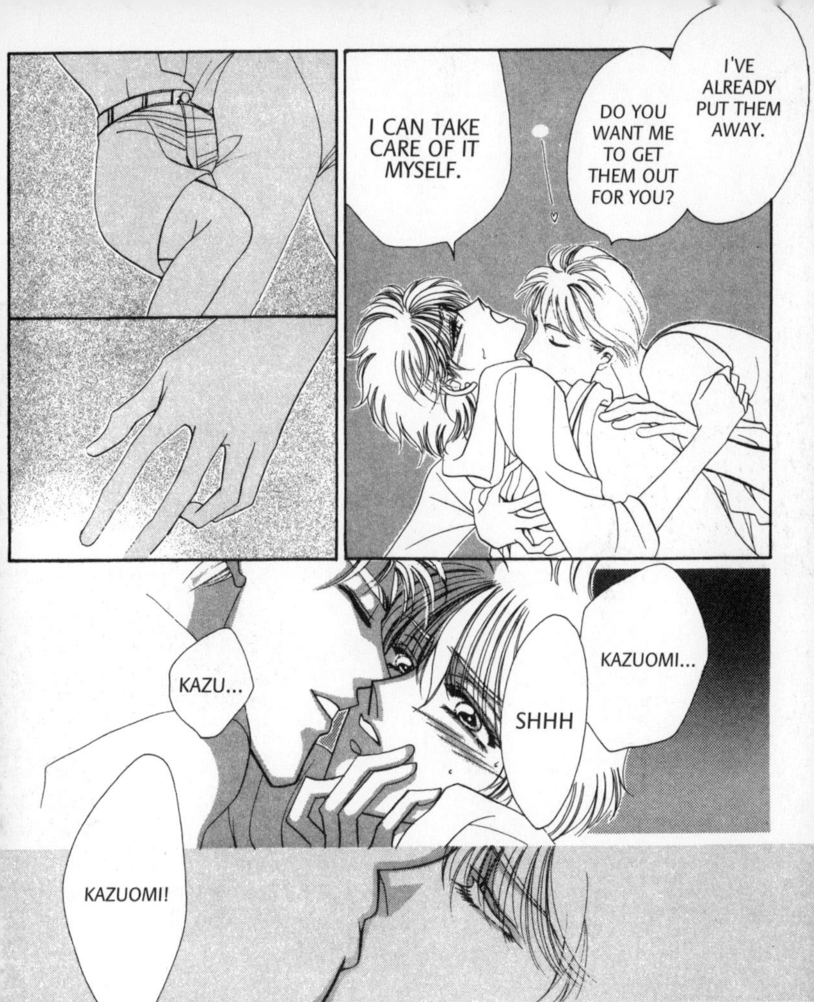
I'VE ALREADY PUT THEM AWAY.
DO YOU WANT ME TO GET THEM OUT FOR YOU?
I CAN TAKE CARE OF IT MYSELF.
KAZUOMI...
SHHH
KAZU...
KAZUOMI!

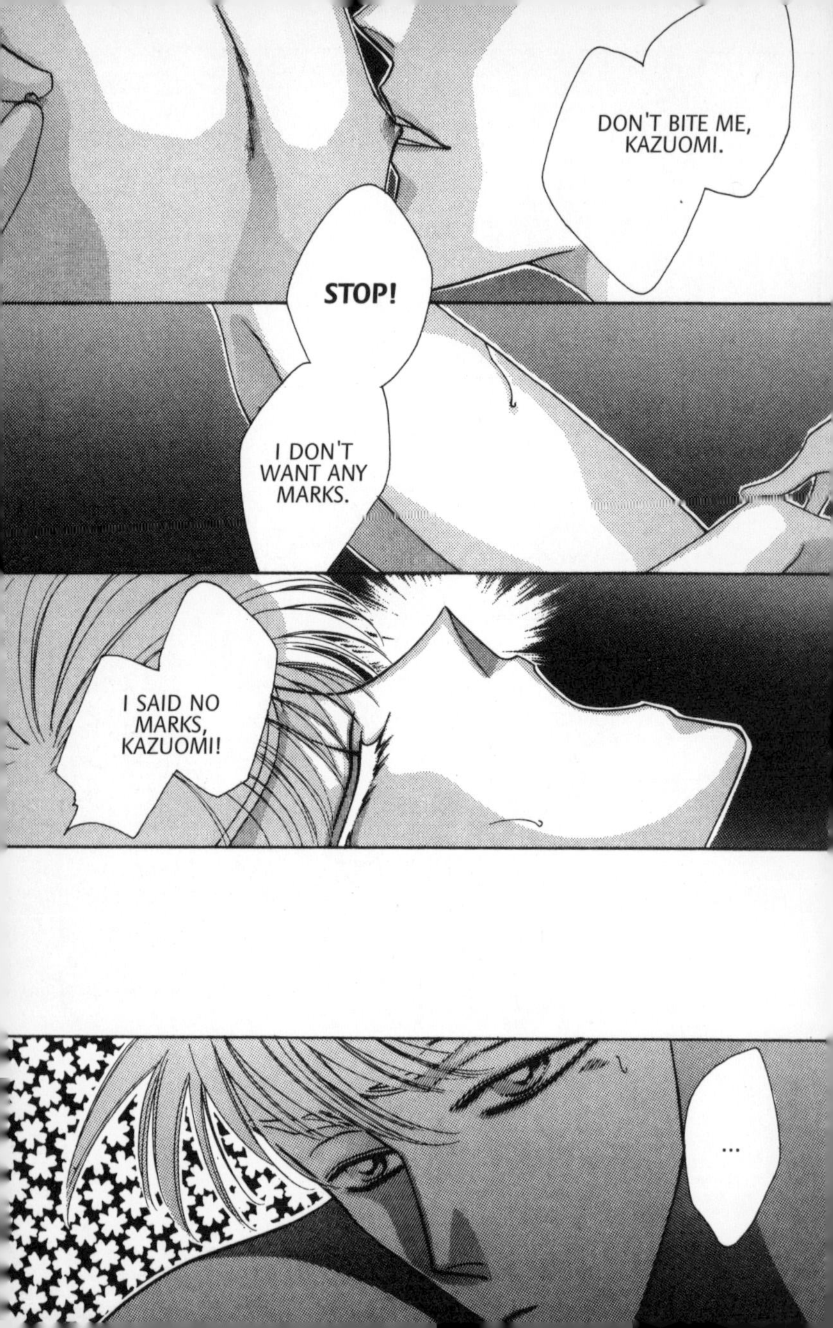
DON'T BITE ME, KAZUOMI.
STOP!
I DON'T WANT ANY MARKS.
I SAID NO MARKS, KAZUOMI!
...

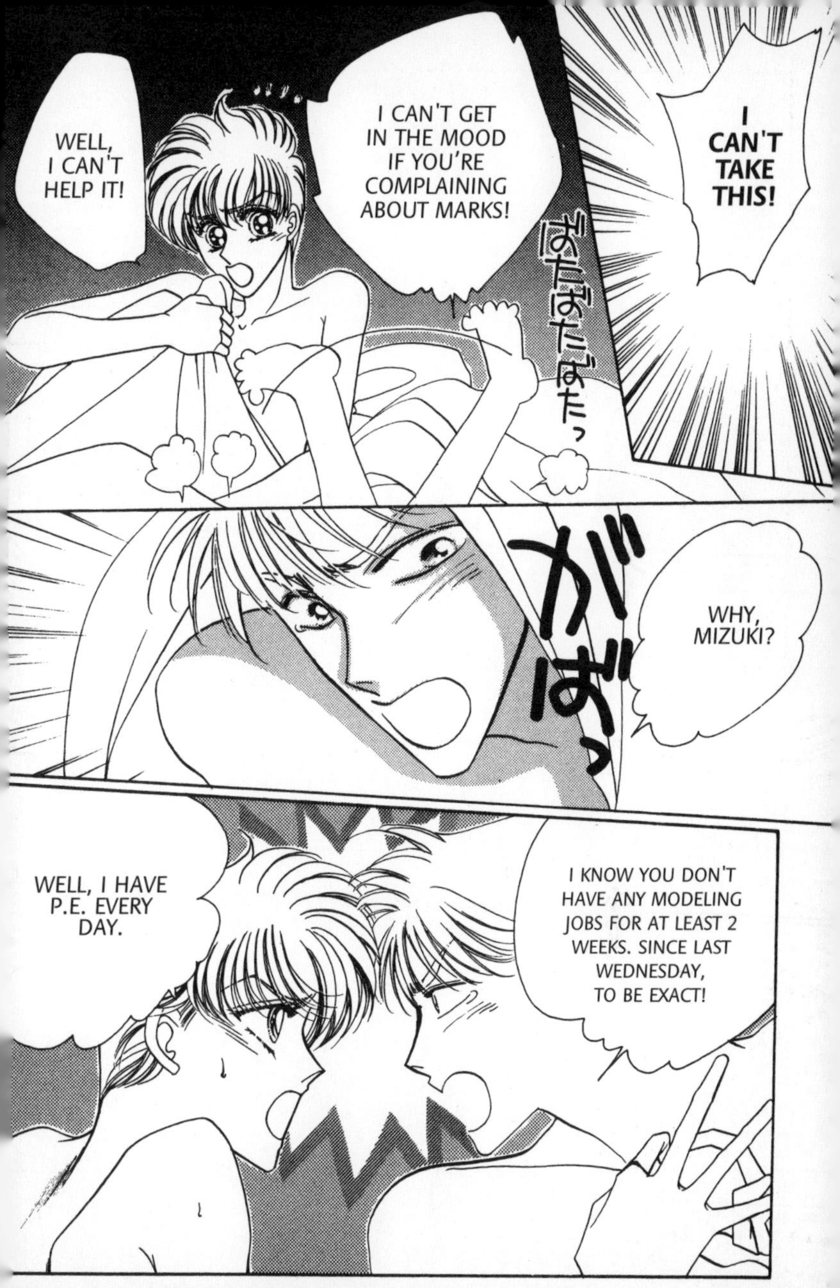
I CAN'T TAKE THIS!
I CAN'T GET IN THE MOOD IF YOU'RE COMPLAINING ABOUT MARKS!
ぱたぱたぱたっ
WELL, I CAN'T HELP IT!
WHY, MIZUKI?
がばっ
I KNOW YOU DON'T HAVE ANY MODELING JOBS FOR AT LEAST 2 WEEKS. SINCE LAST WEDNESDAY, TO BE EXACT!
WELL, I HAVE P.E. EVERY DAY.

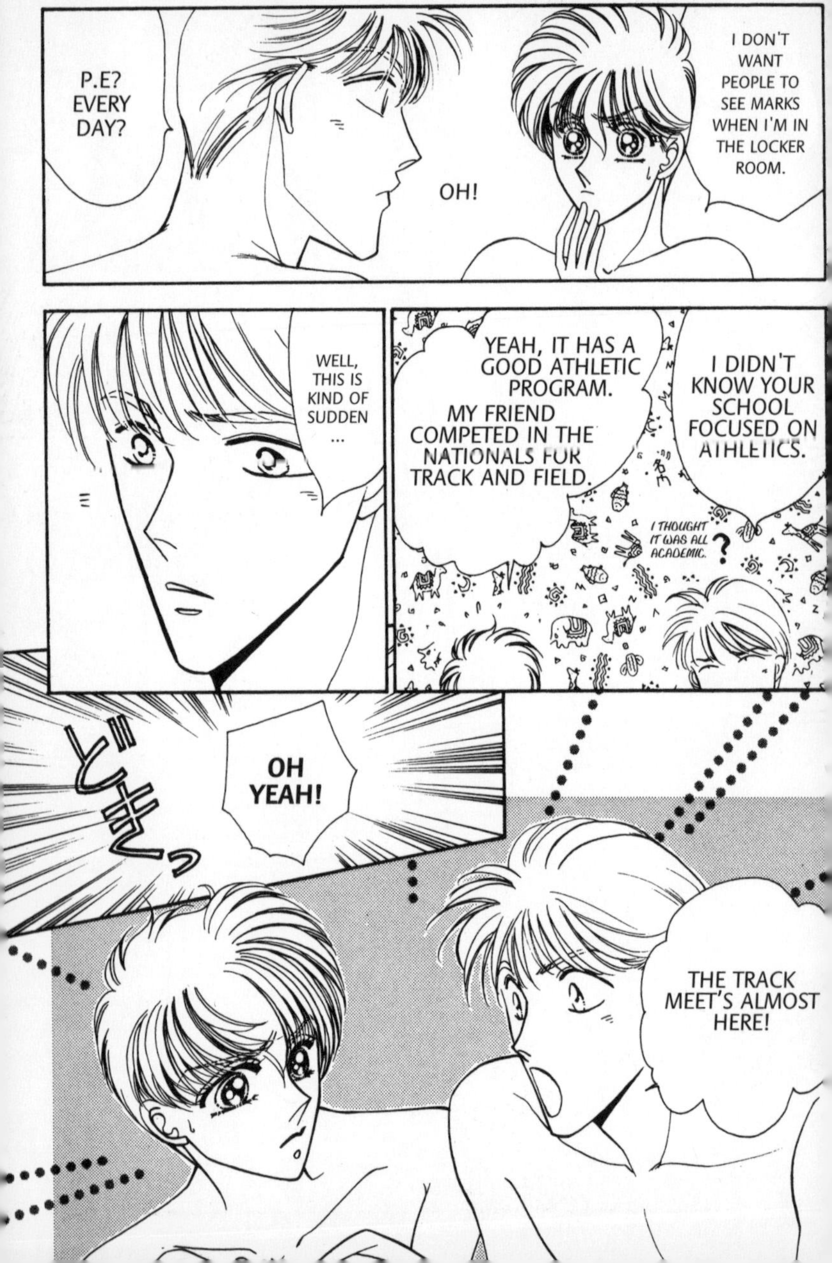
I DON'T WANT PEOPLE TO SEE MARKS WHEN I'M IN THE LOCKER ROOM.
OH!
P.E? EVERY DAY?
I DIDN'T KNOW YOUR SCHOOL FOCUSED ON ATHLETICS.
YEAH, IT HAS A GOOD ATHLETIC PROGRAM.
MY FRIEND COMPETED IN THE NATIONALS FOR TRACK AND FIELD.
I THOUGHT IT WAS ALL ACADEMIC.
?
WELL, THIS IS KIND OF SUDDEN ...
THE TRACK MEET'S ALMOST HERE!
どきっ
OH YEAH!

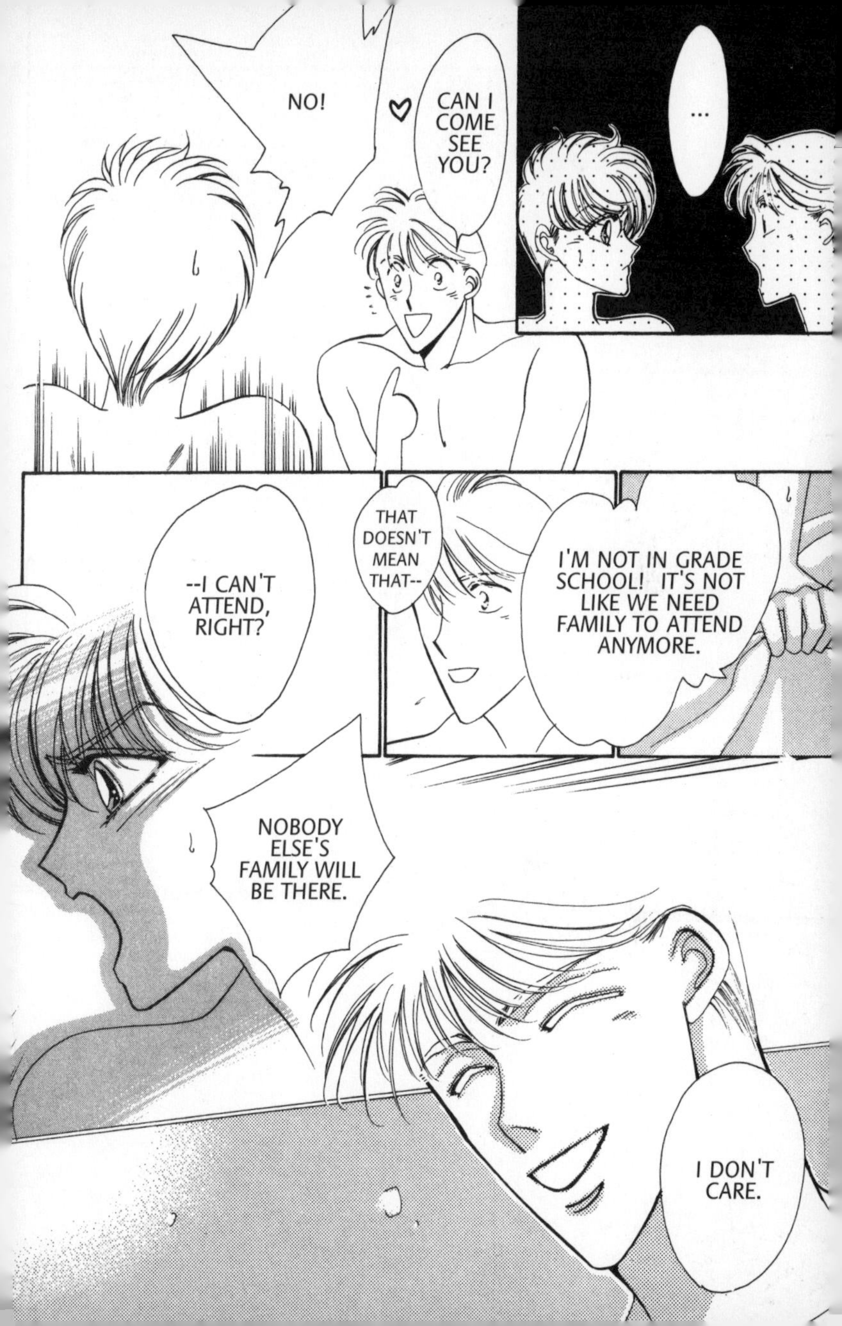
...
CAN I COME SEE YOU?
NO!
I'M NOT IN GRADE SCHOOL! IT'S NOT LIKE WE NEED FAMILY TO ATTEND ANYMORE.
THAT DOESN'T MEAN THAT--
--I CAN'T ATTEND, RIGHT?
NOBODY ELSE'S FAMILY WILL BE THERE.
I DON'T CARE.

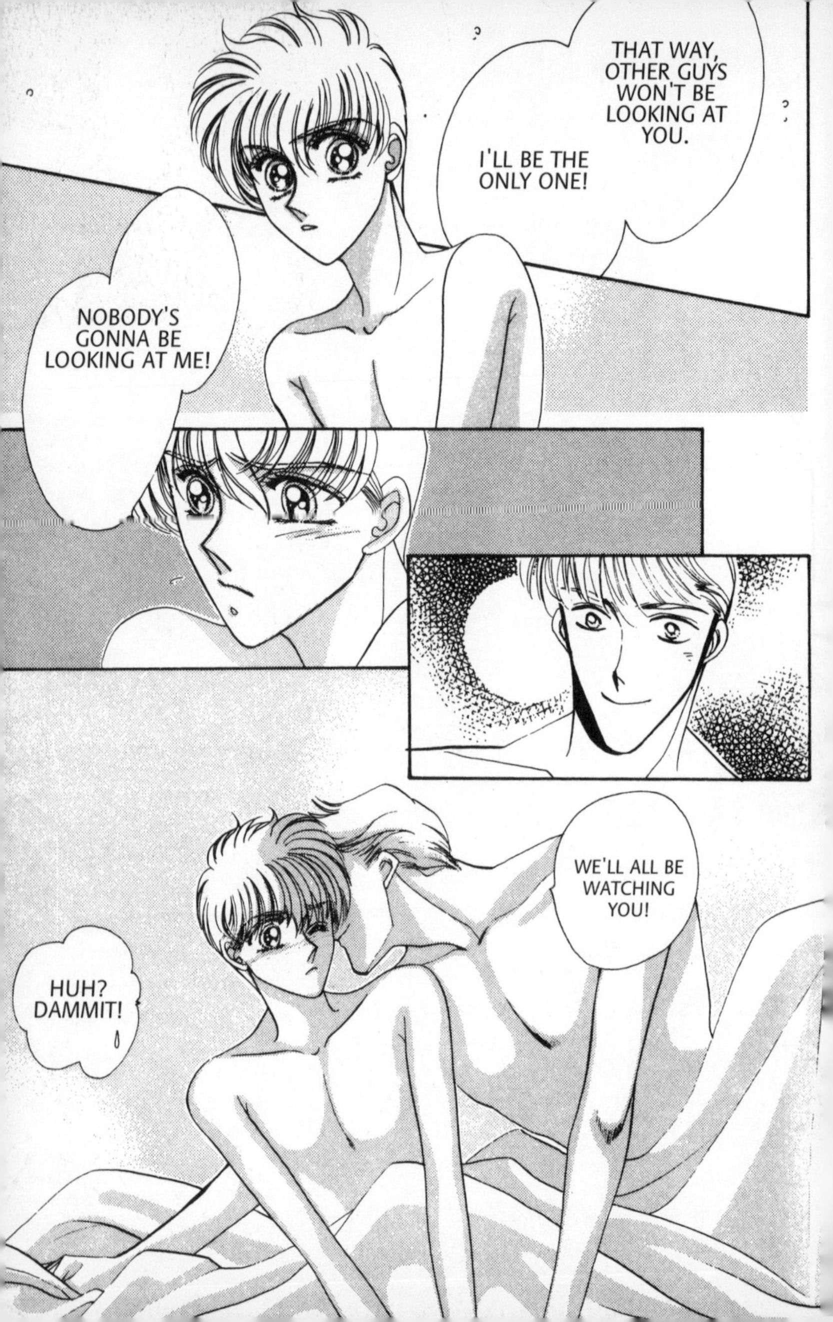
THAT WAY, OTHER GUYS WON'T BE LOOKING AT YOU.
I'LL BE THE ONLY ONE!
NOBODY'S GONNA BE LOOKING AT ME!
WE'LL ALL BE WATCHING YOU!
HUH? DAMMIT!

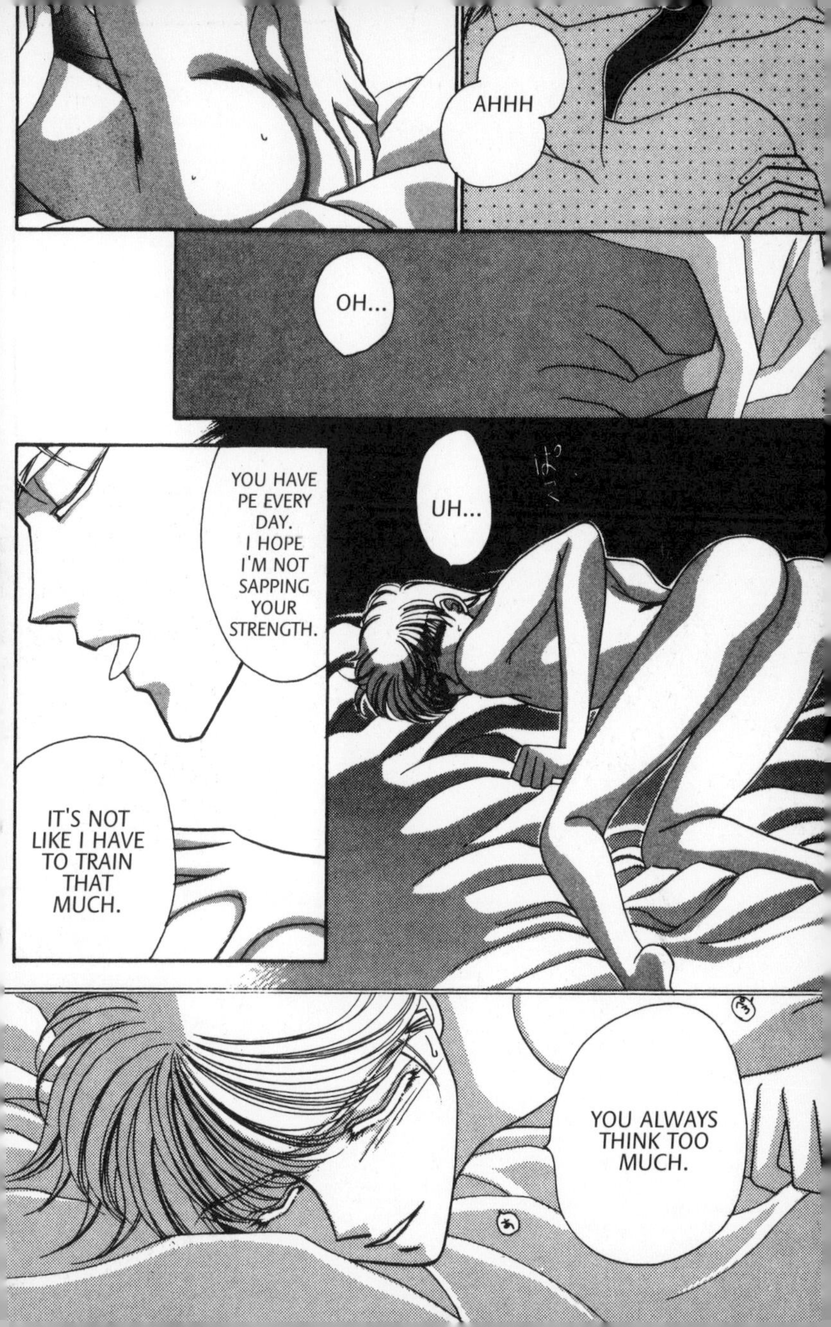
AHHH
OH...
UH...
YOU HAVE PE EVERY DAY. I HOPE I'M NOT SAPPING YOUR STRENGTH.
IT'S NOT LIKE I HAVE TO TRAIN THAT MUCH.
YOU ALWAYS THINK TOO MUCH.

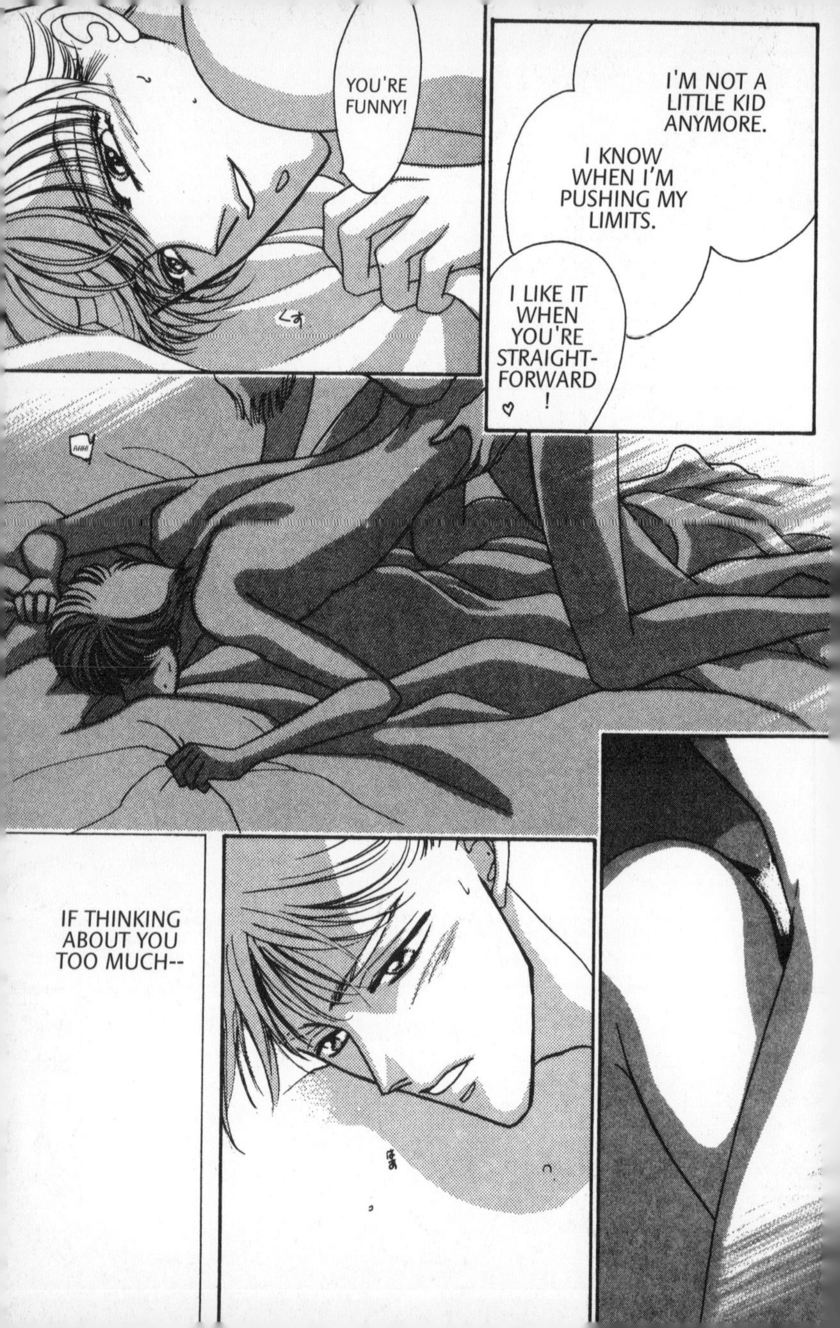
I'M NOT A LITTLE KID ANYMORE.
I KNOW WHEN I'M PUSHING MY LIMITS.
I LIKE IT WHEN YOU'RE STRAIGHT-FORWARD ♡ !
YOU'RE FUNNY!
IF THINKING ABOUT YOU TOO MUCH--

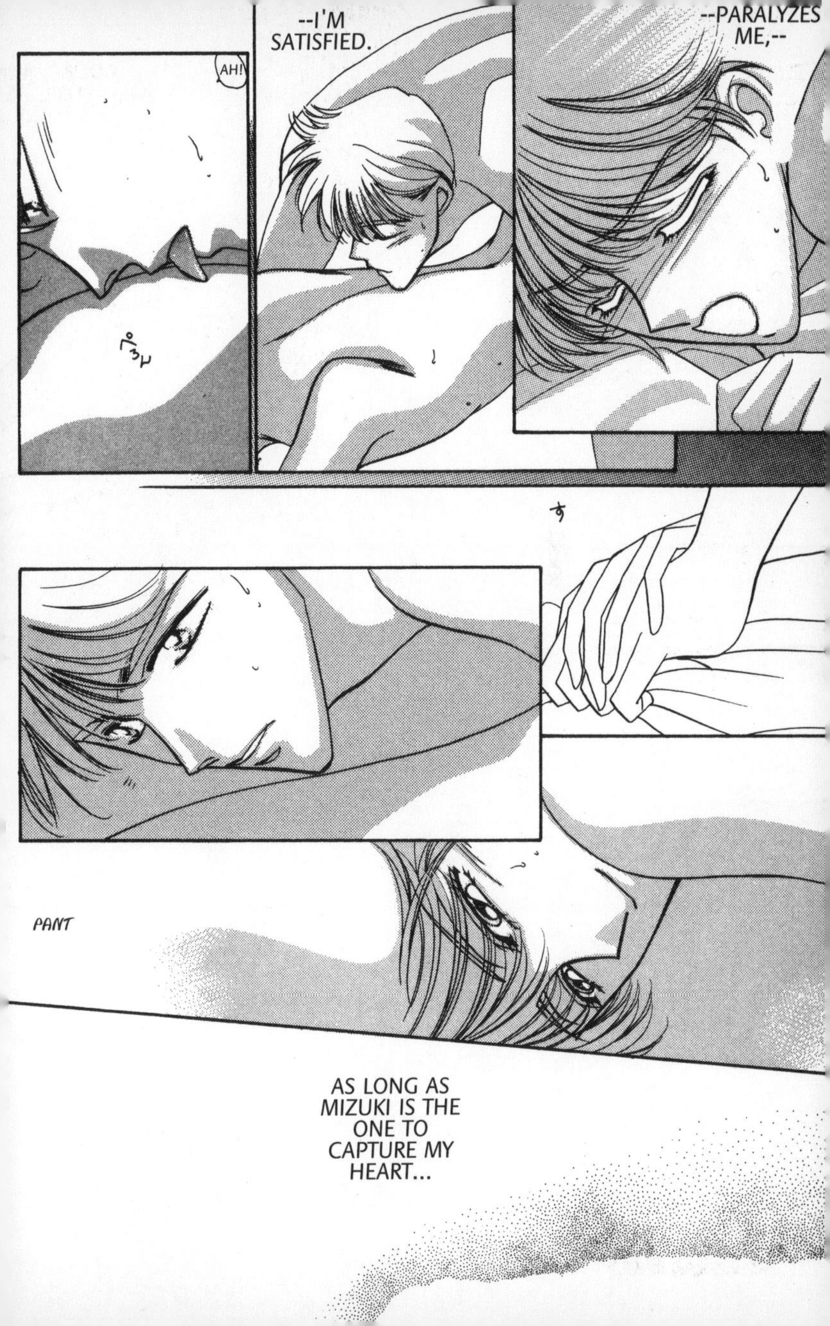
--PARALYZES ME,--
--I'M SATISFIED.
AH!
す
PANT
AS LONG AS MIZUKI IS THE ONE TO CAPTURE MY HEART...

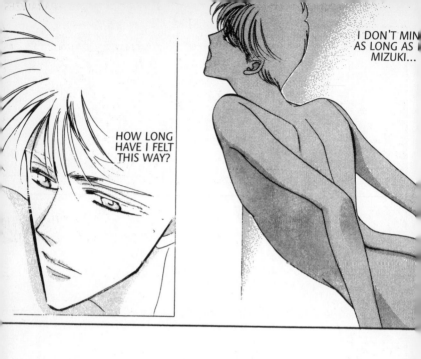

I DON'T MIND
AS LONG AS
MIZUKI...

HOW LONG
HAVE I FELT
THIS WAY?

FOR A LONG
TIME...

LEVEL-C END

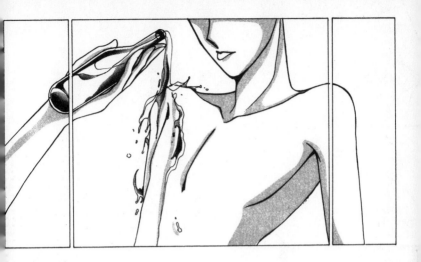

WHEN VOLUME 1 WAS RELEASED, I DIDN'T THINK THAT THIS SERIES WOULD CONTINUE! WELL, HERE'S TO VOLUME 2 (GIGGLE). I FIGURED I WOULD CONTINUE THIS SERIES ON MY OWN IN A DOUJINSHI, AND I ACTUALLY RELEASED SEVERAL EPISODES IN A DOUJINSHI. AS A RESULT, THERE ARE TWO VERSIONS OF LEVEL C PROGRESSING AT THE SAME TIME, THE COMMERCIAL AND THE DOUJINSHI VERSION. I THINK AT THIS POINT, I FEEL THAT THE STORY HAS A SOLID DIRECTION, COMPARATIVELY SPEAKING. THIS SERIES LOOKS LIKE IT'S STILL GOING STRONG, SO I APPRECIATE YOUR SUPPORT!

COMMENT. 1

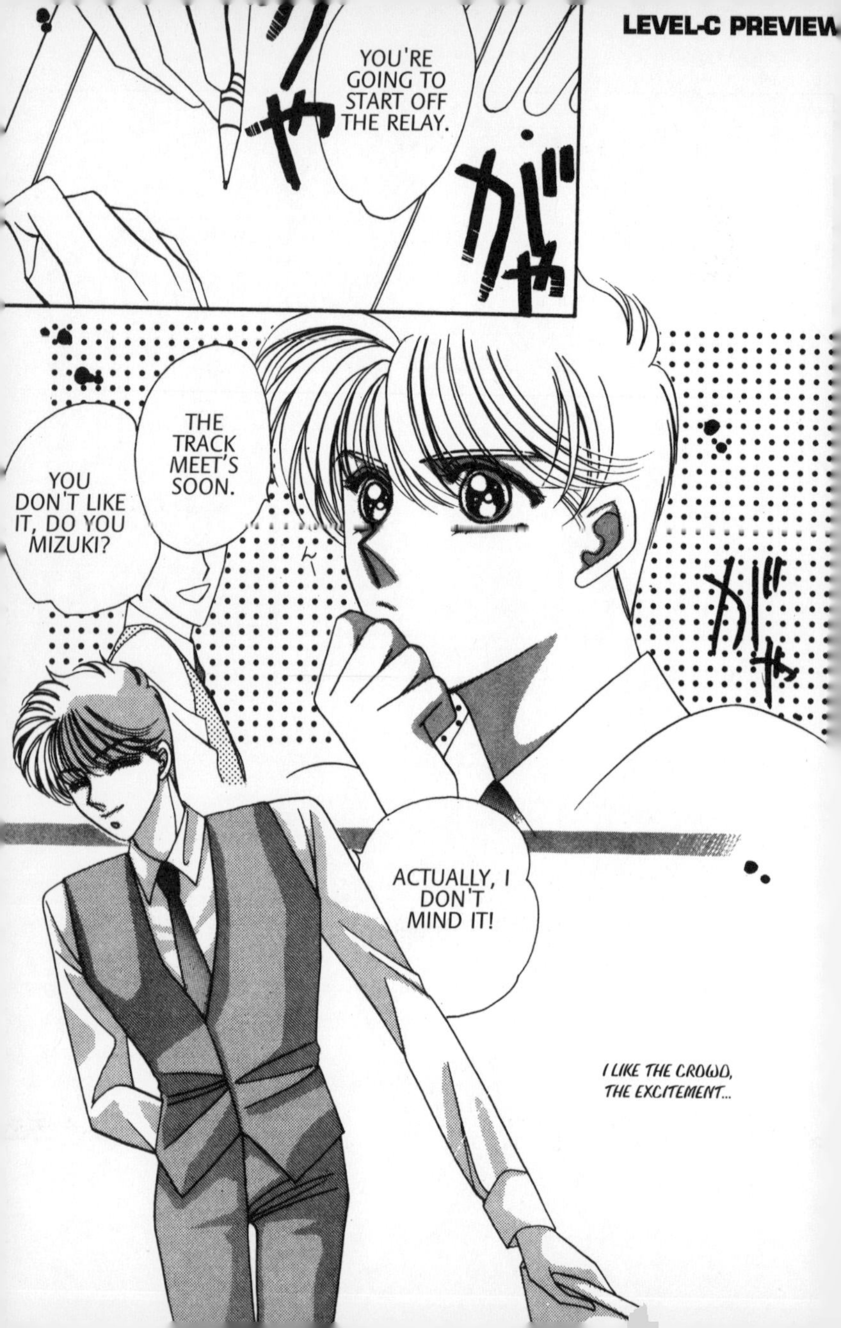
YOU'RE GOING TO START OFF THE RELAY.
THE TRACK MEET'S SOON.
YOU DON'T LIKE IT, DO YOU MIZUKI?
ACTUALLY, I DON'T MIND IT!
I LIKE THE CROWD, THE EXCITEMENT...

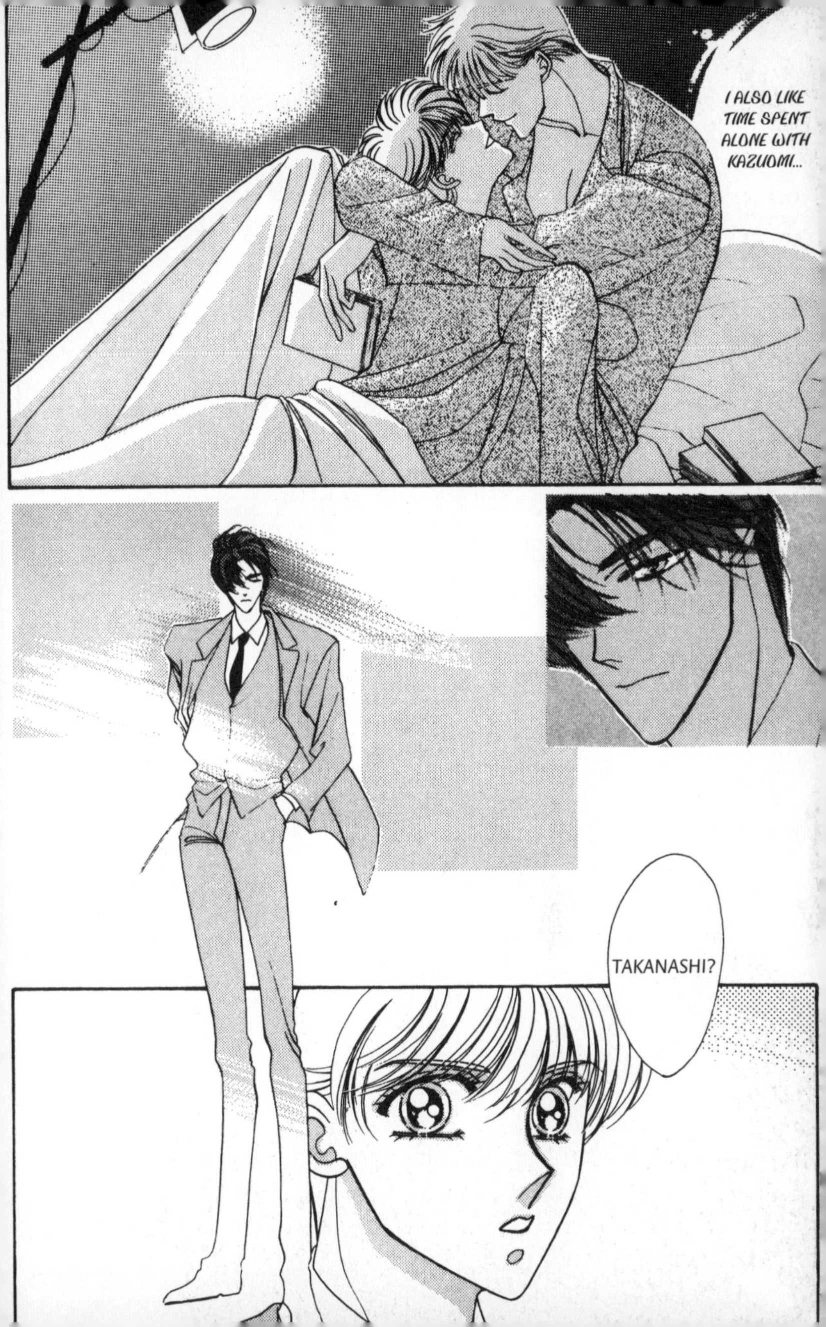
I ALSO LIKE TIME SPENT ALONE WITH KAZUOMI...
TAKANASHI?

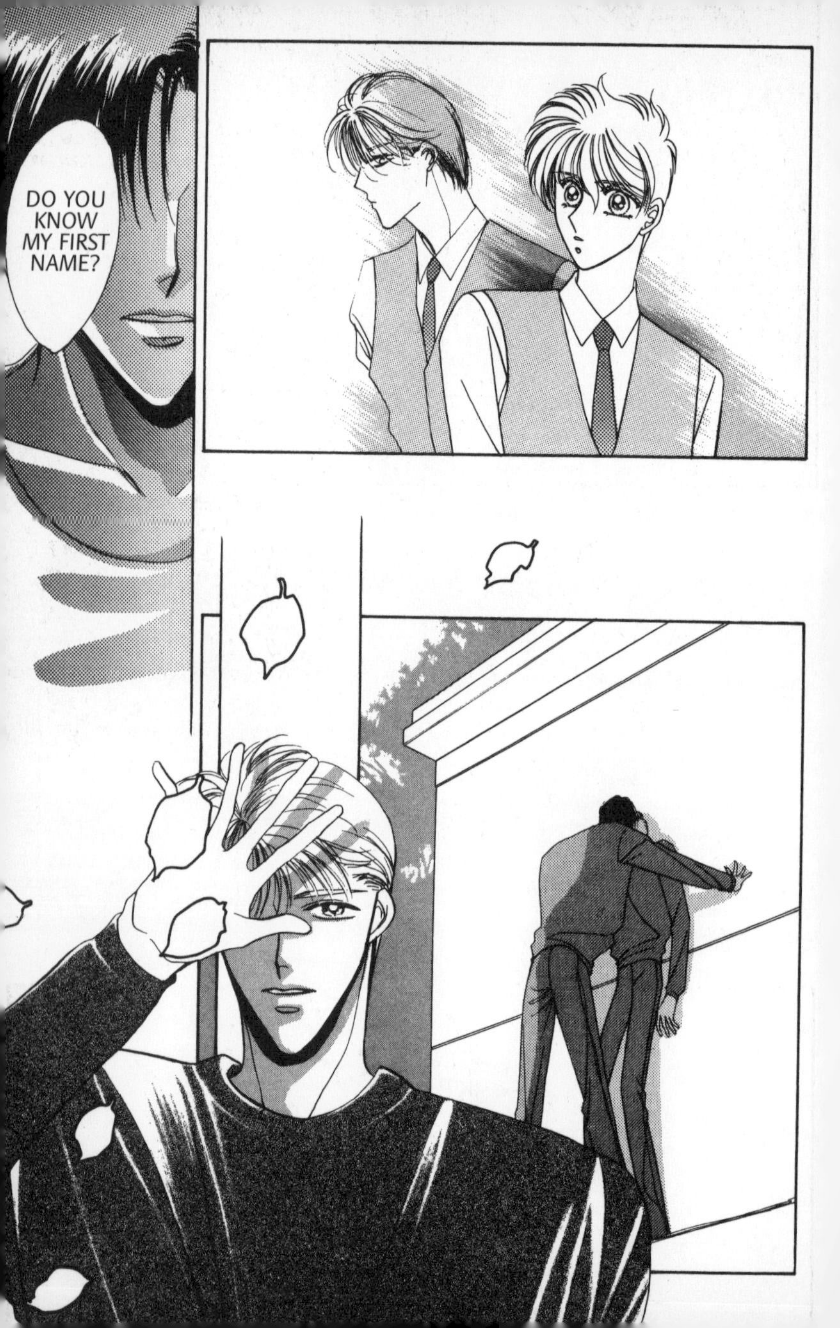
DO YOU KNOW MY FIRST NAME?

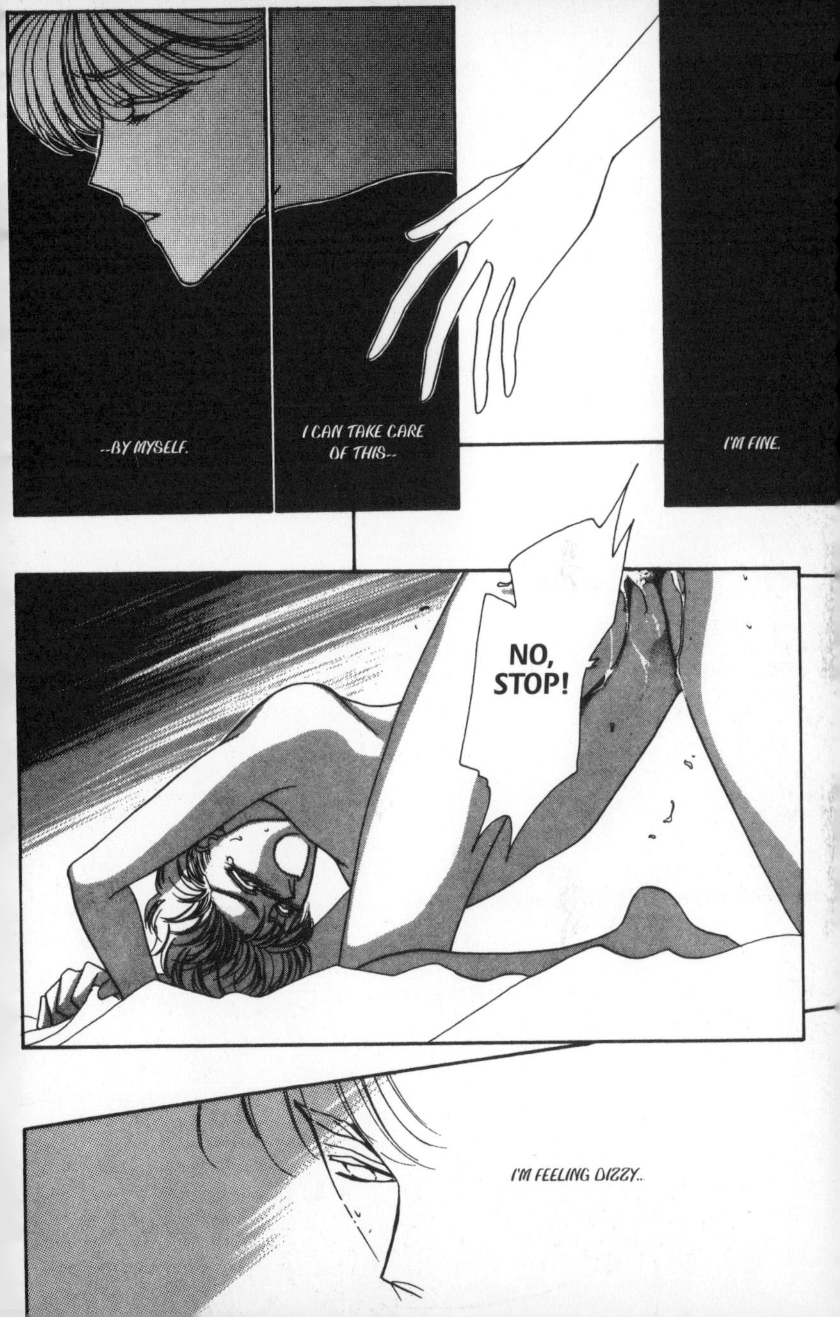
I'M FINE.
I CAN TAKE CARE OF THIS--
--BY MYSELF.
NO, STOP!
I'M FEELING DIZZY..

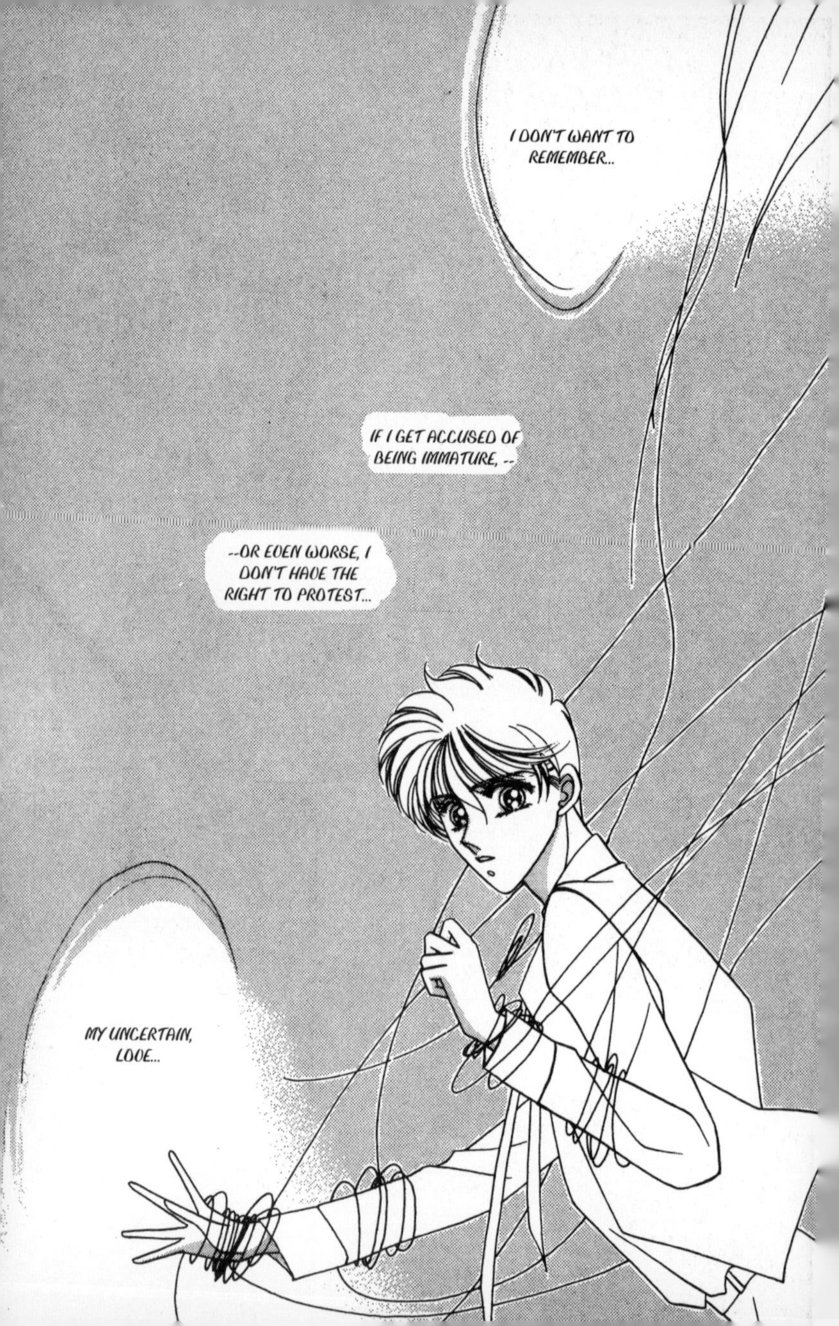
I DON'T WANT TO REMEMBER...
IF I GET ACCUSED OF BEING IMMATURE, --
--OR EVEN WORSE, I DON'T HAVE THE RIGHT TO PROTEST...
MY UNCERTAIN, LOVE...

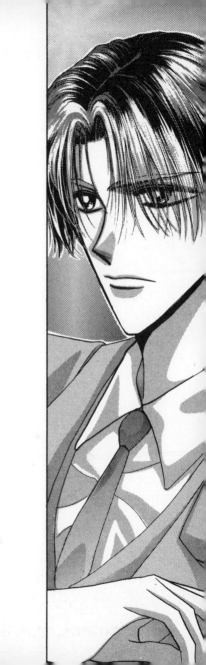

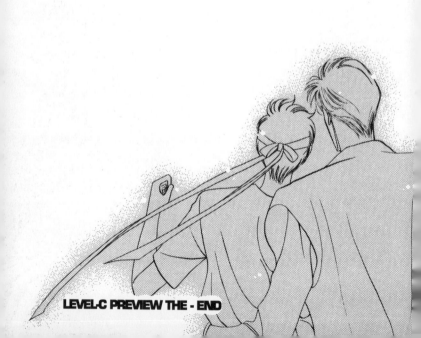

LEVEL-C PREVIEW THE - END

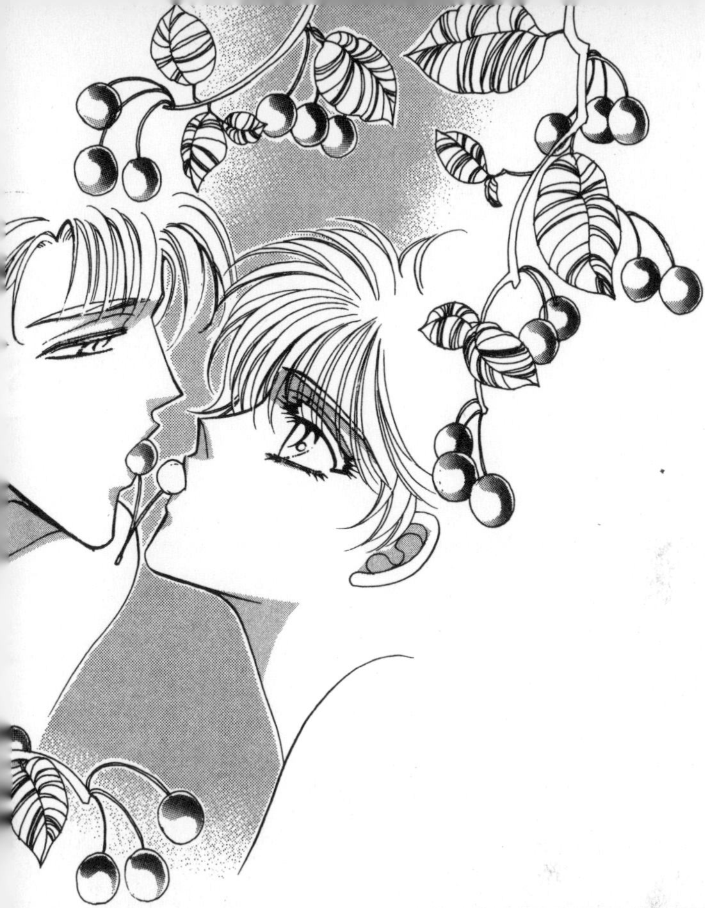

COMMENT.2

IN THIS VOLUME, THERE IS A STORY THAT I BORROWED FROM MY ROUGH DRAFT FOR THE DOUJINSHI VERSION. (IT'S NOT "SUMMER VACATION." THAT'S A BONUS FOR YOU GUYS!) I WAS RELUCTANT ABOUT IT, BUT IT IS MY RESPONSIBILITY. I APOLOGIZE. WE WILL REMEMBER THIS, AND WE WILL VOW TO FOCUS EVERY DAY (LAUGH)! (THIS TIME, I'D LIKE TO THANK MR. YOSHIDA, MY EDITOR AND PRINTING DEPARTMENT. THANK YOU SO MUCH FOR PUTTING UP WITH ME!)

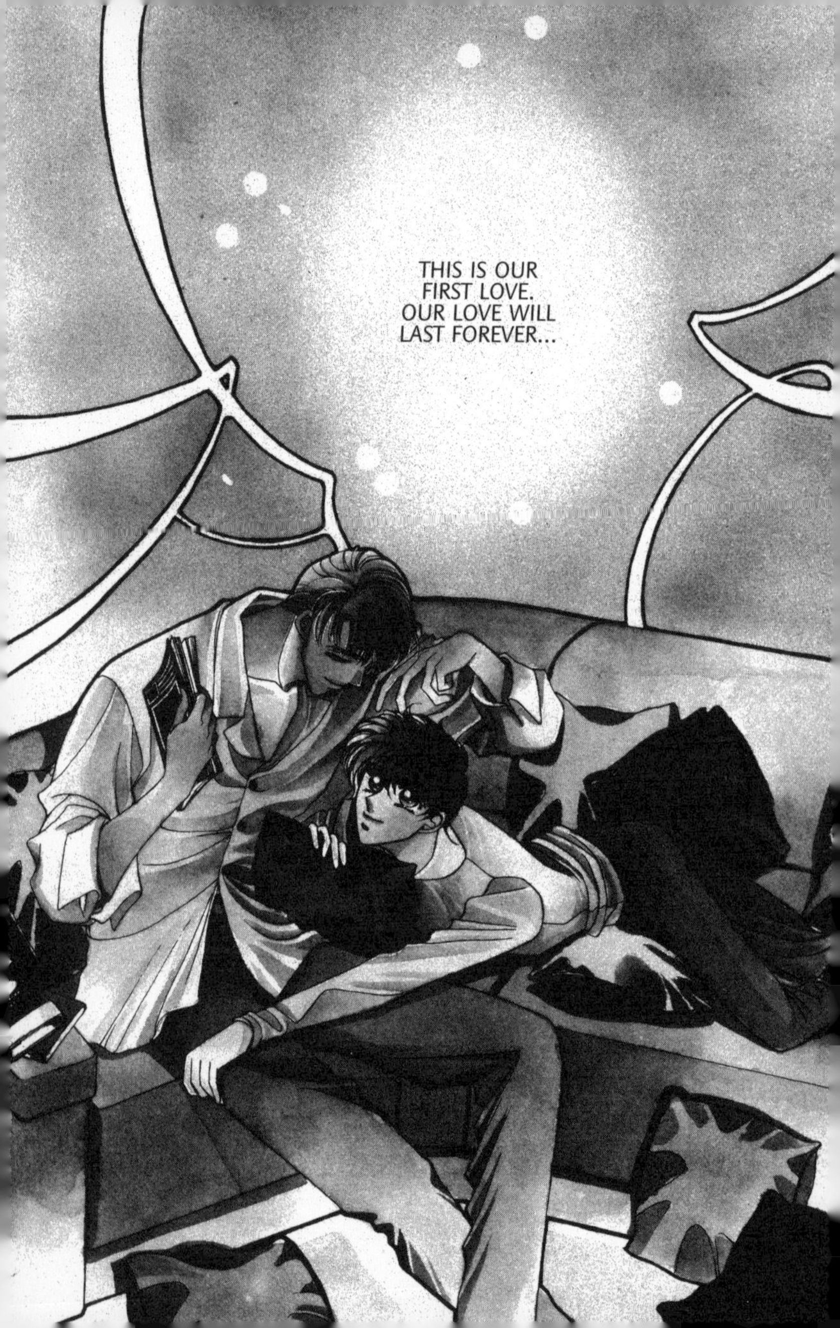
THIS IS OUR FIRST LOVE. OUR LOVE WILL LAST FOREVER...

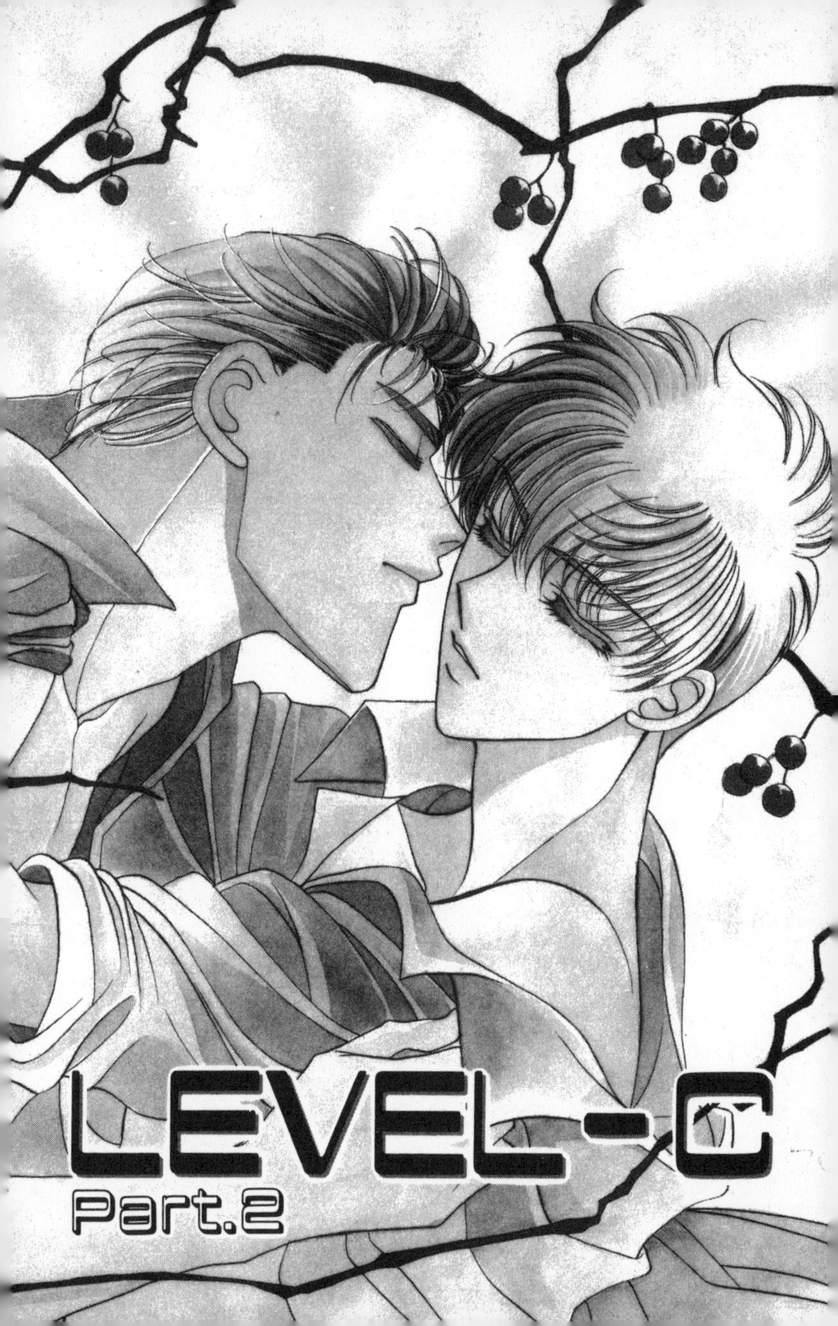
LEVEL-C
Part.2

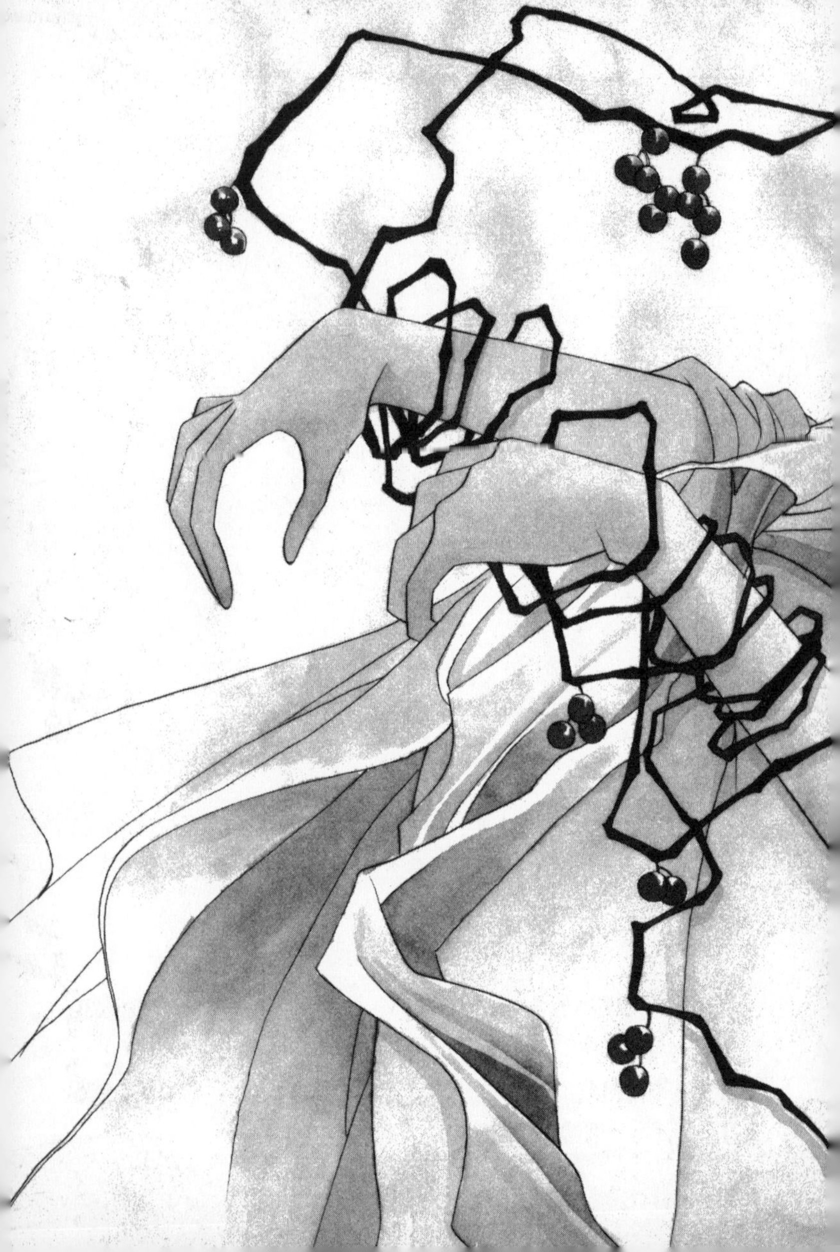

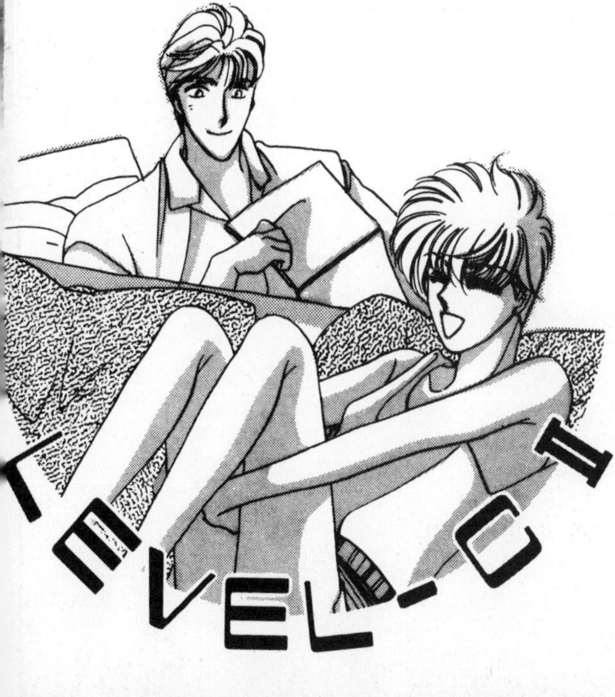
LEVEL-C II

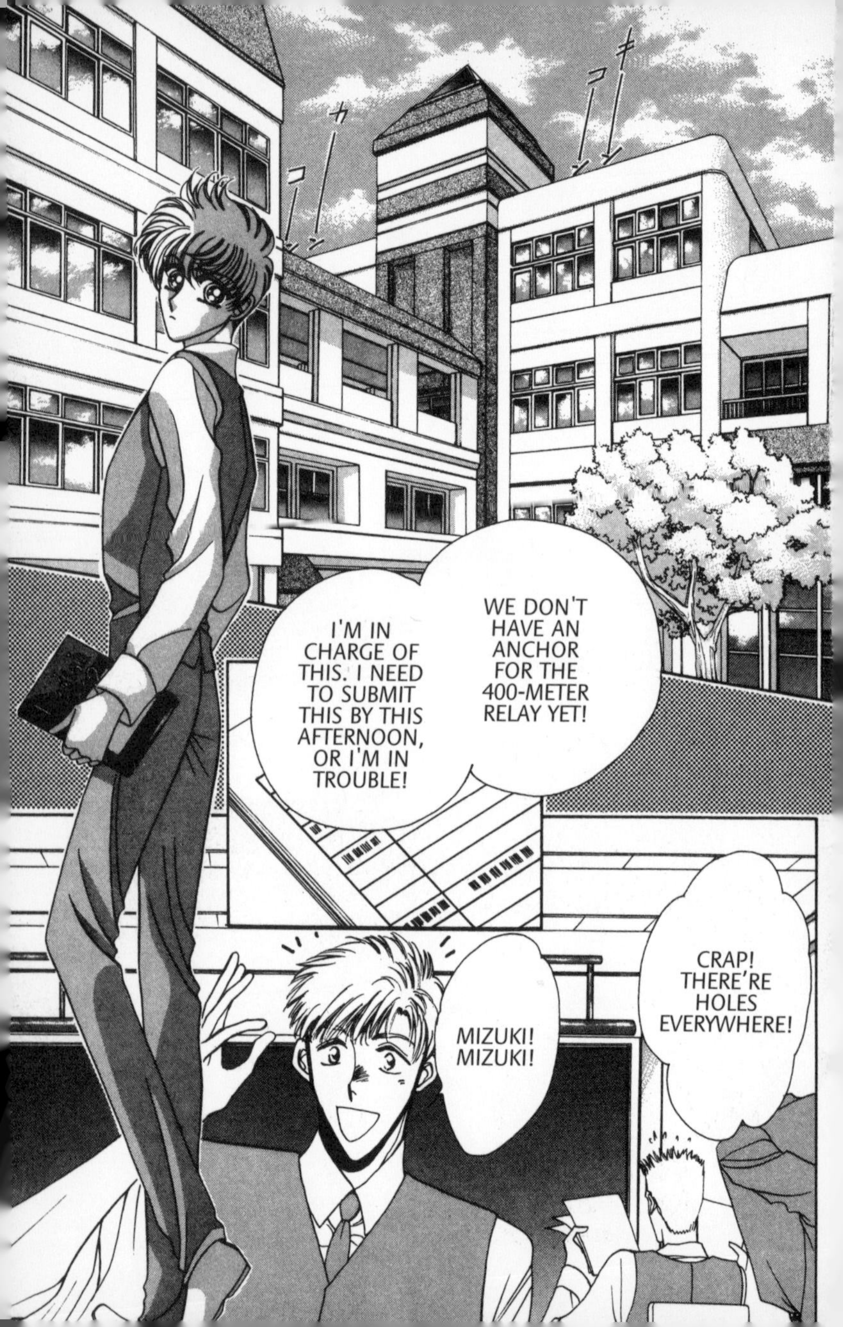
WE DON'T HAVE AN ANCHOR FOR THE 400-METER RELAY YET!
I'M IN CHARGE OF THIS. I NEED TO SUBMIT THIS BY THIS AFTERNOON, OR I'M IN TROUBLE!
CRAP! THERE'RE HOLES EVERYWHERE!
MIZUKI! MIZUKI!

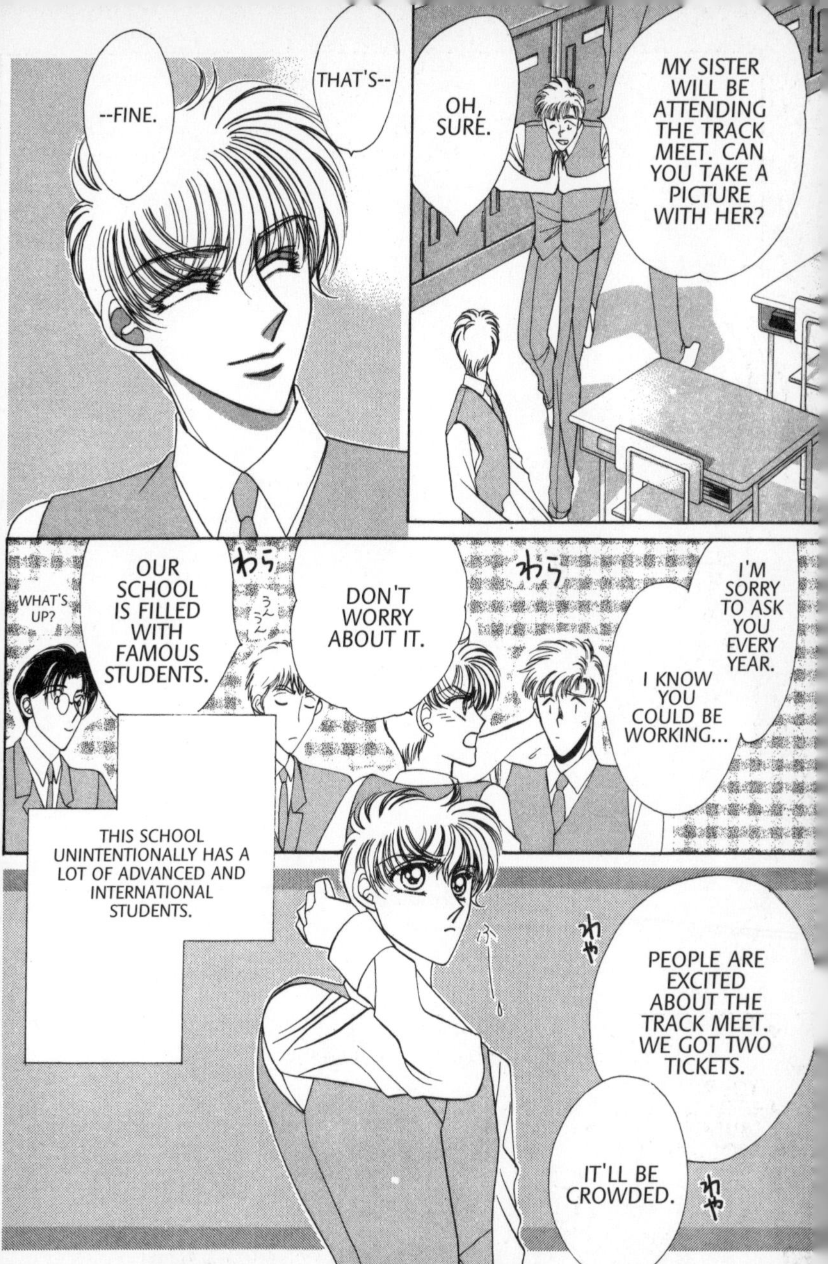

MY SISTER WILL BE ATTENDING THE TRACK MEET. CAN YOU TAKE A PICTURE WITH HER?
OH, SURE.
THAT'S--
--FINE.
I'M SORRY TO ASK YOU EVERY YEAR.
I KNOW YOU COULD BE WORKING...
わら
DON'T WORRY ABOUT IT.
わら
OUR SCHOOL IS FILLED WITH FAMOUS STUDENTS.
WHAT'S UP?
わや
PEOPLE ARE EXCITED ABOUT THE TRACK MEET. WE GOT TWO TICKETS.
IT'LL BE CROWDED.
わや
THIS SCHOOL UNINTENTIONALLY HAS A LOT OF ADVANCED AND INTERNATIONAL STUDENTS.

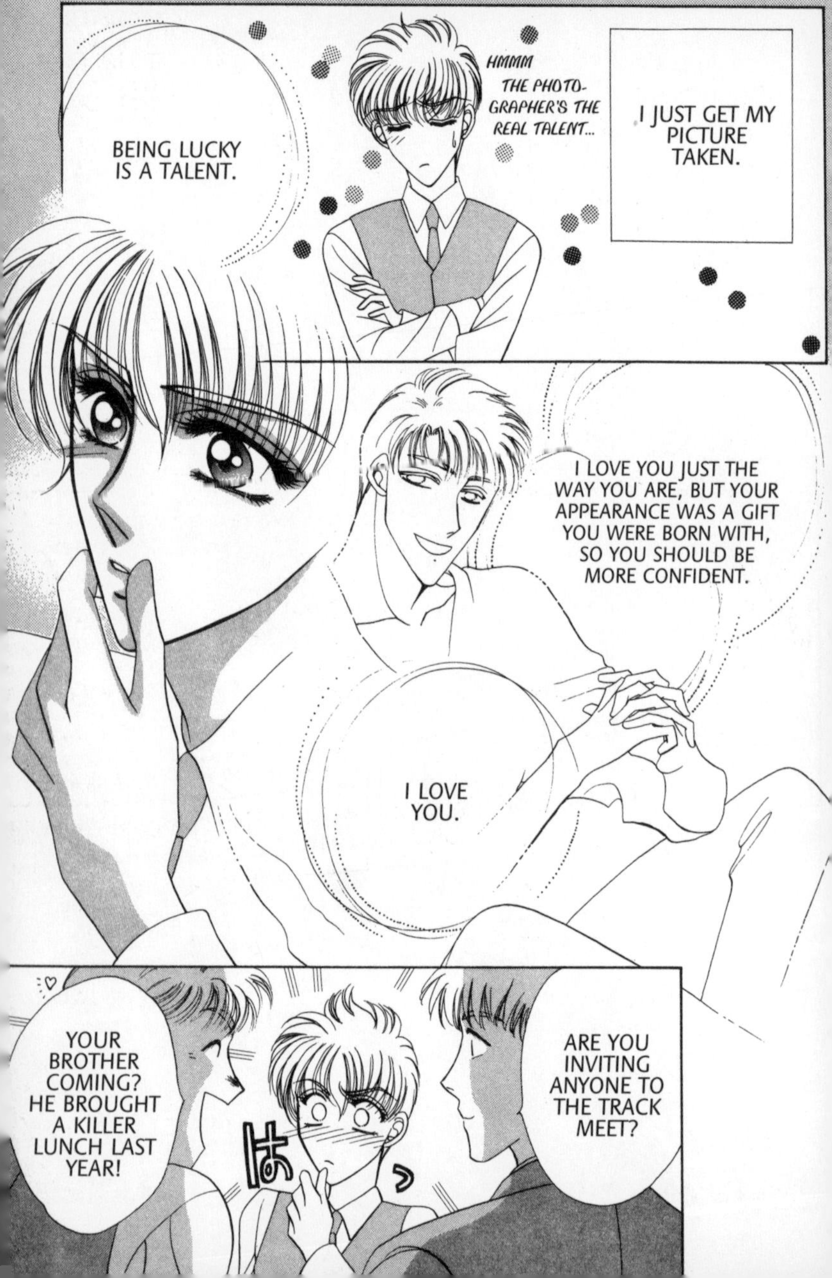
I JUST GET MY PICTURE TAKEN.
HMMM THE PHOTO-GRAPHER'S THE REAL TALENT...
BEING LUCKY IS A TALENT.
I LOVE YOU JUST THE WAY YOU ARE, BUT YOUR APPEARANCE WAS A GIFT YOU WERE BORN WITH, SO YOU SHOULD BE MORE CONFIDENT.
I LOVE YOU.
ARE YOU INVITING ANYONE TO THE TRACK MEET?
YOUR BROTHER COMING? HE BROUGHT A KILLER LUNCH LAST YEAR!
はっ

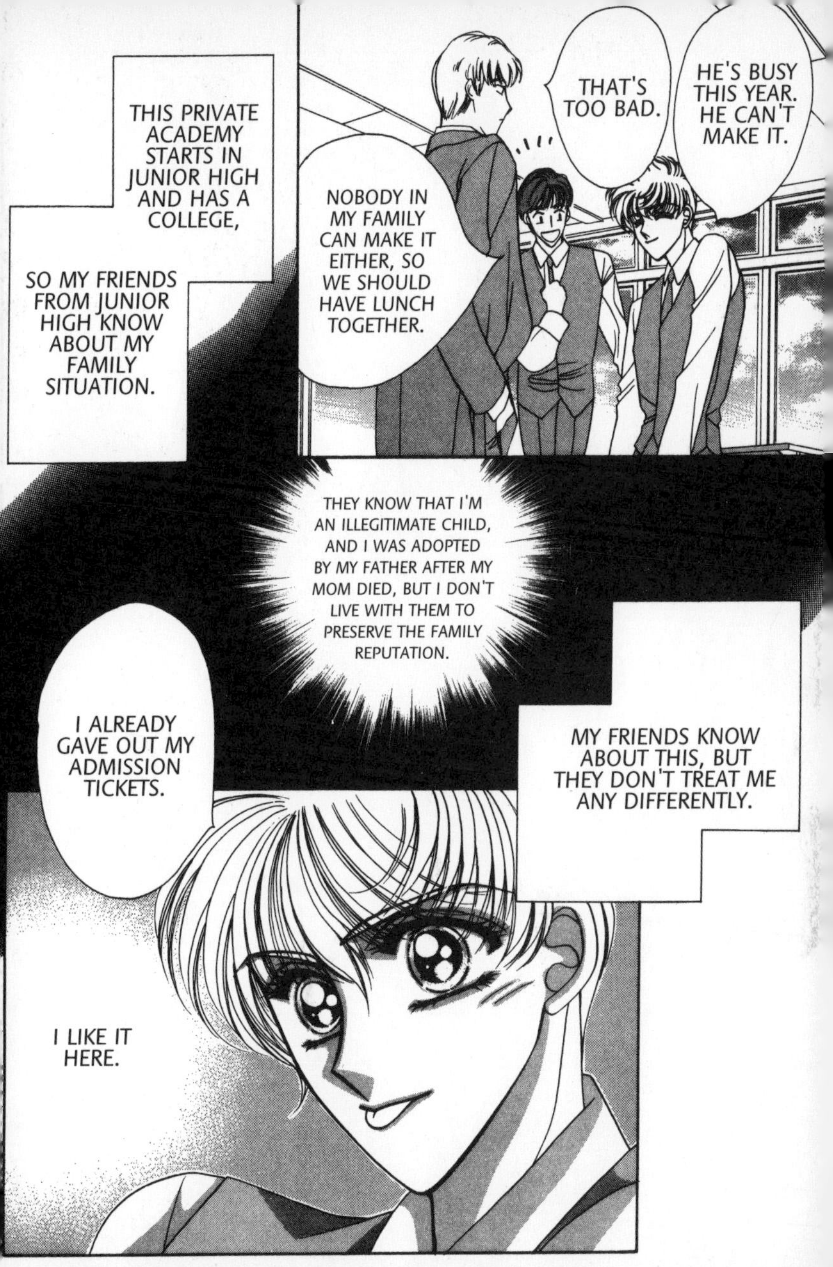
HE'S BUSY THIS YEAR. HE CAN'T MAKE IT.
THAT'S TOO BAD.
NOBODY IN MY FAMILY CAN MAKE IT EITHER, SO WE SHOULD HAVE LUNCH TOGETHER.
THIS PRIVATE ACADEMY STARTS IN JUNIOR HIGH AND HAS A COLLEGE,
SO MY FRIENDS FROM JUNIOR HIGH KNOW ABOUT MY FAMILY SITUATION.
THEY KNOW THAT I'M AN ILLEGITIMATE CHILD, AND I WAS ADOPTED BY MY FATHER AFTER MY MOM DIED, BUT I DON'T LIVE WITH THEM TO PRESERVE THE FAMILY REPUTATION.
MY FRIENDS KNOW ABOUT THIS, BUT THEY DON'T TREAT ME ANY DIFFERENTLY.
I ALREADY GAVE OUT MY ADMISSION TICKETS.
I LIKE IT HERE.

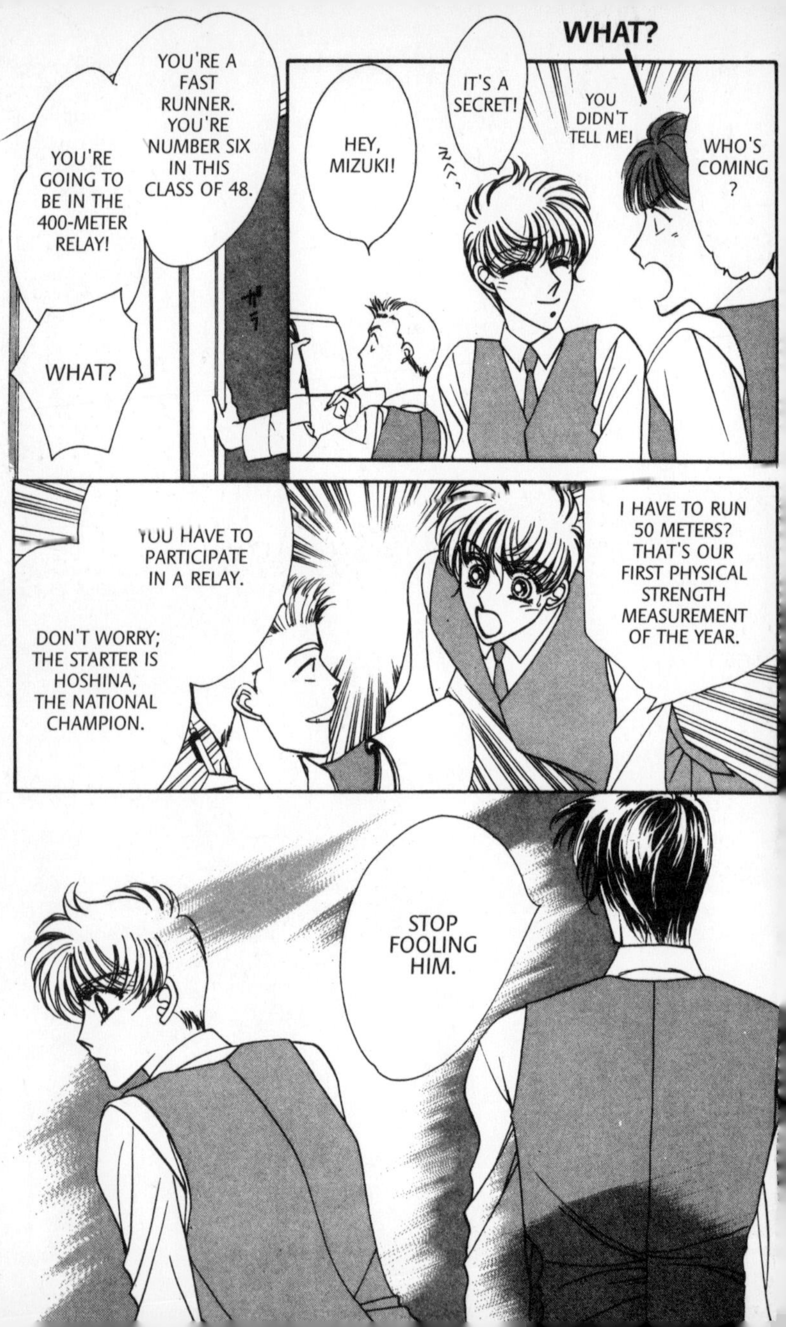
WHAT?
WHO'S COMING?
YOU DIDN'T TELL ME!
IT'S A SECRET!
HEY, MIZUKI!
YOU'RE A FAST RUNNER. YOU'RE NUMBER SIX IN THIS CLASS OF 48.
YOU'RE GOING TO BE IN THE 400-METER RELAY!
WHAT?
I HAVE TO RUN 50 METERS? THAT'S OUR FIRST PHYSICAL STRENGTH MEASUREMENT OF THE YEAR.
YOU HAVE TO PARTICIPATE IN A RELAY.
DON'T WORRY; THE STARTER IS HOSHINA, THE NATIONAL CHAMPION.
STOP FOOLING HIM.

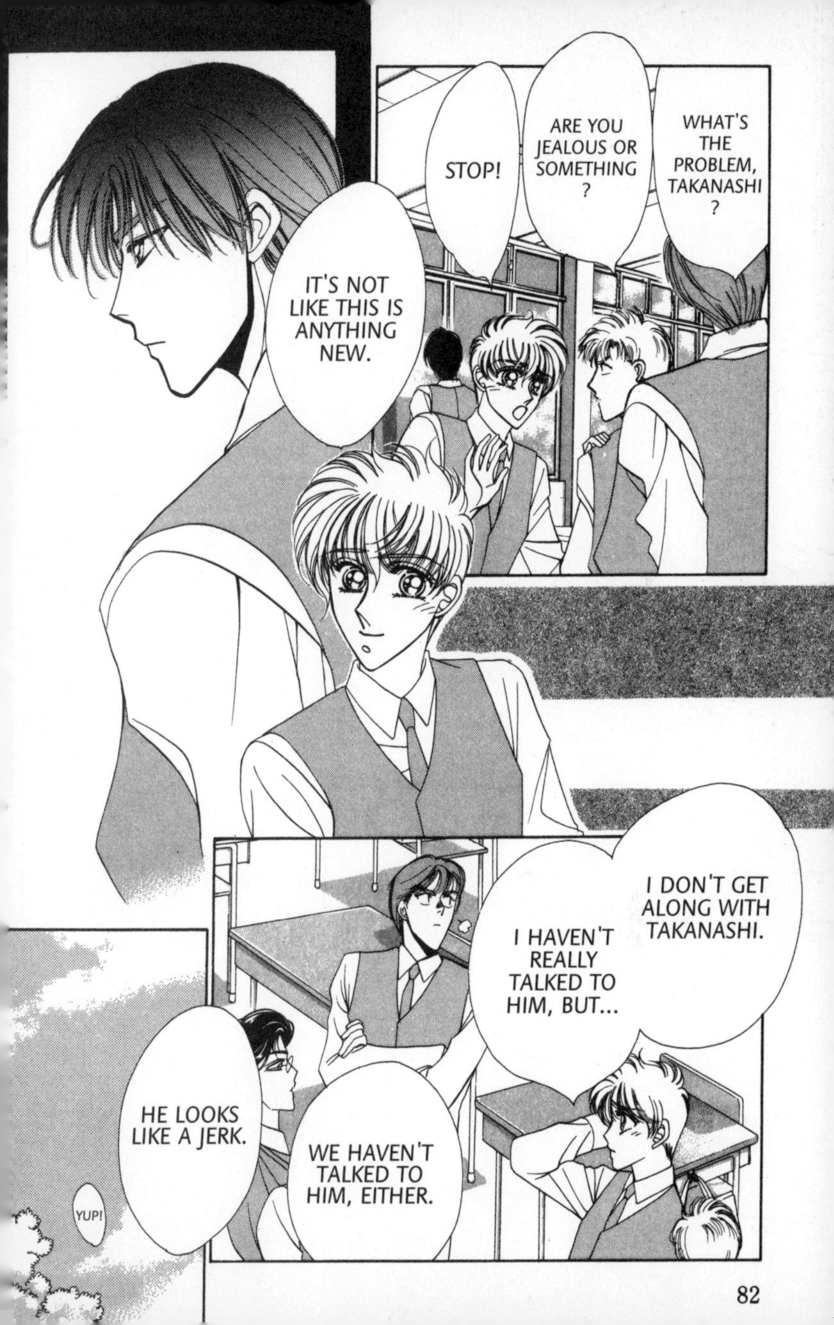
WHAT'S THE PROBLEM, TAKANASHI?
ARE YOU JEALOUS OR SOMETHING?
STOP!
IT'S NOT LIKE THIS IS ANYTHING NEW.
I DON'T GET ALONG WITH TAKANASHI.
I HAVEN'T REALLY TALKED TO HIM, BUT...
WE HAVEN'T TALKED TO HIM, EITHER.
HE LOOKS LIKE A JERK.
YUP!

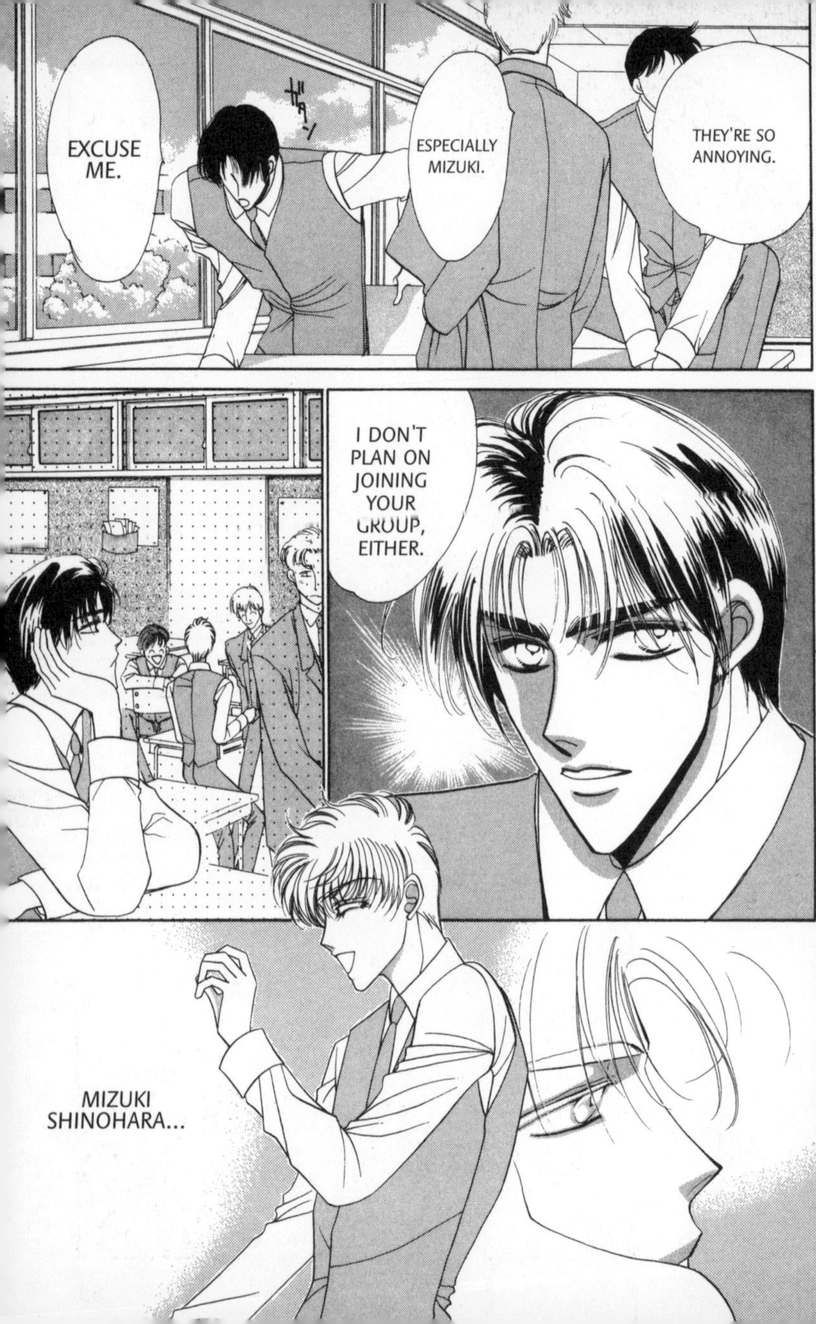
THEY'RE SO ANNOYING.
ESPECIALLY MIZUKI.
EXCUSE ME.
I DON'T PLAN ON JOINING YOUR GROUP, EITHER.
MIZUKI SHINOHARA...

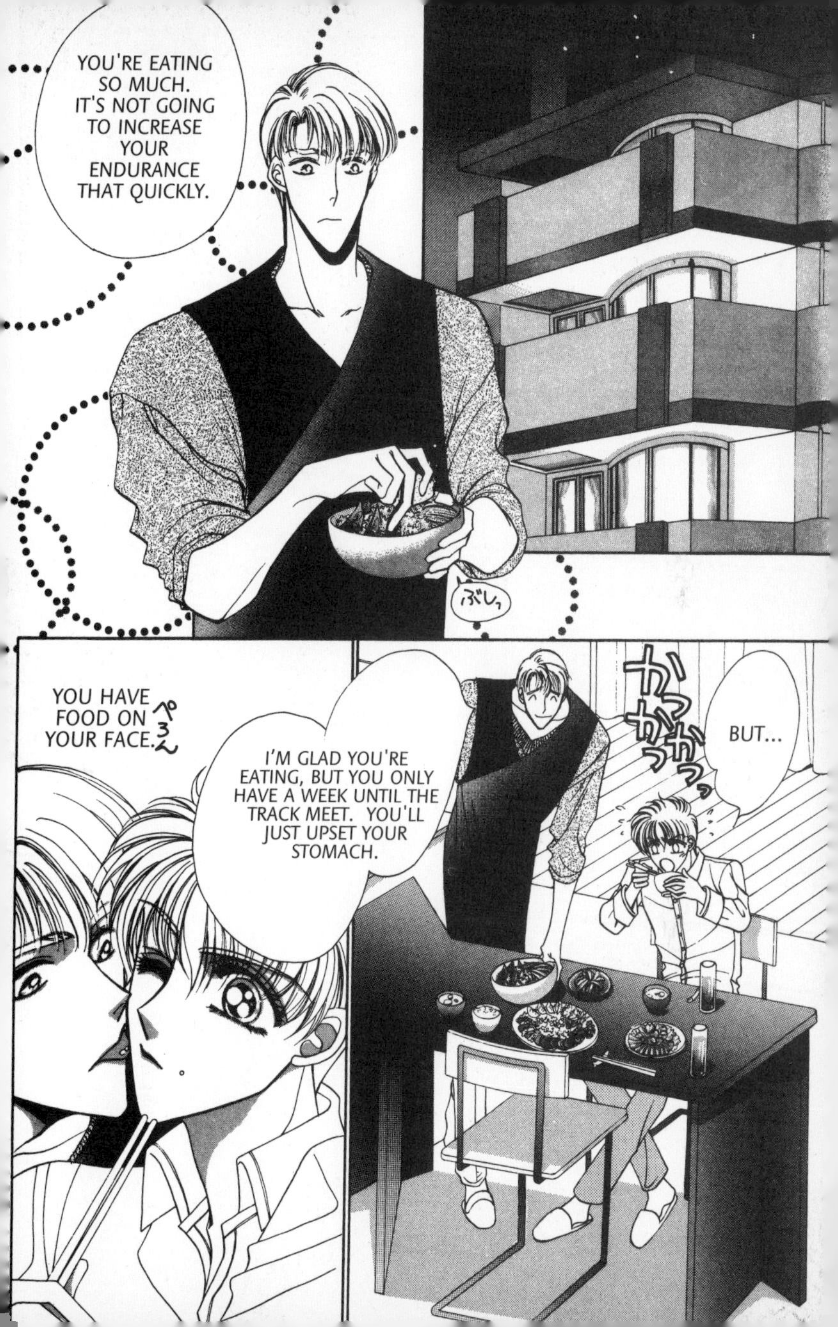
YOU'RE EATING SO MUCH. IT'S NOT GOING TO INCREASE YOUR ENDURANCE THAT QUICKLY.
ぶしっ
かっかっかっ
BUT...
I'M GLAD YOU'RE EATING, BUT YOU ONLY HAVE A WEEK UNTIL THE TRACK MEET. YOU'LL JUST UPSET YOUR STOMACH.
YOU HAVE FOOD ON YOUR FACE.
ぺろん

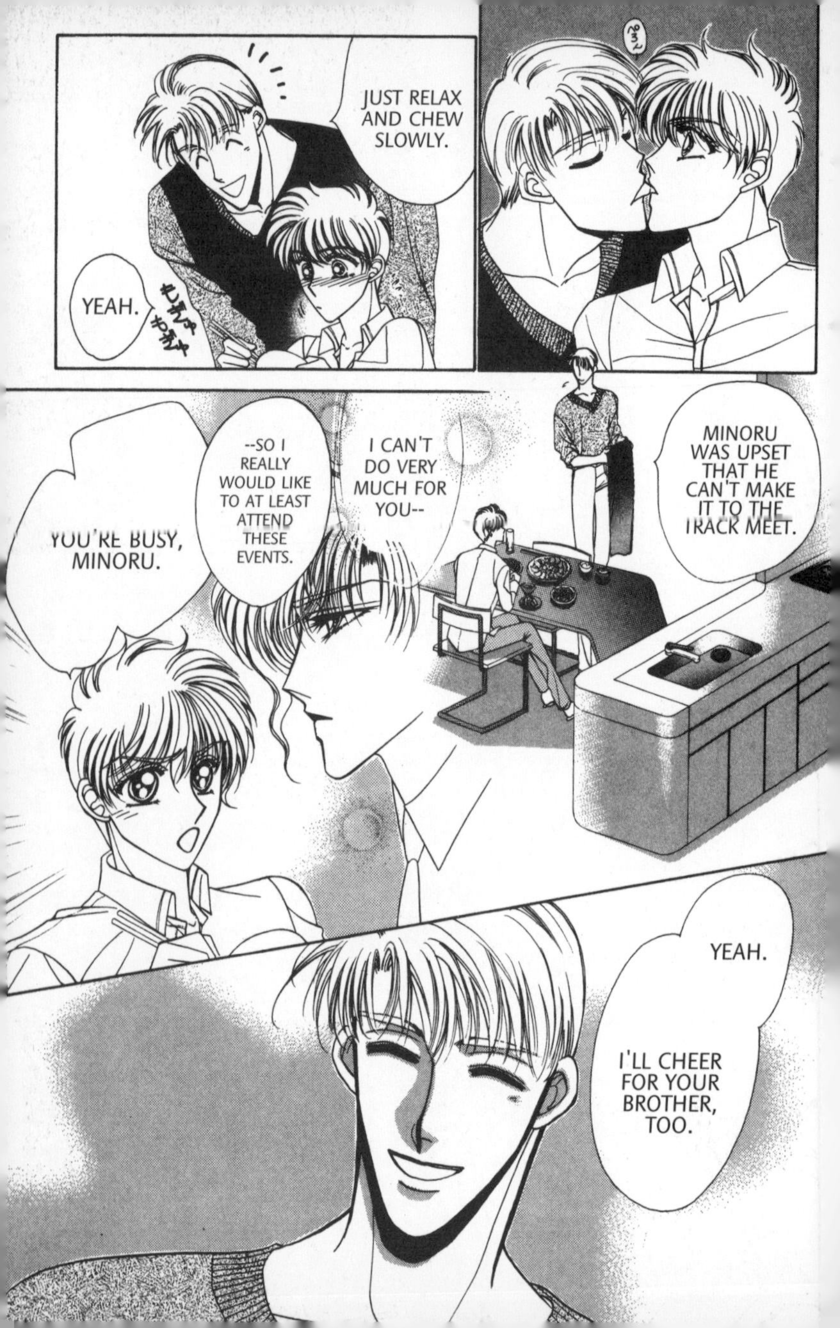
ぺろん
JUST RELAX AND CHEW SLOWLY.
YEAH.
もぎゅもぎゅ
MINORU WAS UPSET THAT HE CAN'T MAKE IT TO THE TRACK MEET.
I CAN'T DO VERY MUCH FOR YOU--
--SO I REALLY WOULD LIKE TO AT LEAST ATTEND THESE EVENTS.
YOU'RE BUSY, MINORU.
YEAH.
I'LL CHEER FOR YOUR BROTHER, TOO.

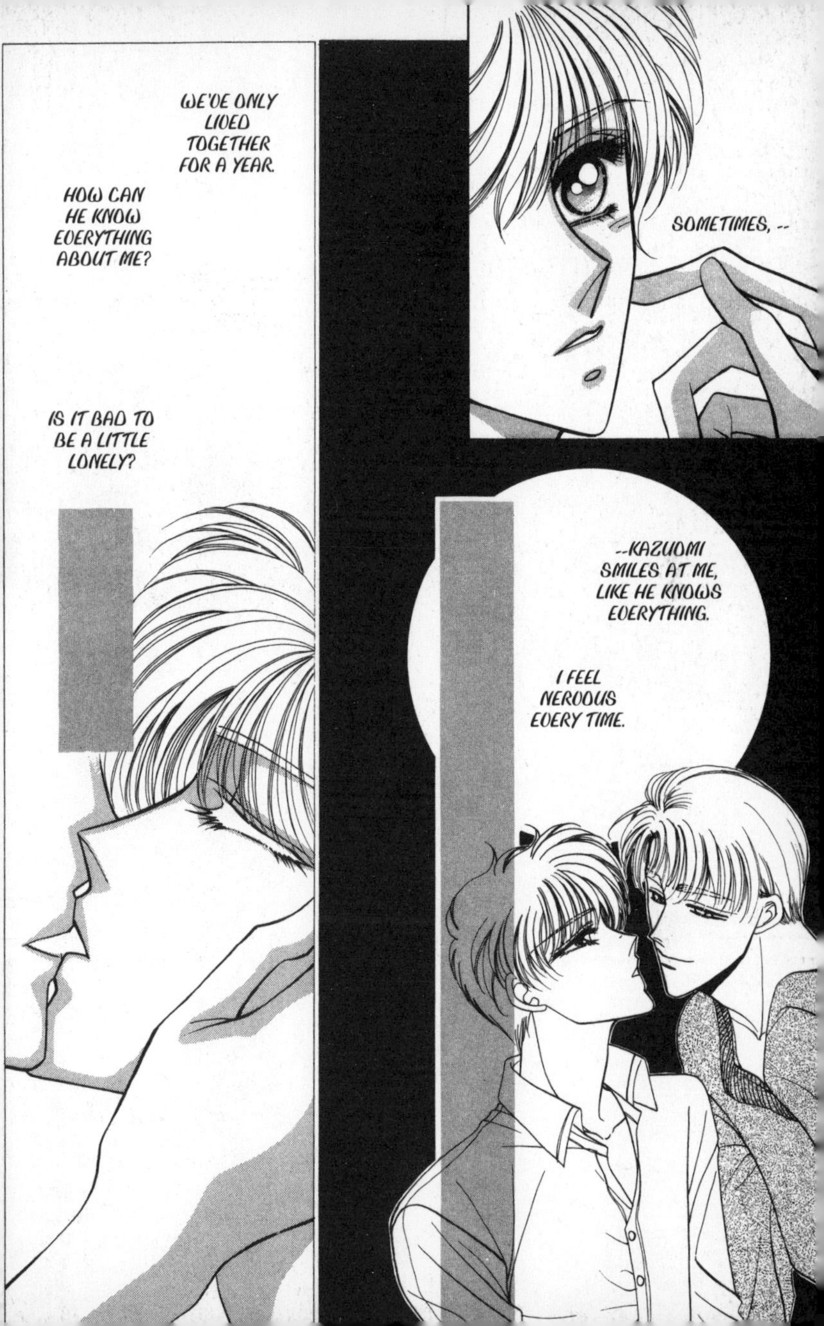
SOMETIMES, --
--KAZUOMI SMILES AT ME, LIKE HE KNOWS EVERYTHING.
I FEEL NERVOUS EVERY TIME.
WE'VE ONLY LIVED TOGETHER FOR A YEAR.
HOW CAN HE KNOW EVERYTHING ABOUT ME?
IS IT BAD TO BE A LITTLE LONELY?

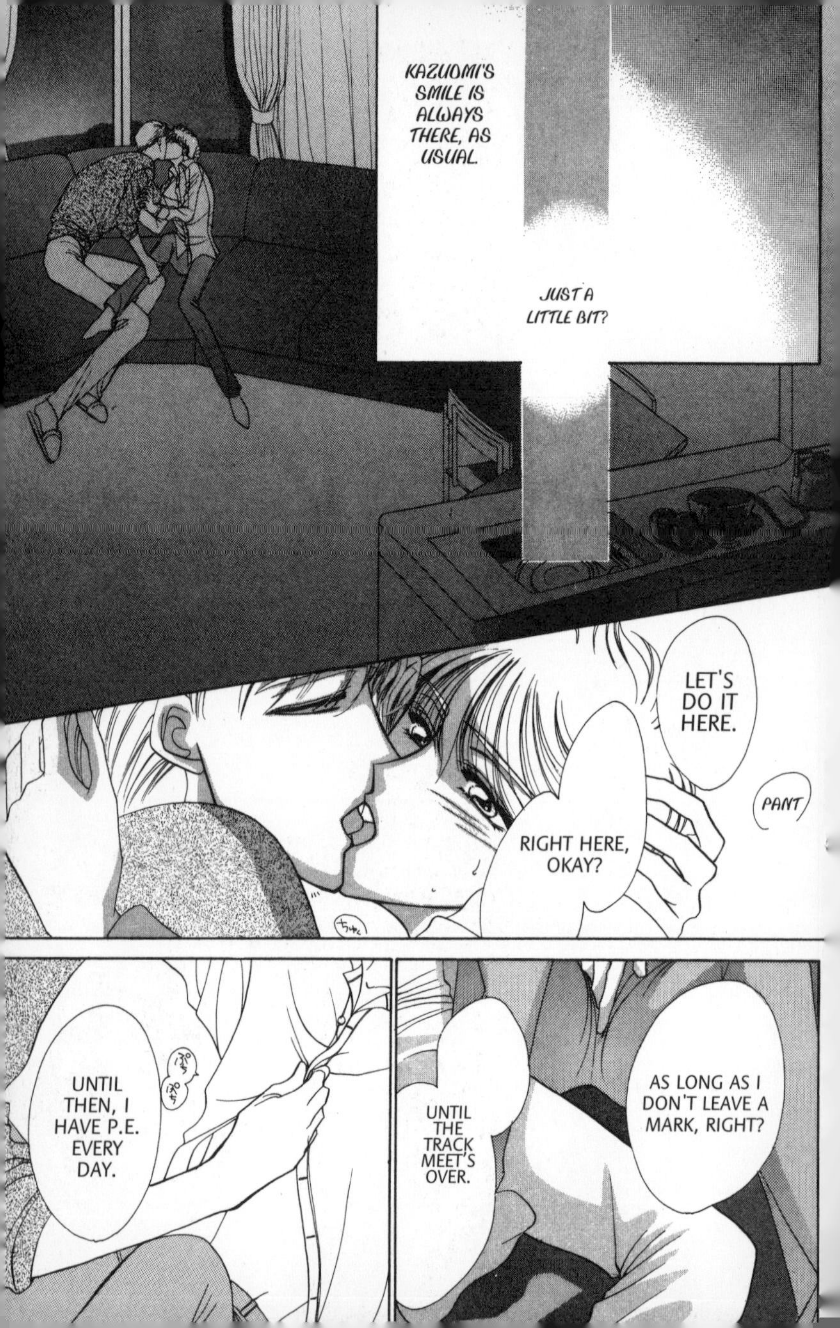
KAZUOMI'S SMILE IS ALWAYS THERE, AS USUAL.
JUST A LITTLE BIT?
LET'S DO IT HERE.
PANT
RIGHT HERE, OKAY?
AS LONG AS I DON'T LEAVE A MARK, RIGHT?
UNTIL THE TRACK MEET'S OVER.
UNTIL THEN, I HAVE P.E. EVERY DAY.

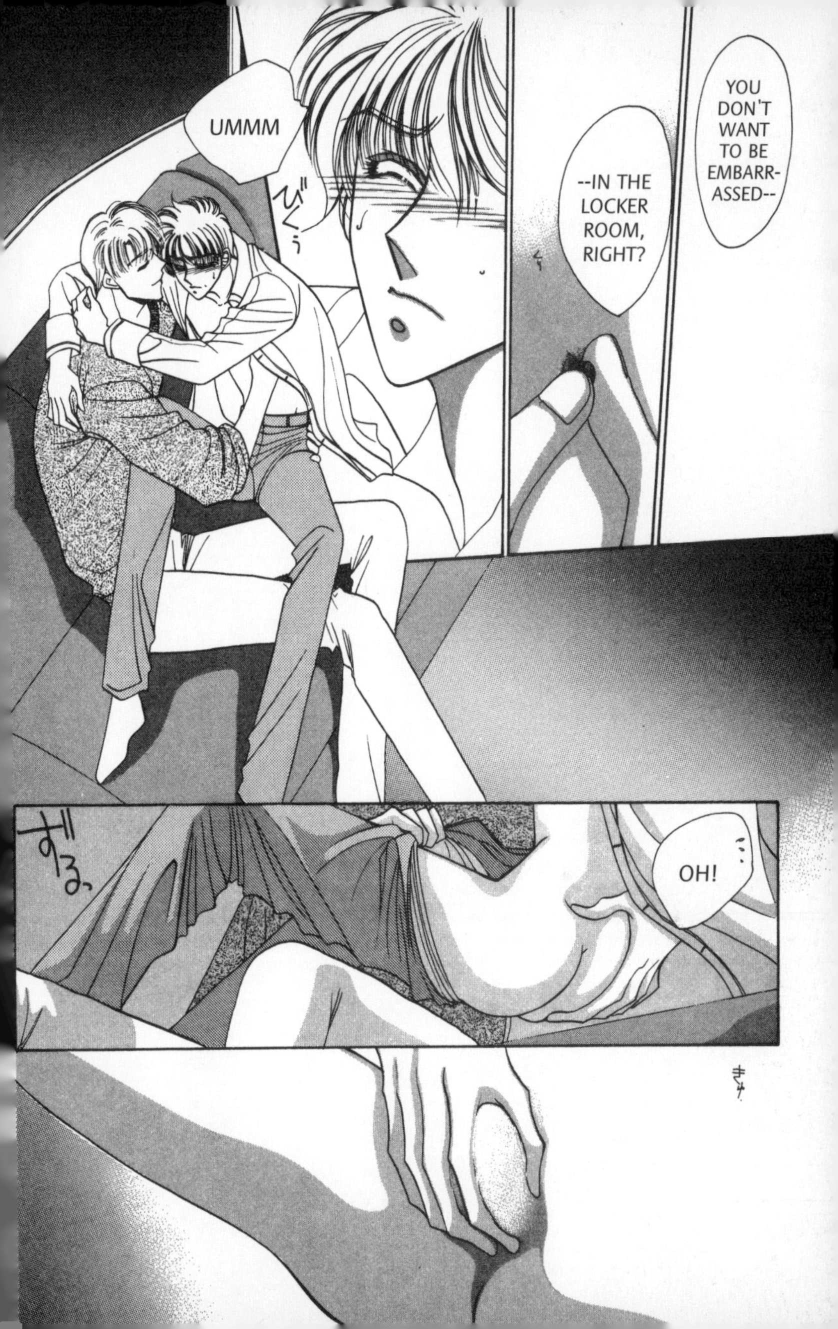
YOU DON'T WANT TO BE EMBARR-ASSED--
--IN THE LOCKER ROOM, RIGHT?
UMMM
びくぅ
OH!
ずるっ

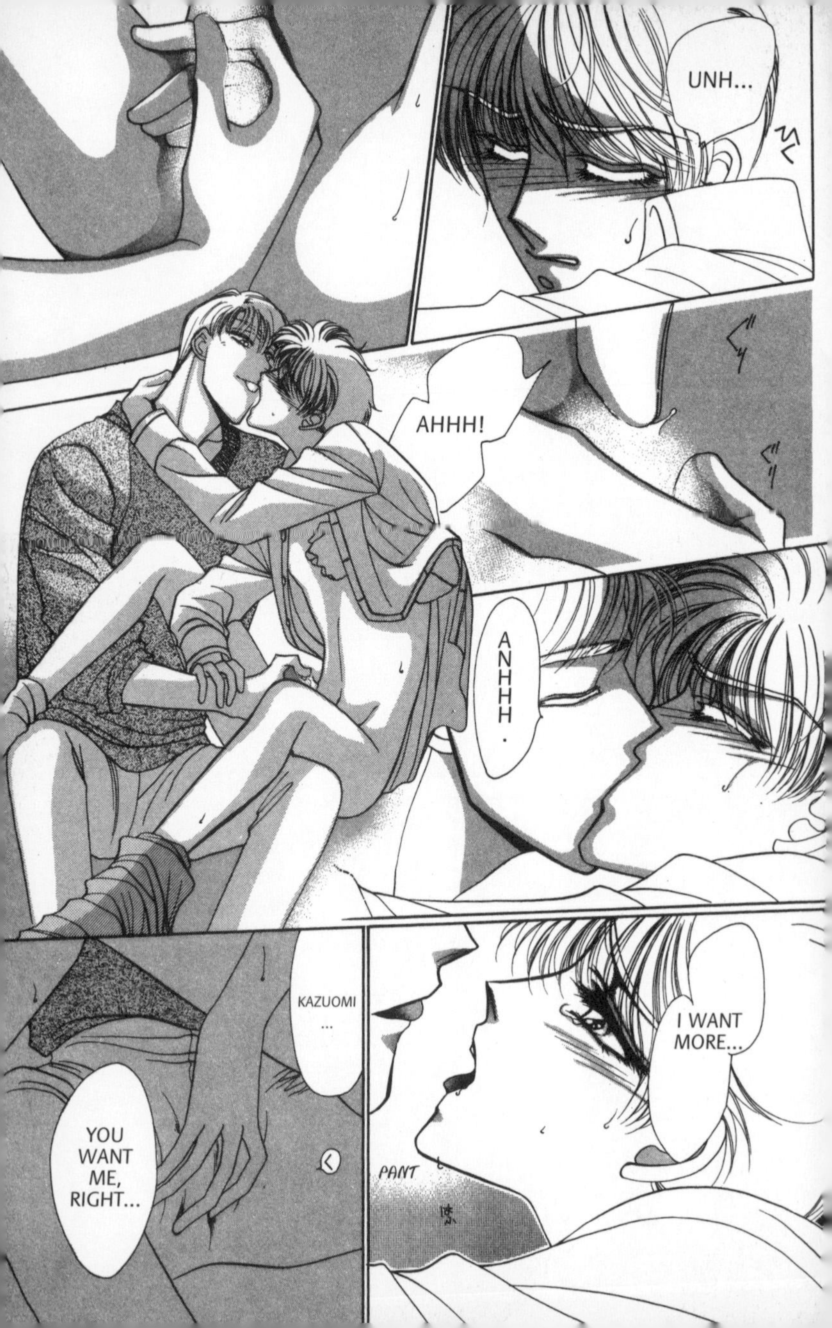

UNH...
AHHH!
ANHHH.
I WANT MORE...
PANT
KAZUOMI ...
YOU WANT ME, RIGHT...

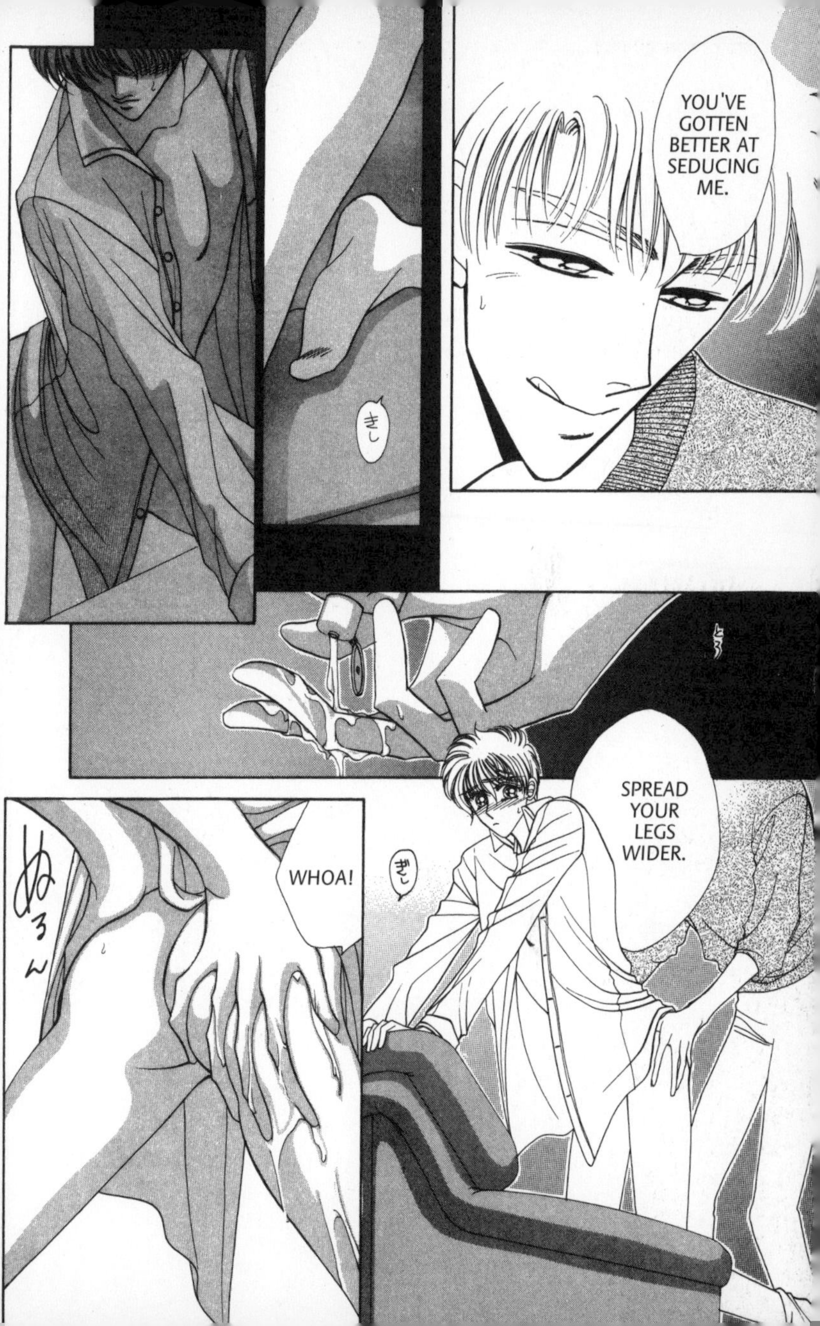
YOU'VE GOTTEN BETTER AT SEDUCING ME.
きし
SPREAD YOUR LEGS WIDER.
ぎし
WHOA!
ぬるん

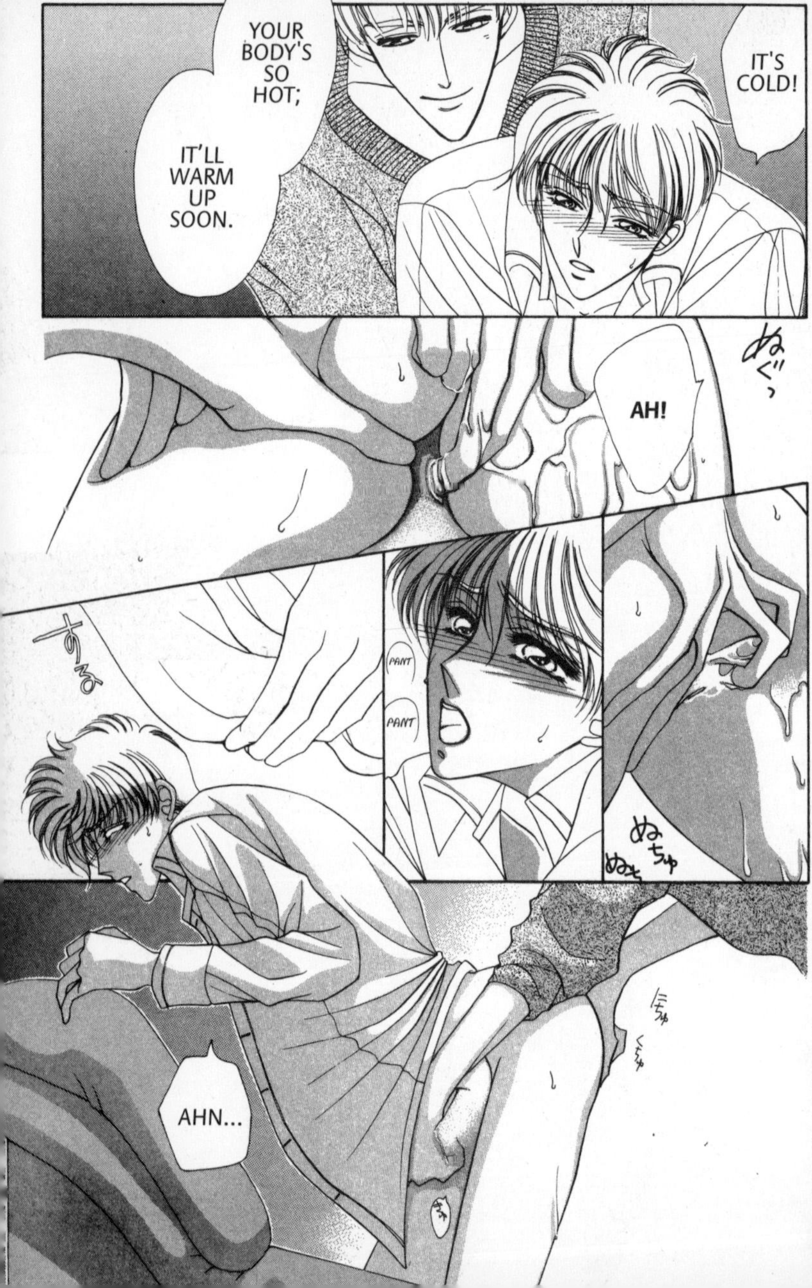
IT'S COLD!
YOUR BODY'S SO HOT;
IT'LL WARM UP SOON.
ぬぐっ
AH!
ぬちゅ
ぬちゅ
PANT
PANT
するる
にちゅ
くちゅ
AHN...

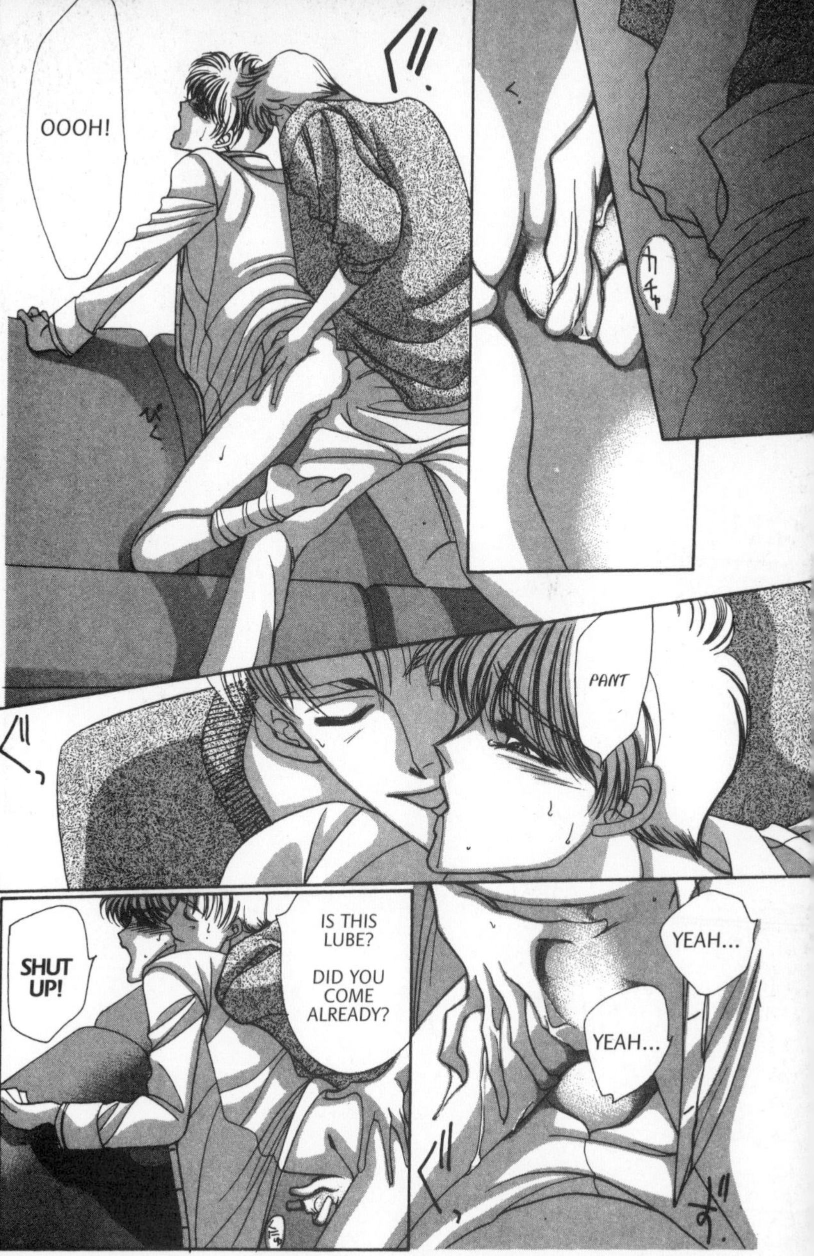
カチャ
OOOH!
PANT
YEAH...
YEAH...
IS THIS LUBE?
DID YOU COME ALREADY?
SHUT UP!

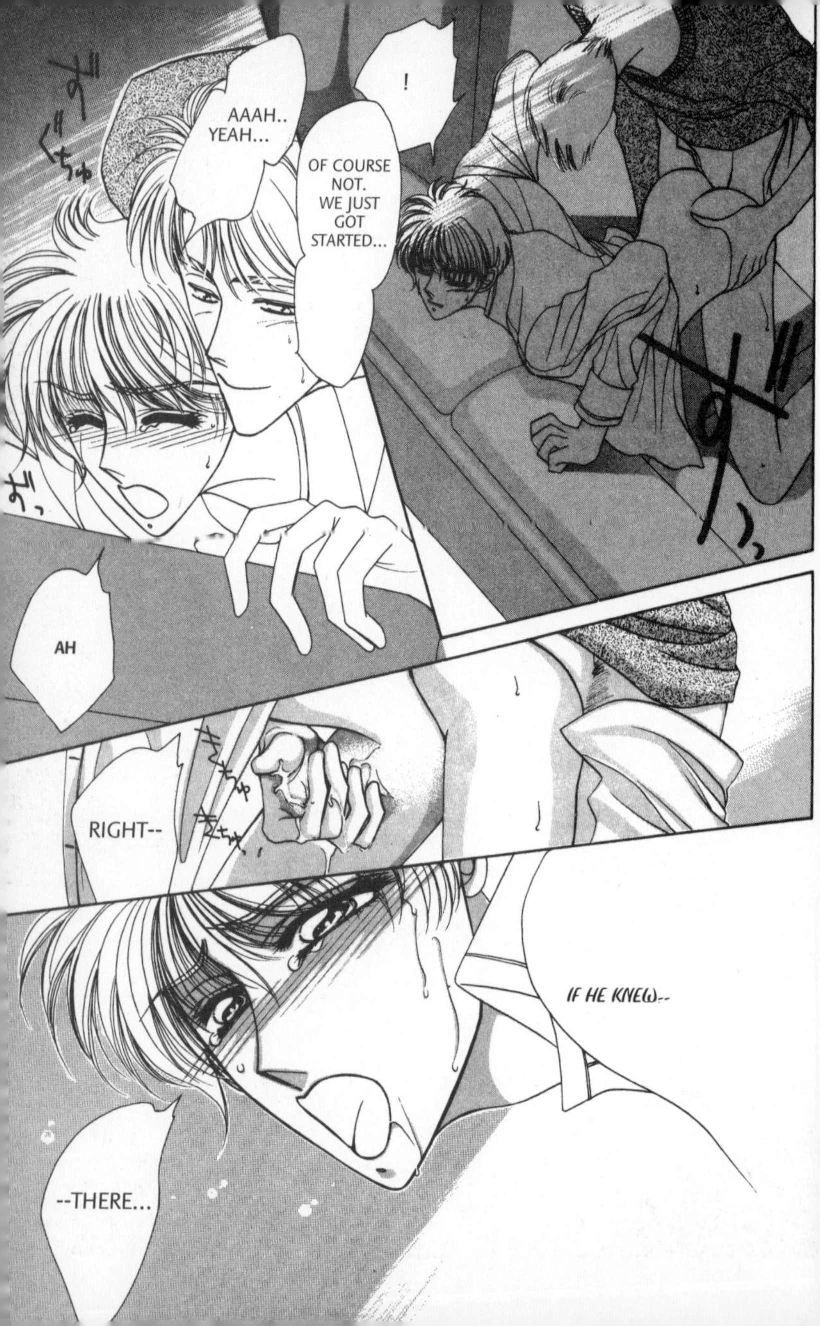
!
OF COURSE NOT. WE JUST GOT STARTED...
AAAH.. YEAH...
AH
RIGHT--
IF HE KNEW--
--THERE...

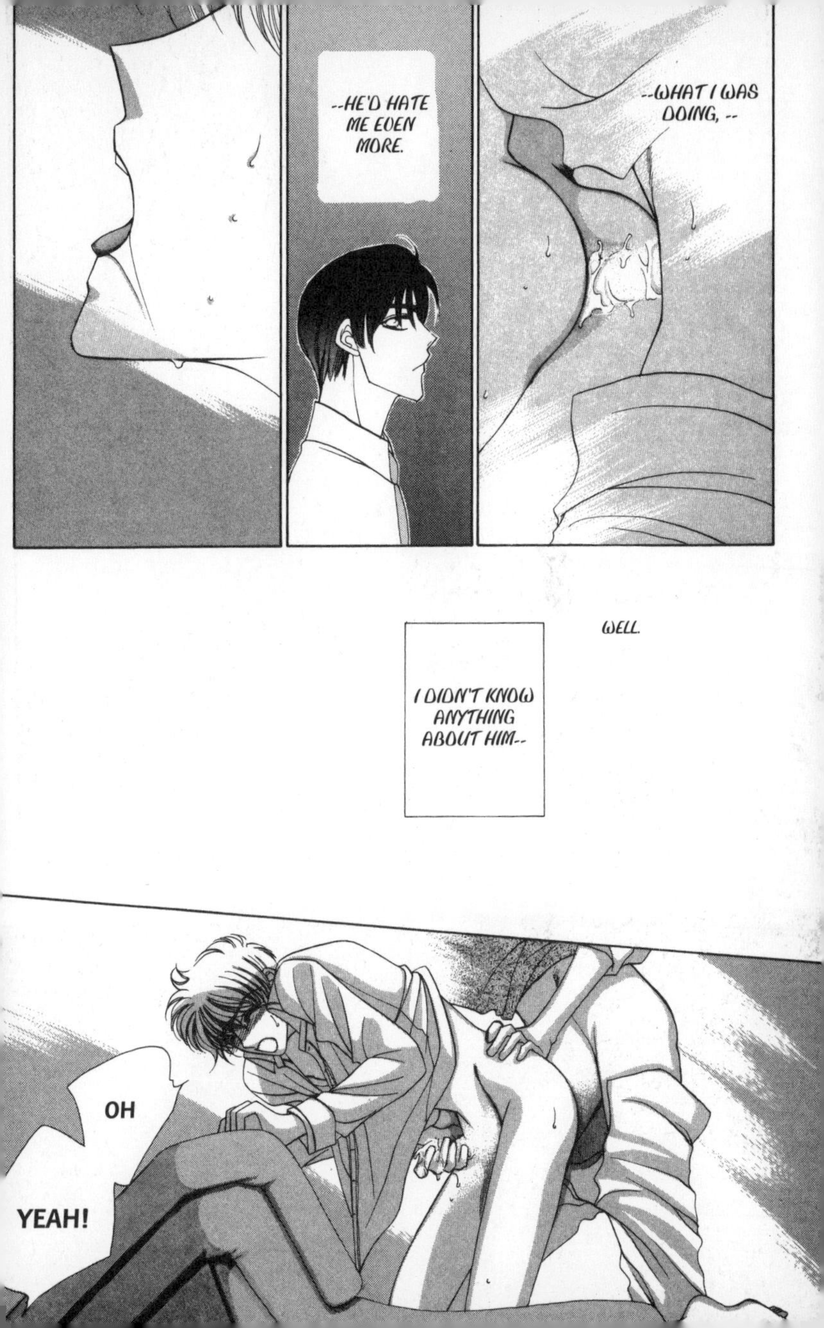
--WHAT I WAS DOING, --
--HE'D HATE ME EVEN MORE.
WELL.
I DIDN'T KNOW ANYTHING ABOUT HIM--
OH YEAH!

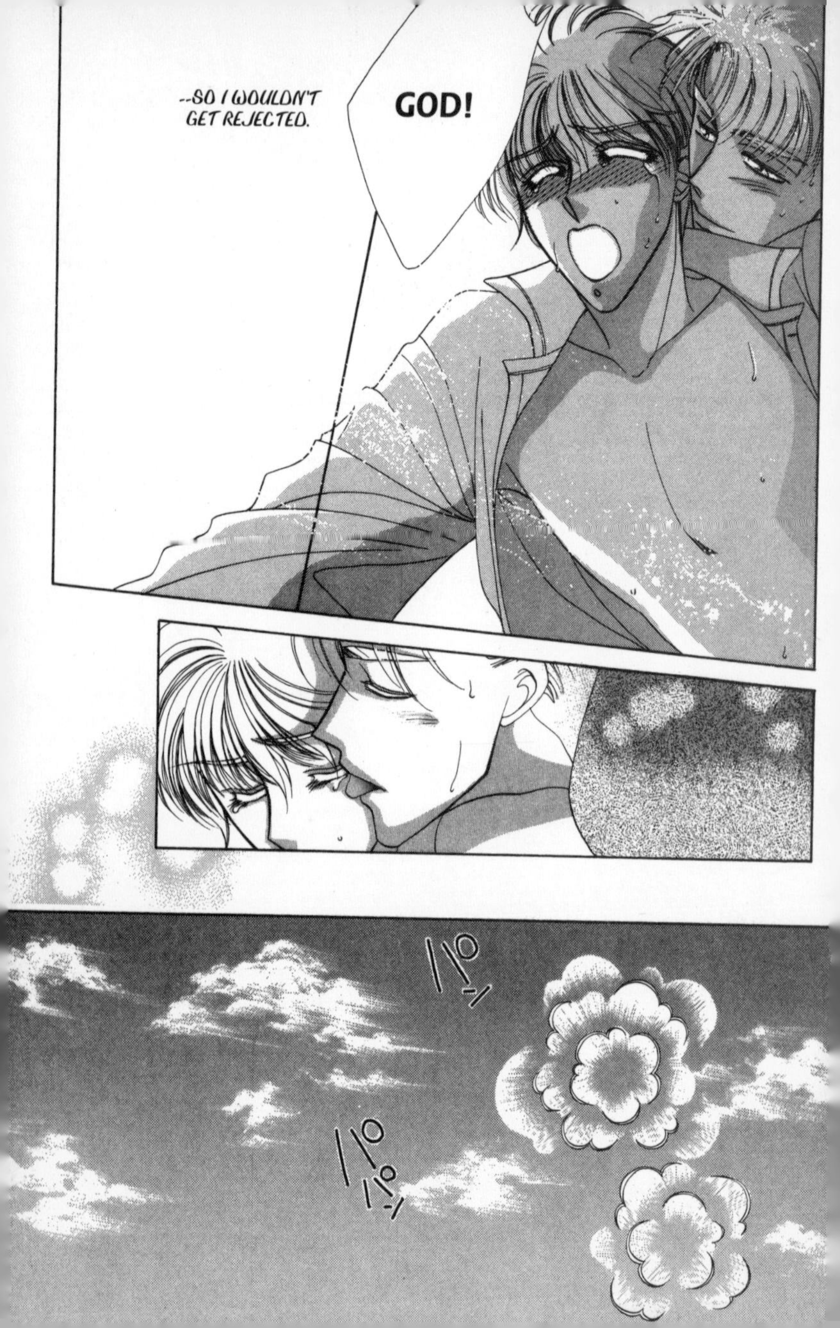
GOD!
--SO I WOULDN'T GET REJECTED.

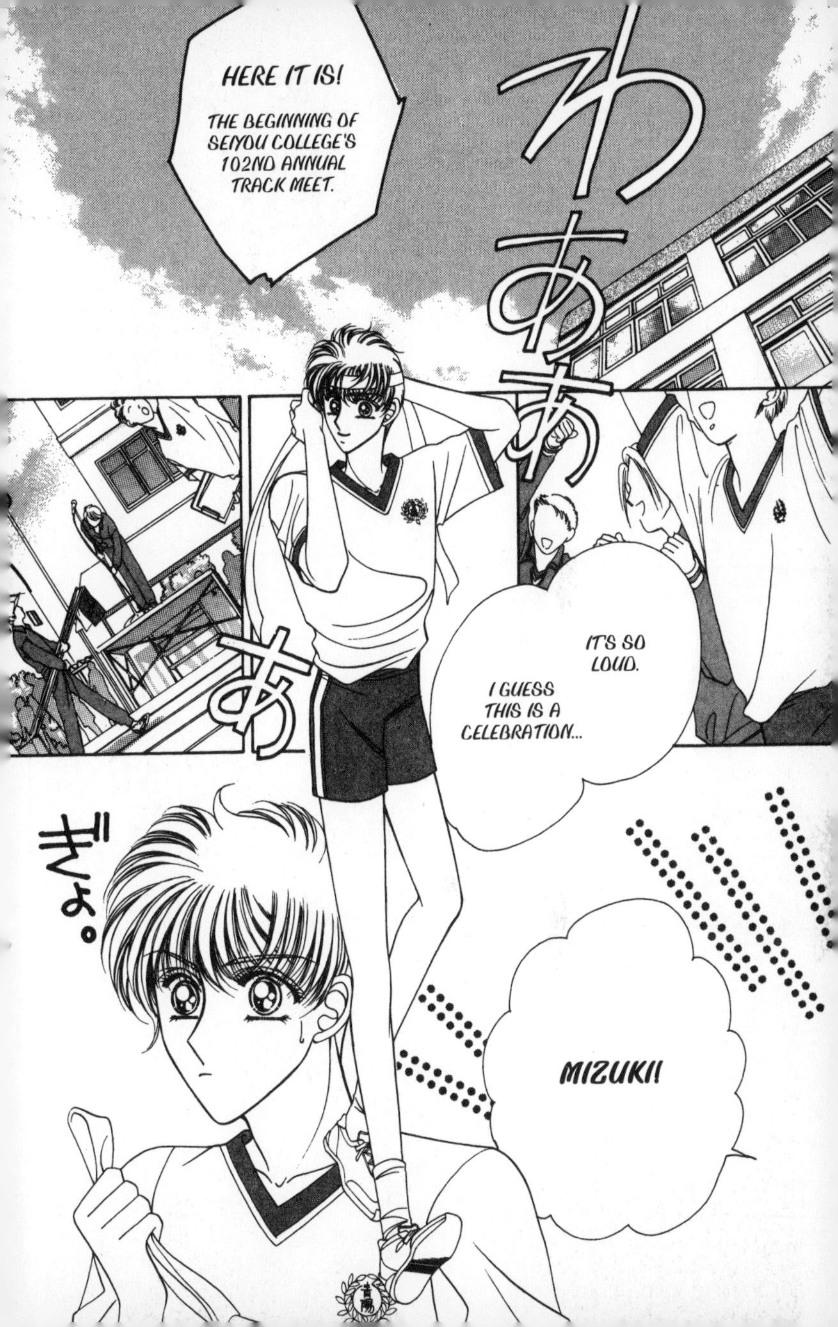
わああ
HERE IT IS!
THE BEGINNING OF SEIYOU COLLEGE'S 102ND ANNUAL TRACK MEET.
あ
IT'S SO LOUD.
I GUESS THIS IS A CELEBRATION...
MIZUKI!
ぎょ。

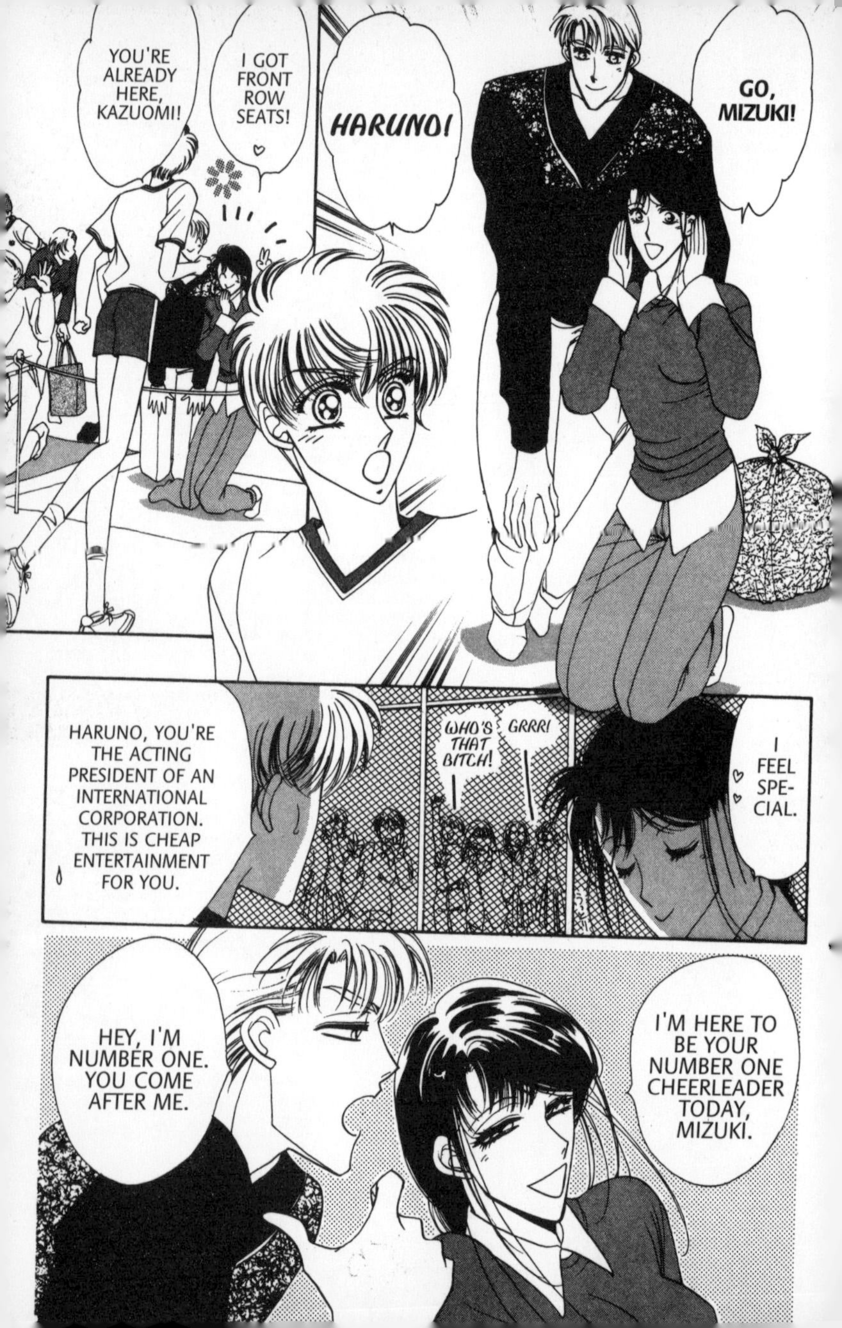
GO, MIZUKI!
HARUNO!
I GOT FRONT ROW SEATS!
YOU'RE ALREADY HERE, KAZUOMI!
I FEEL SPECIAL.
GRRR!
WHO'S THAT BITCH!
HARUNO, YOU'RE THE ACTING PRESIDENT OF AN INTERNATIONAL CORPORATION. THIS IS CHEAP ENTERTAINMENT FOR YOU.
I'M HERE TO BE YOUR NUMBER ONE CHEERLEADER TODAY, MIZUKI.
HEY, I'M NUMBER ONE. YOU COME AFTER ME.

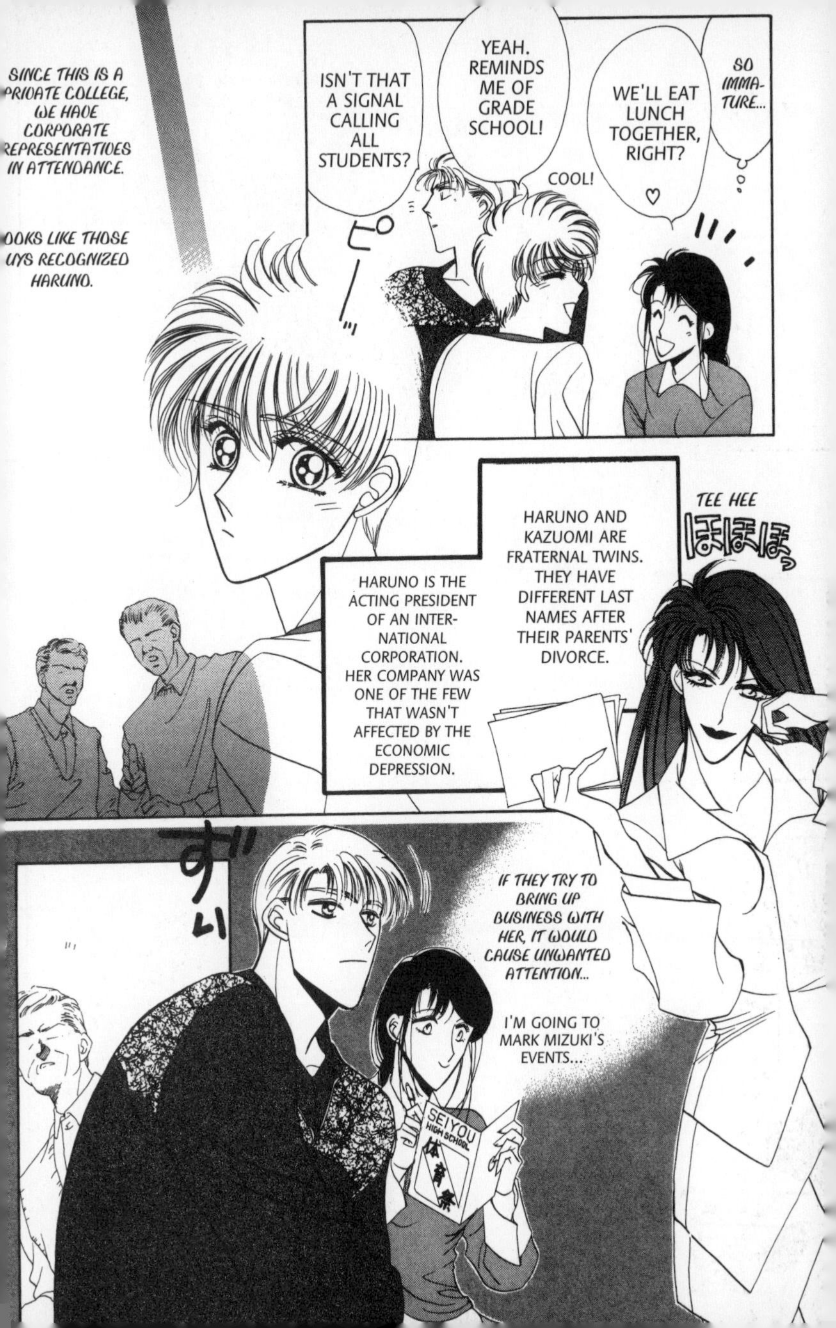
SO IMMATURE...
WE'LL EAT LUNCH TOGETHER, RIGHT? ♡
COOL!
YEAH. REMINDS ME OF GRADE SCHOOL!
ISN'T THAT A SIGNAL CALLING ALL STUDENTS?
ピー
TEE HEE
ほほほっ
HARUNO AND KAZUOMI ARE FRATERNAL TWINS. THEY HAVE DIFFERENT LAST NAMES AFTER THEIR PARENTS' DIVORCE.
HARUNO IS THE ACTING PRESIDENT OF AN INTERNATIONAL CORPORATION. HER COMPANY WAS ONE OF THE FEW THAT WASN'T AFFECTED BY THE ECONOMIC DEPRESSION.
SINCE THIS IS A PRIVATE COLLEGE, WE HAVE CORPORATE REPRESENTATIVES IN ATTENDANCE.
OOKS LIKE THOSE UYS RECOGNIZED HARUNO.
IF THEY TRY TO BRING UP BUSINESS WITH HER, IT WOULD CAUSE UNWANTED ATTENTION...
I'M GOING TO MARK MIZUKI'S EVENTS...
ずい
SEIYOU HIGH SCHOOL
体育祭

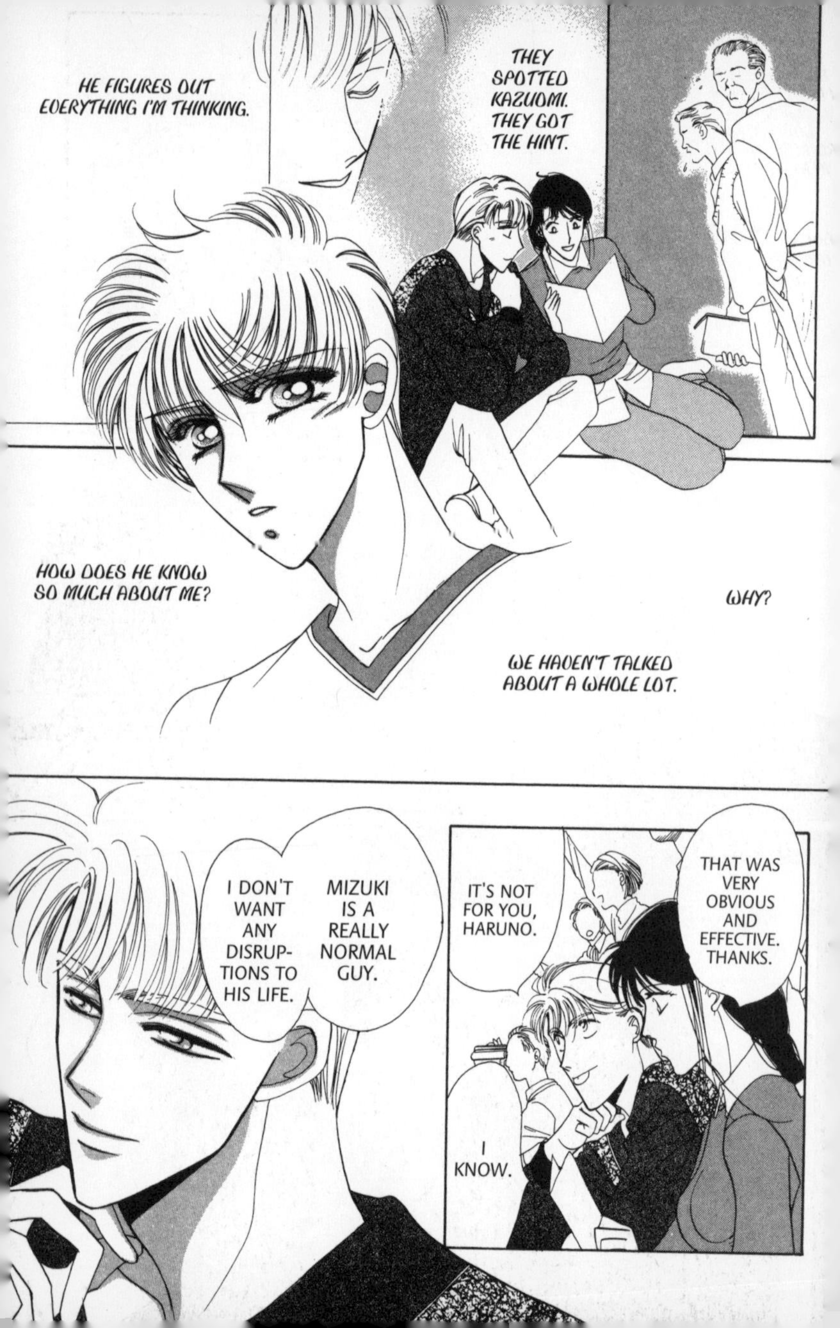
THEY SPOTTED KAZUOMI. THEY GOT THE HINT.
HE FIGURES OUT EVERYTHING I'M THINKING.
WHY?
HOW DOES HE KNOW SO MUCH ABOUT ME?
WE HAVEN'T TALKED ABOUT A WHOLE LOT.
THAT WAS VERY OBVIOUS AND EFFECTIVE. THANKS.
IT'S NOT FOR YOU, HARUNO.
I KNOW.
MIZUKI IS A REALLY NORMAL GUY.
I DON'T WANT ANY DISRUPTIONS TO HIS LIFE.

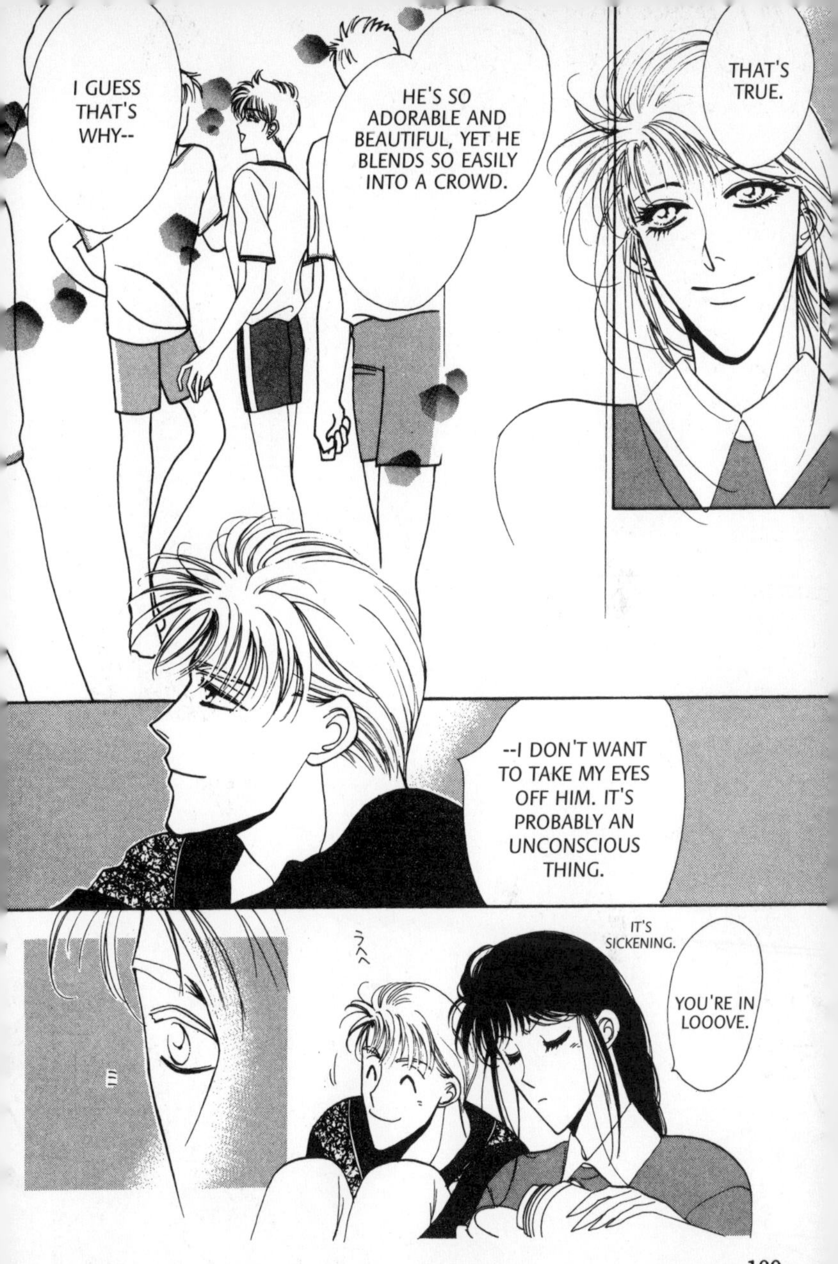
THAT'S TRUE.
HE'S SO ADORABLE AND BEAUTIFUL, YET HE BLENDS SO EASILY INTO A CROWD.
I GUESS THAT'S WHY--
--I DON'T WANT TO TAKE MY EYES OFF HIM. IT'S PROBABLY AN UNCONSCIOUS THING.
YOU'RE IN LOOOVE.
IT'S SICKENING.

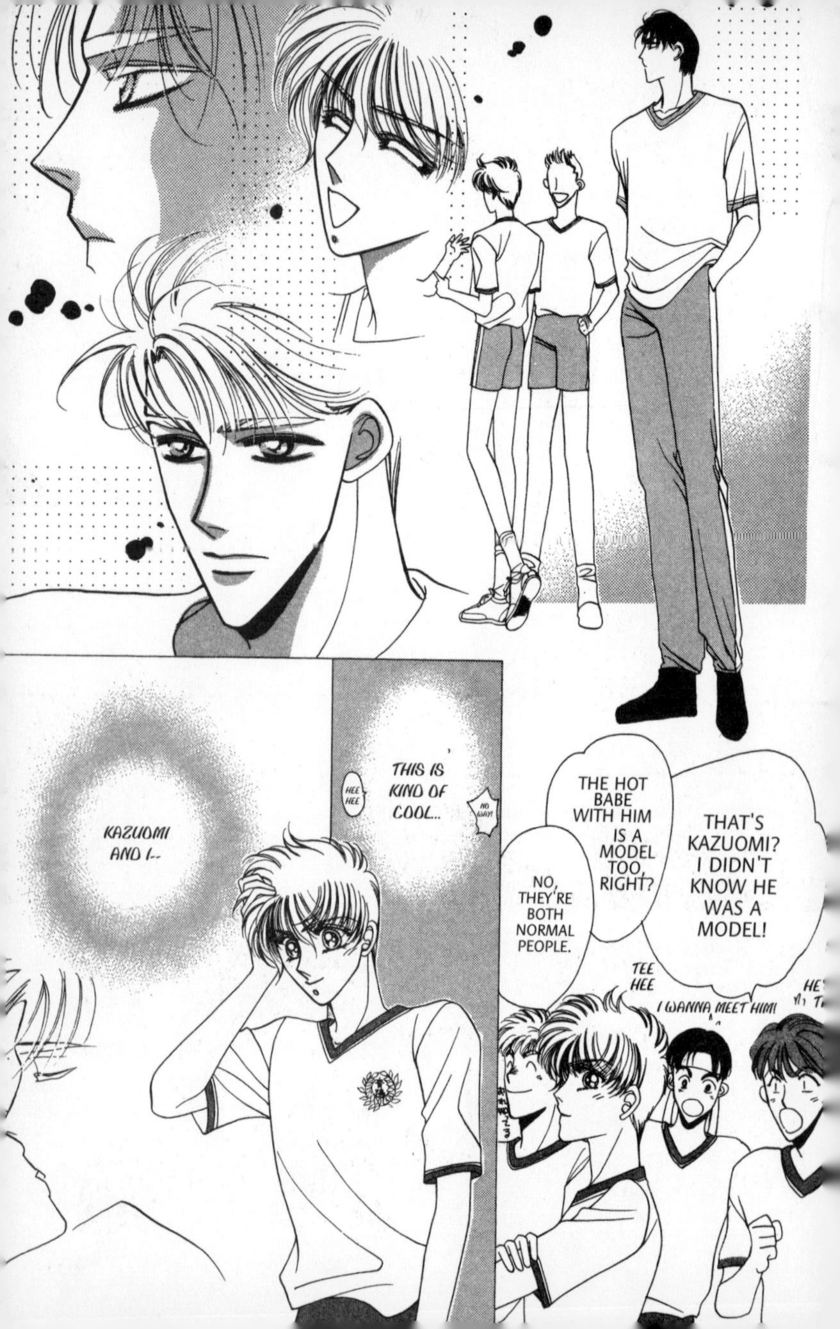
THAT'S KAZUOMI? I DIDN'T KNOW HE WAS A MODEL!
THE HOT BABE WITH HIM IS A MODEL TOO, RIGHT?
NO, THEY'RE BOTH NORMAL PEOPLE.
I WANNA MEET HIM!
TEE HEE
NO WAY!
THIS IS KIND OF COOL...
HEE HEE
KAZUOMI AND I--

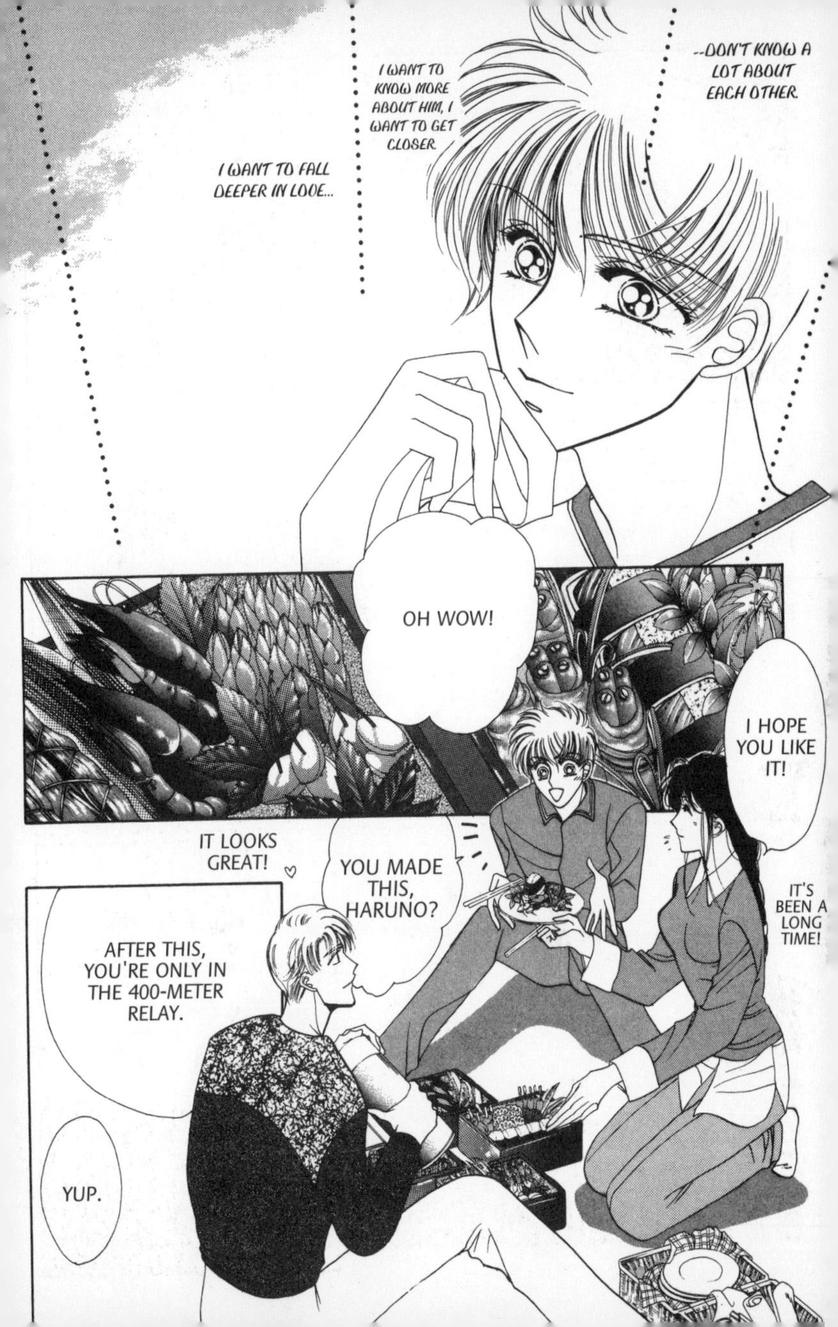
--DON'T KNOW A LOT ABOUT EACH OTHER.
I WANT TO KNOW MORE ABOUT HIM, I WANT TO GET CLOSER.
I WANT TO FALL DEEPER IN LOVE...
OH WOW!
I HOPE YOU LIKE IT!
IT'S BEEN A LONG TIME!
YOU MADE THIS, HARUNO?
IT LOOKS GREAT!
AFTER THIS, YOU'RE ONLY IN THE 400-METER RELAY.
YUP.

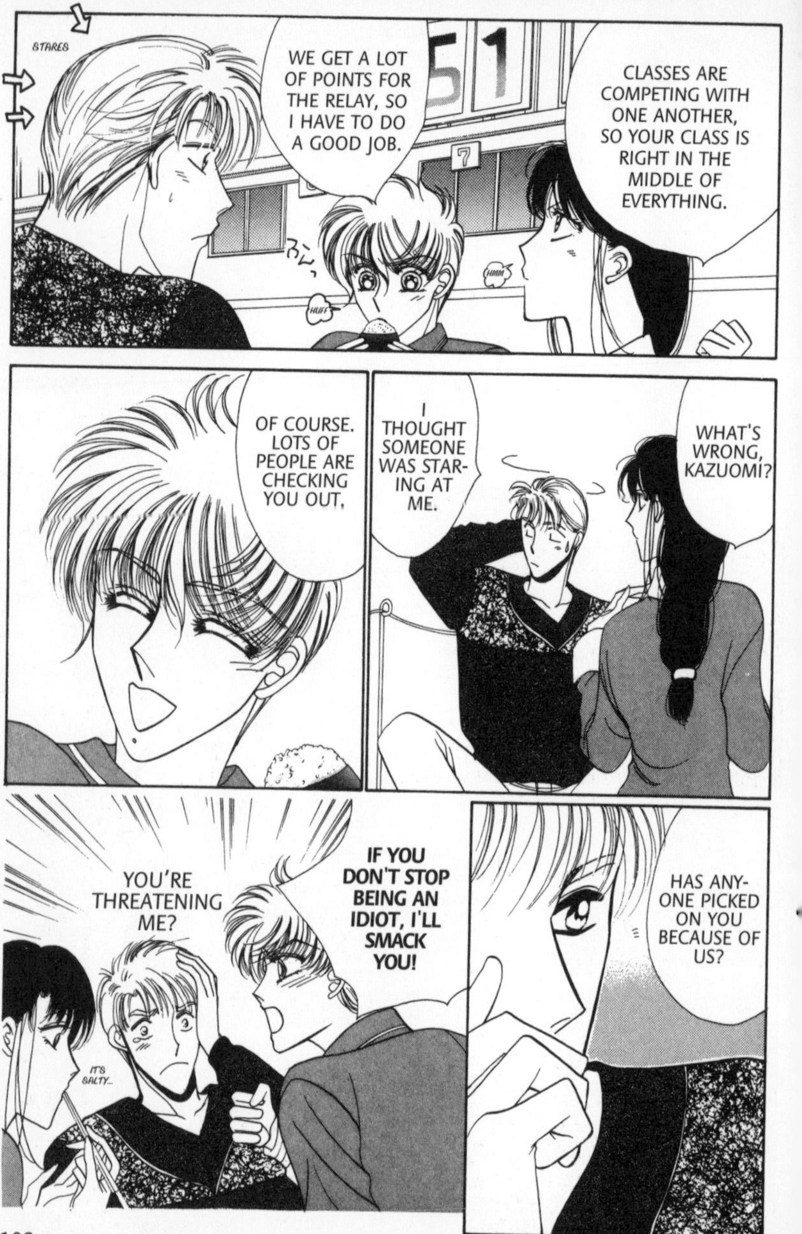
CLASSES ARE COMPETING WITH ONE ANOTHER, SO YOUR CLASS IS RIGHT IN THE MIDDLE OF EVERYTHING.
HMM
WE GET A LOT OF POINTS FOR THE RELAY, SO I HAVE TO DO A GOOD JOB.
HUFF
ふん
STARES
WHAT'S WRONG, KAZUOMI?
I THOUGHT SOMEONE WAS STAR-ING AT ME.
OF COURSE. LOTS OF PEOPLE ARE CHECKING YOU OUT.
HAS ANY-ONE PICKED ON YOU BECAUSE OF US?
IF YOU DON'T STOP BEING AN IDIOT, I'LL SMACK YOU!
YOU'RE THREATENING ME?
IT'S SALTY...

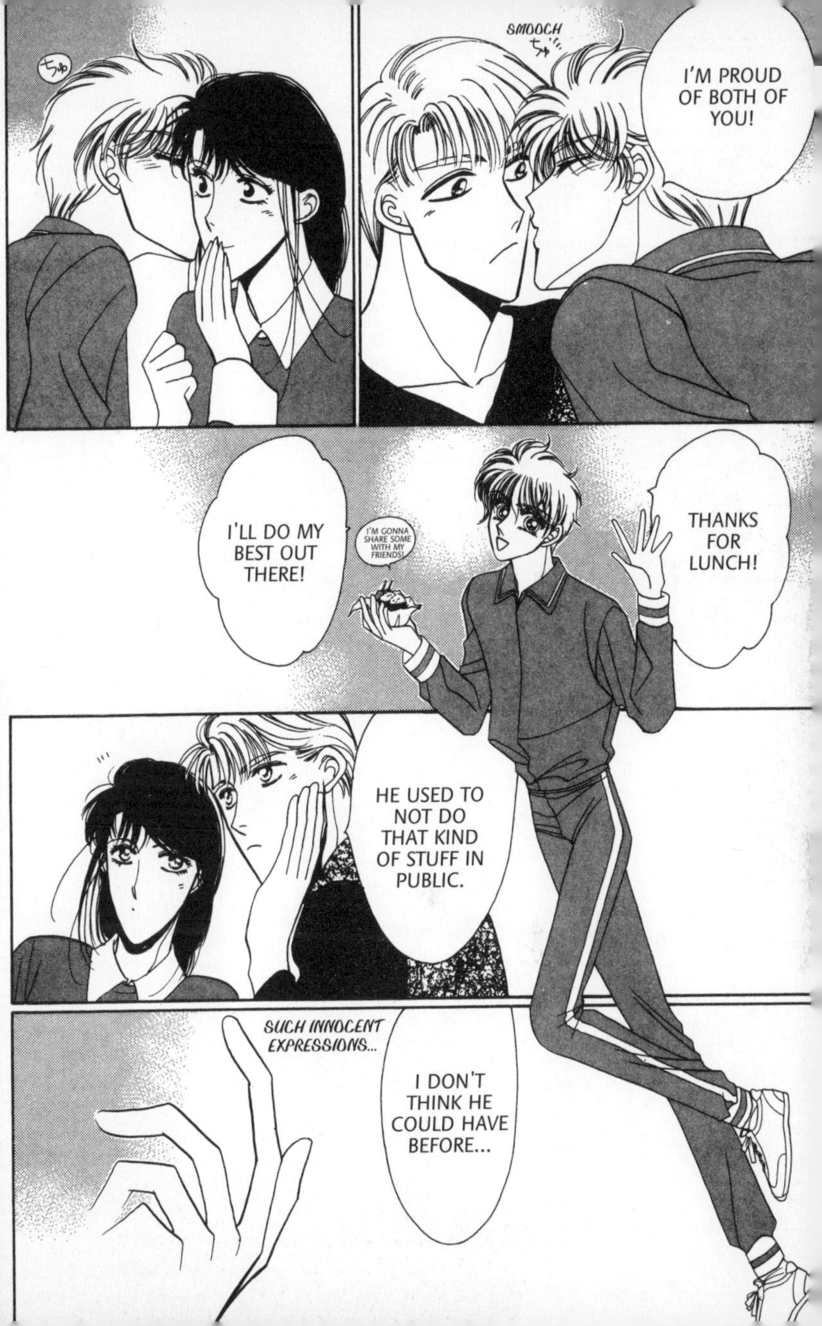
SMOOCH
ちゅ
I'M PROUD OF BOTH OF YOU!
ちゅ
THANKS FOR LUNCH!
I'M GONNA SHARE SOME WITH MY FRIENDS!
I'LL DO MY BEST OUT THERE!
HE USED TO NOT DO THAT KIND OF STUFF IN PUBLIC.
I DON'T THINK HE COULD HAVE BEFORE...
SUCH INNOCENT EXPRESSIONS...

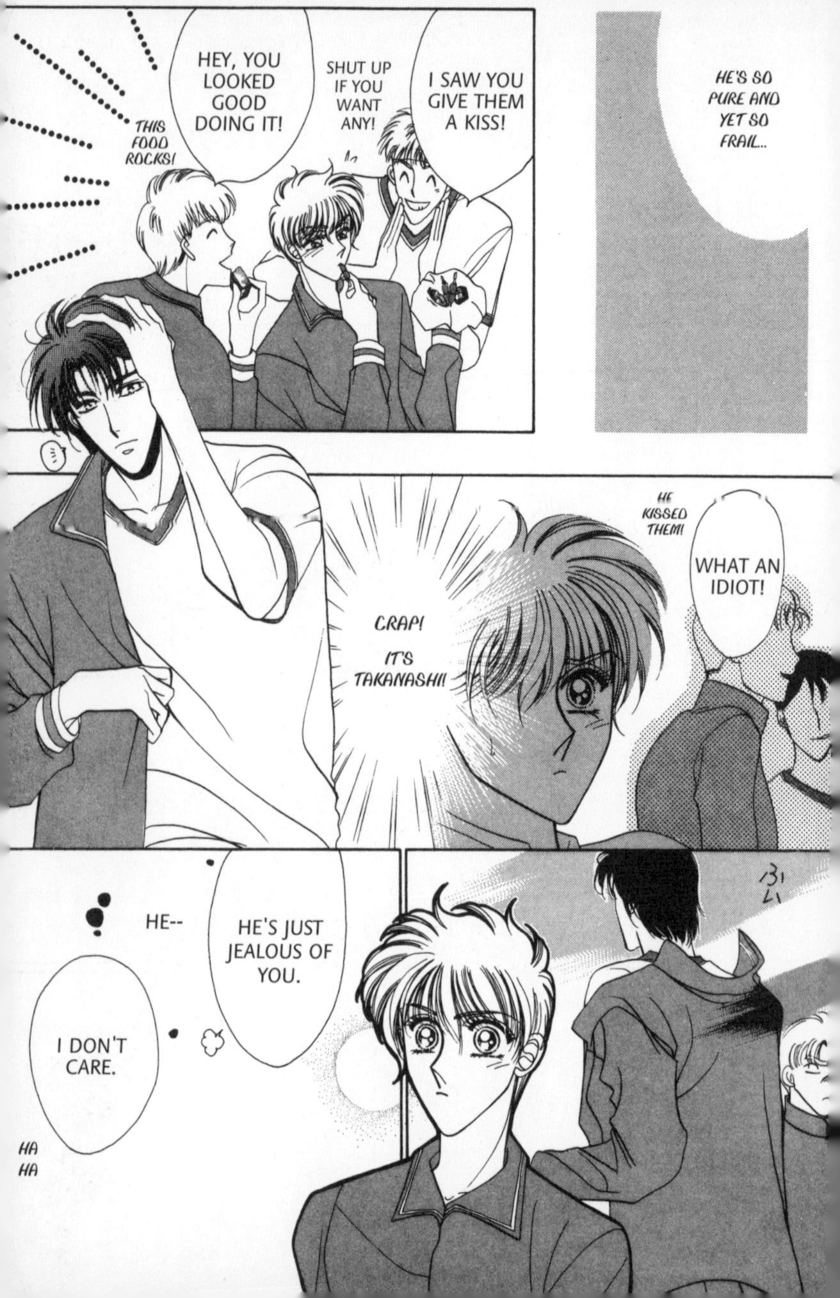
HE'S SO PURE AND YET SO FRAIL...
I SAW YOU GIVE THEM A KISS!
SHUT UP IF YOU WANT ANY!
HEY, YOU LOOKED GOOD DOING IT!
THIS FOOD ROCKS!
HE KISSED THEM!
WHAT AN IDIOT!
CRAP!
IT'S TAKANASHI!
ぷい
HE--
HE'S JUST JEALOUS OF YOU.
I DON'T CARE.
HA HA

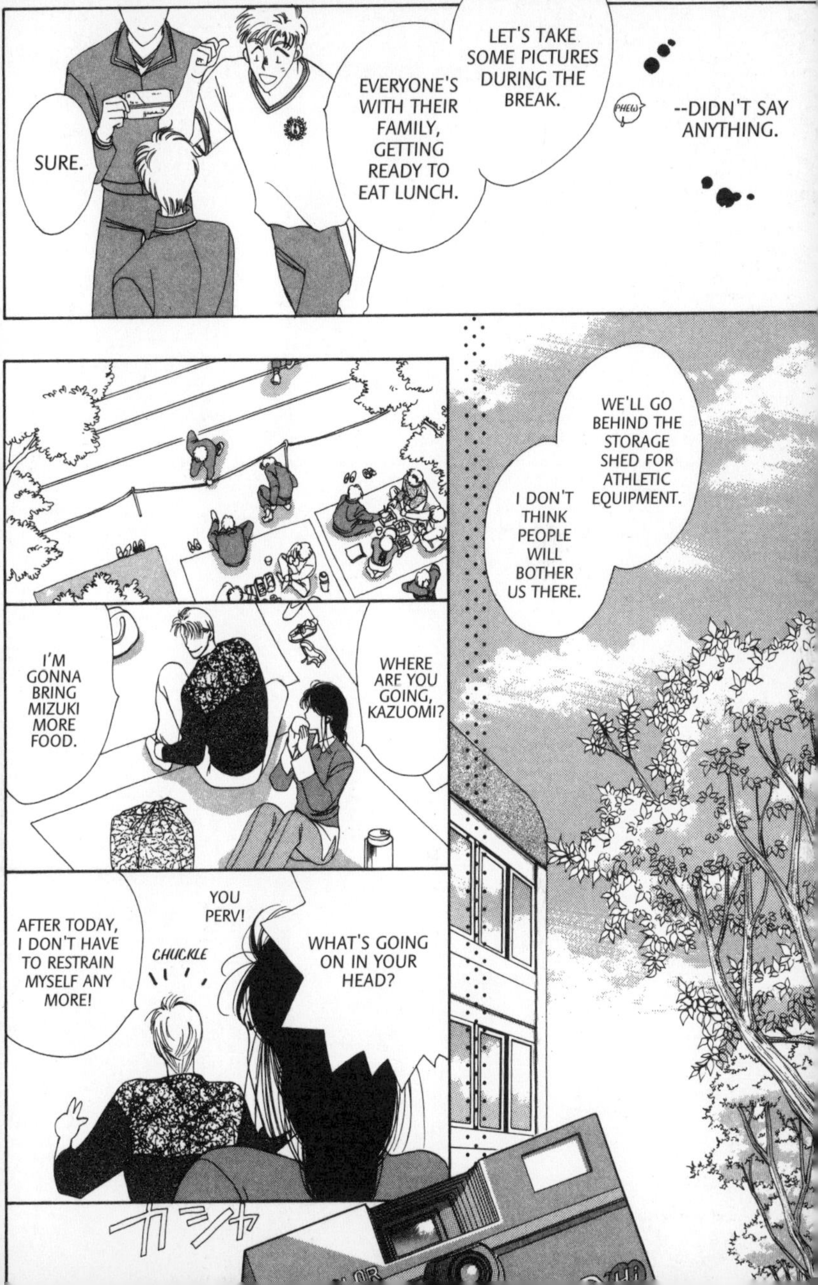
PHEW
--DIDN'T SAY ANYTHING.
LET'S TAKE SOME PICTURES DURING THE BREAK.
EVERYONE'S WITH THEIR FAMILY, GETTING READY TO EAT LUNCH.
SURE.
WE'LL GO BEHIND THE STORAGE SHED FOR ATHLETIC EQUIPMENT.
I DON'T THINK PEOPLE WILL BOTHER US THERE.
WHERE ARE YOU GOING, KAZUOMI?
I'M GONNA BRING MIZUKI MORE FOOD.
YOU PERV!
WHAT'S GOING ON IN YOUR HEAD?
CHUCKLE
AFTER TODAY, I DON'T HAVE TO RESTRAIN MYSELF ANY MORE!
カシャ

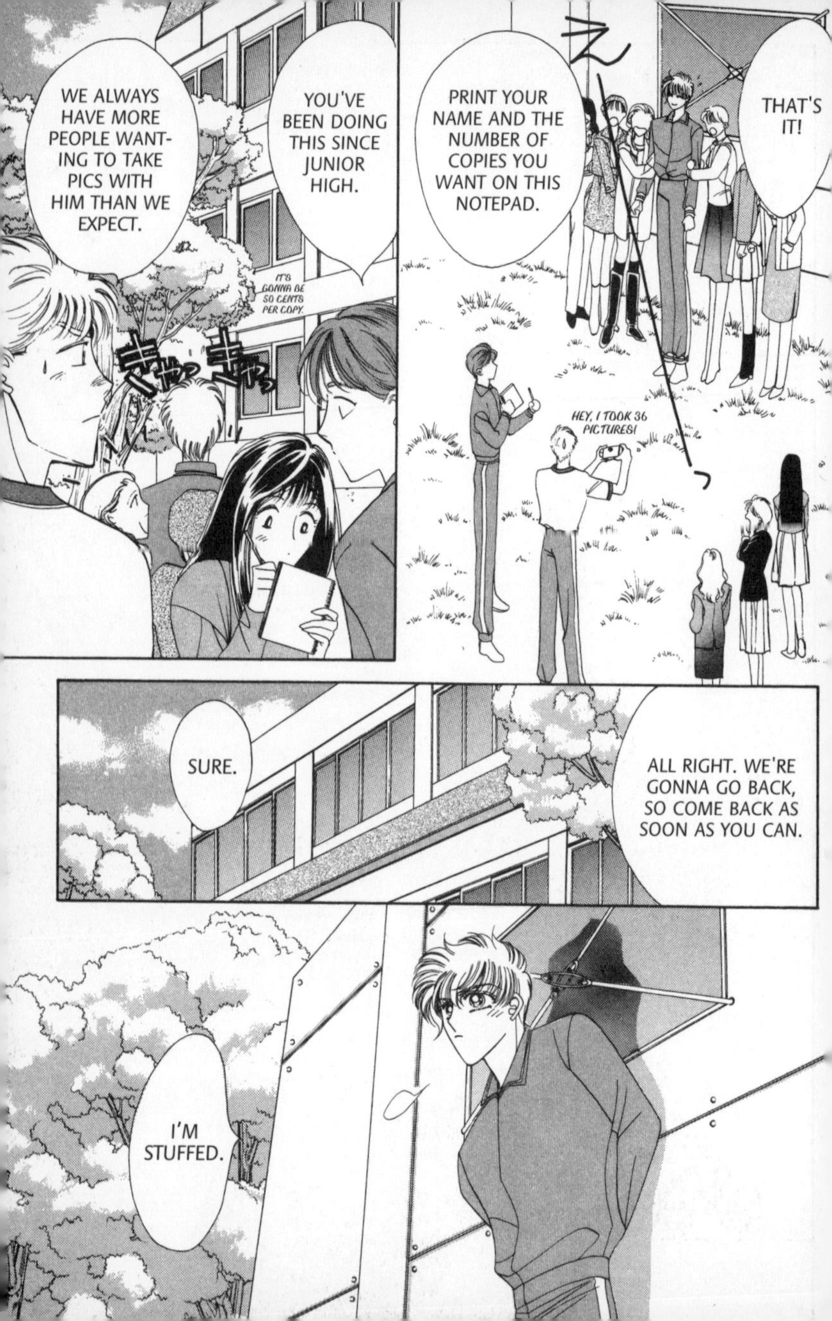
THAT'S IT!
PRINT YOUR NAME AND THE NUMBER OF COPIES YOU WANT ON THIS NOTEPAD.
HEY, I TOOK 36 PICTURES!
YOU'VE BEEN DOING THIS SINCE JUNIOR HIGH.
WE ALWAYS HAVE MORE PEOPLE WANTING TO TAKE PICS WITH HIM THAN WE EXPECT.
IT'S GONNA BE 50 CENTS PER COPY.
ALL RIGHT. WE'RE GONNA GO BACK, SO COME BACK AS SOON AS YOU CAN.
SURE.
I'M STUFFED.

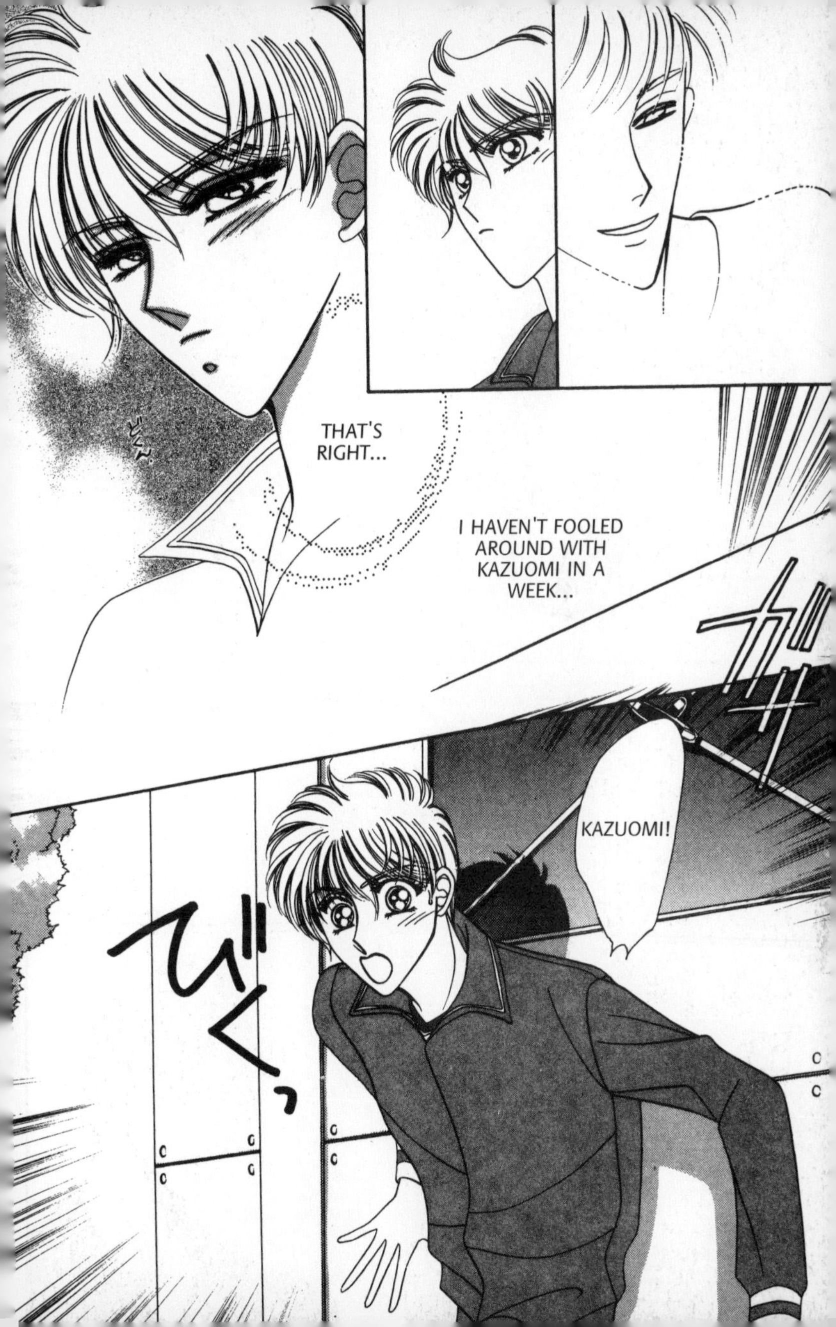
THAT'S RIGHT...
I HAVEN'T FOOLED AROUND WITH KAZUOMI IN A WEEK...
KAZUOMI!
びくっ

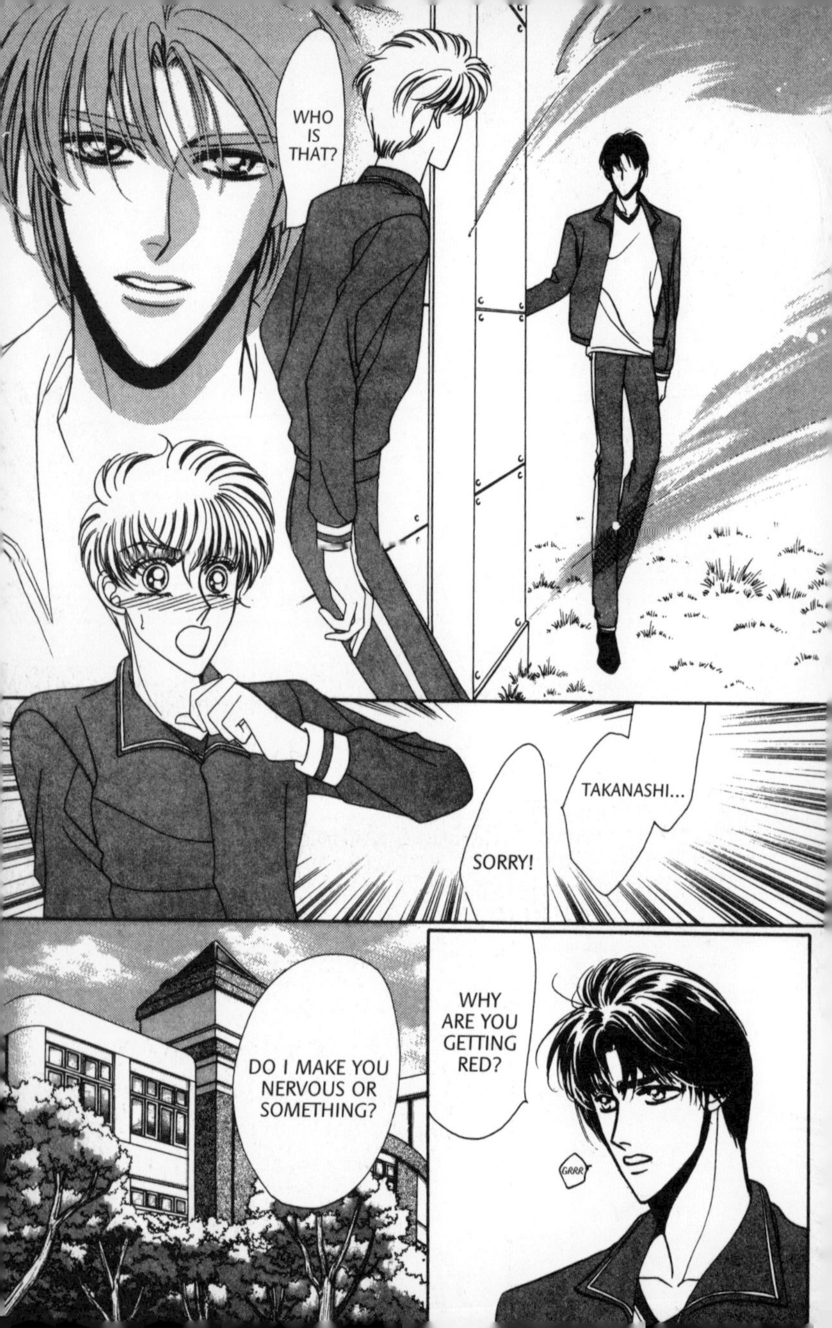
WHO IS THAT?
TAKANASHI...
SORRY!
WHY ARE YOU GETTING RED?
GRRR
DO I MAKE YOU NERVOUS OR SOMETHING?

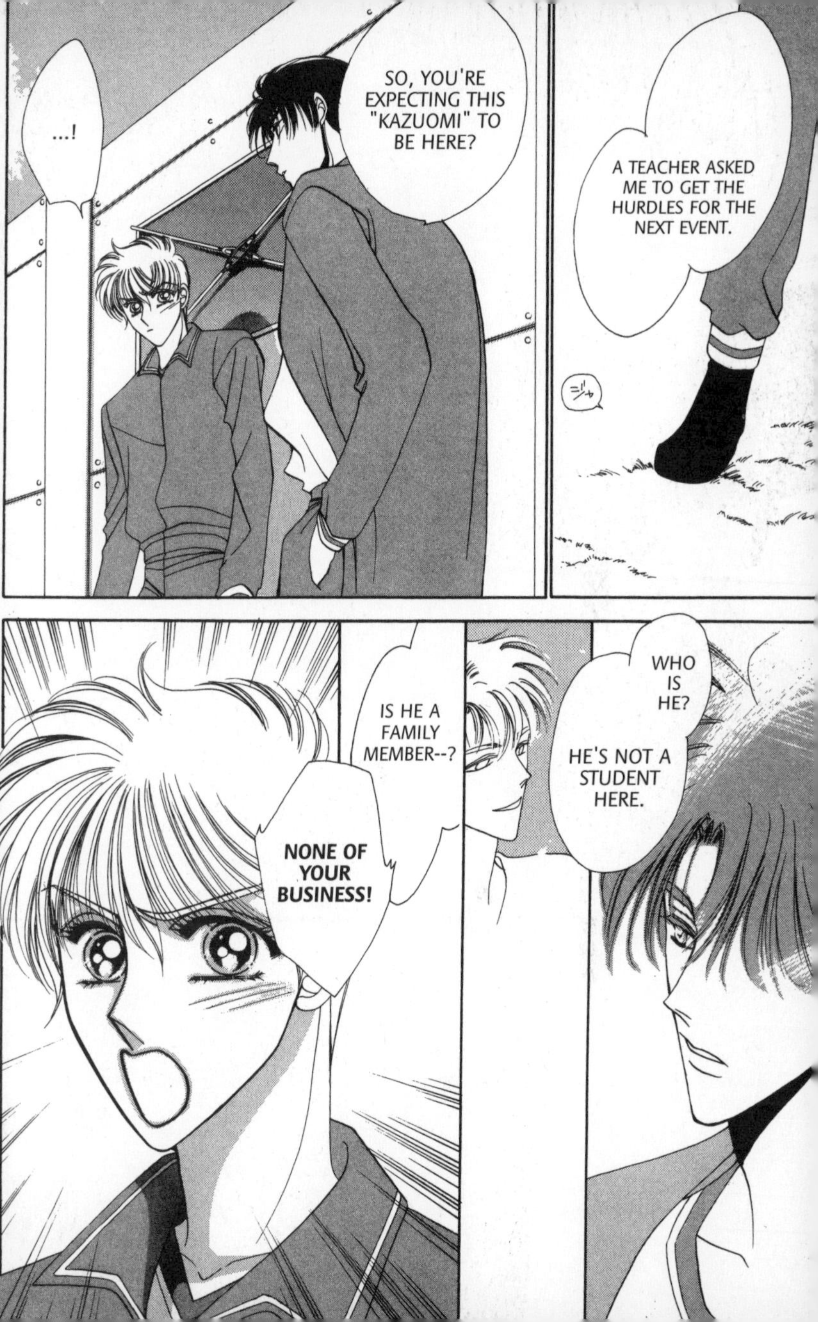
A TEACHER ASKED ME TO GET THE HURDLES FOR THE NEXT EVENT.
SO, YOU'RE EXPECTING THIS "KAZUOMI" TO BE HERE?
...!
WHO IS HE?
HE'S NOT A STUDENT HERE.
IS HE A FAMILY MEMBER--?
NONE OF YOUR BUSINESS!

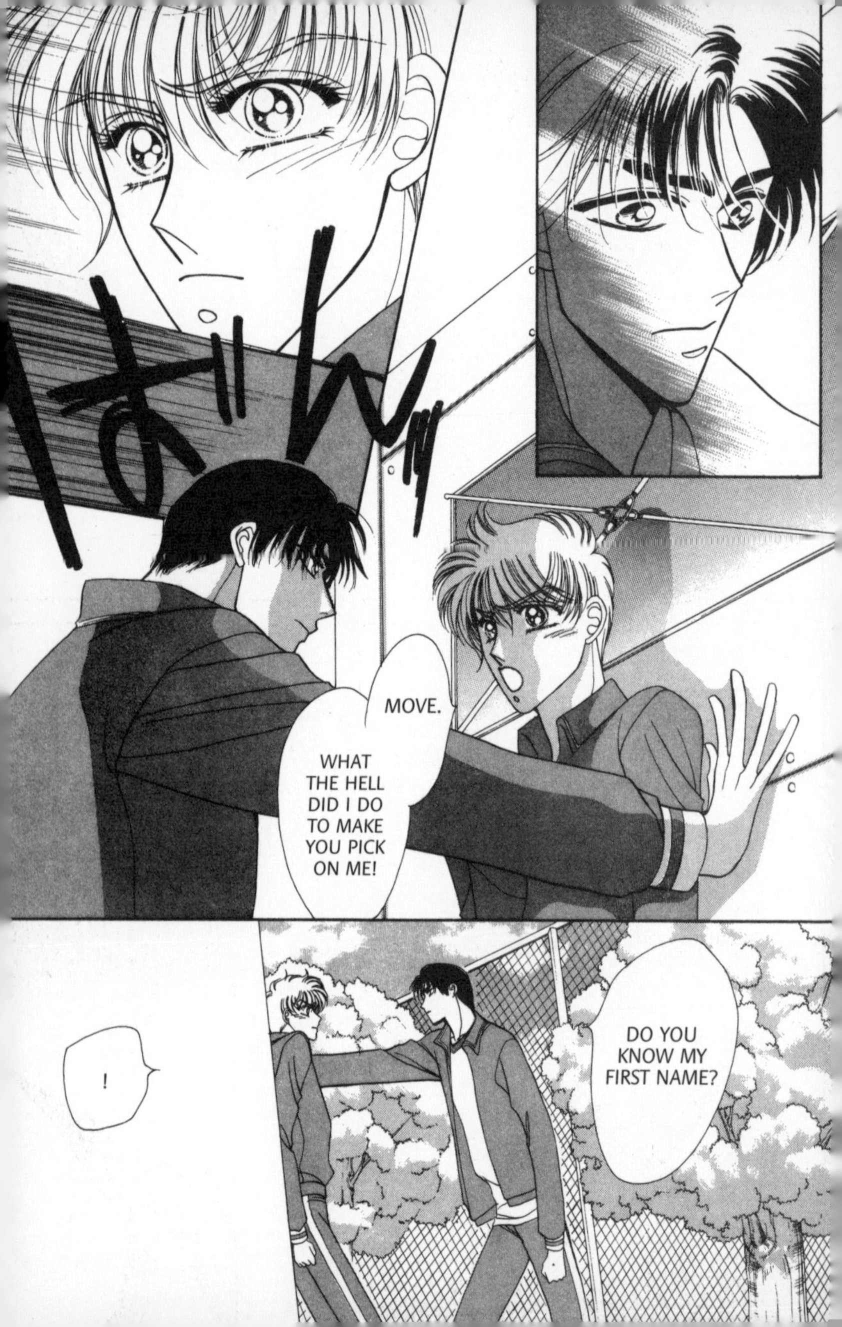
MOVE.
WHAT THE HELL DID I DO TO MAKE YOU PICK ON ME!
DO YOU KNOW MY FIRST NAME?
!

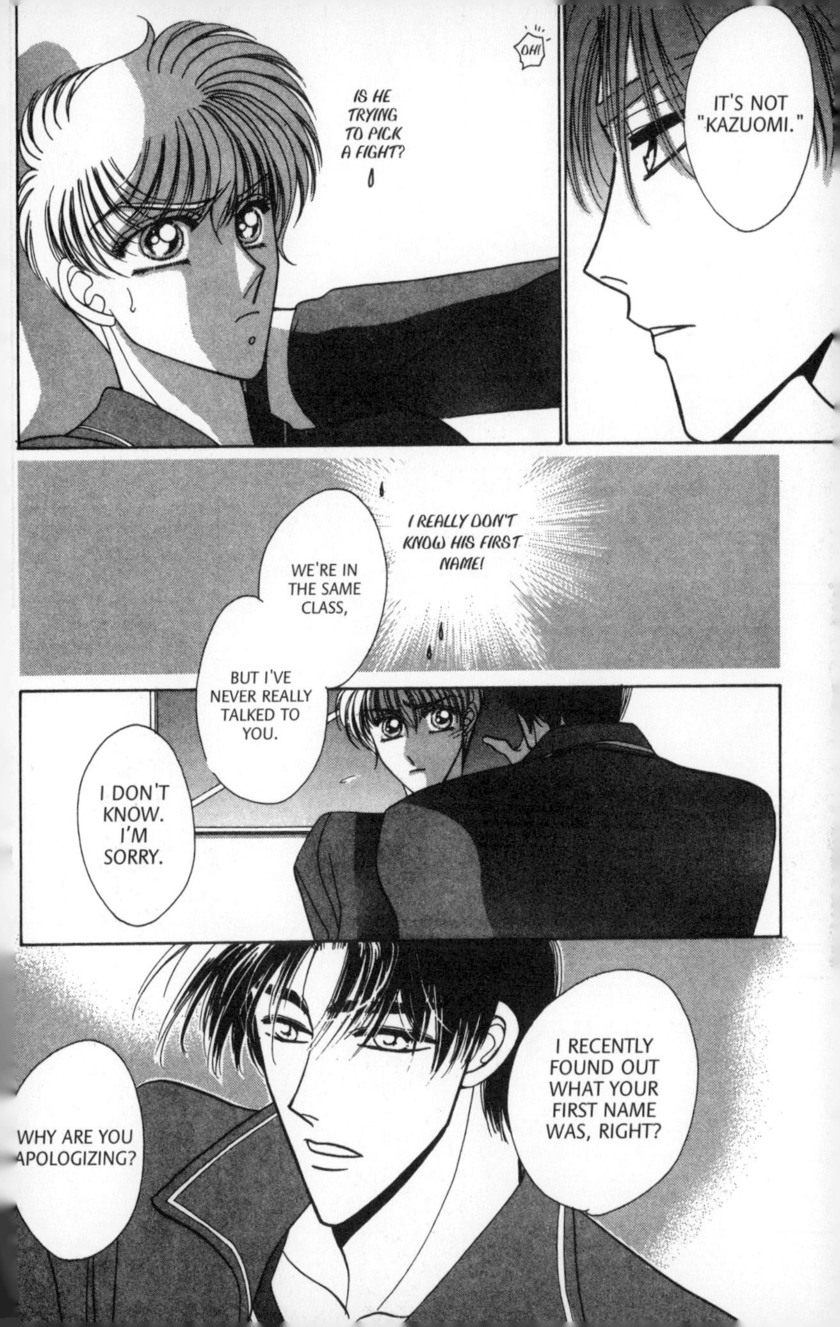
IT'S NOT "KAZUOMI."
OH!
IS HE TRYING TO PICK A FIGHT?
I REALLY DON'T KNOW HIS FIRST NAME!
WE'RE IN THE SAME CLASS,
BUT I'VE NEVER REALLY TALKED TO YOU.
I DON'T KNOW. I'M SORRY.
I RECENTLY FOUND OUT WHAT YOUR FIRST NAME WAS, RIGHT?
WHY ARE YOU APOLOGIZING?

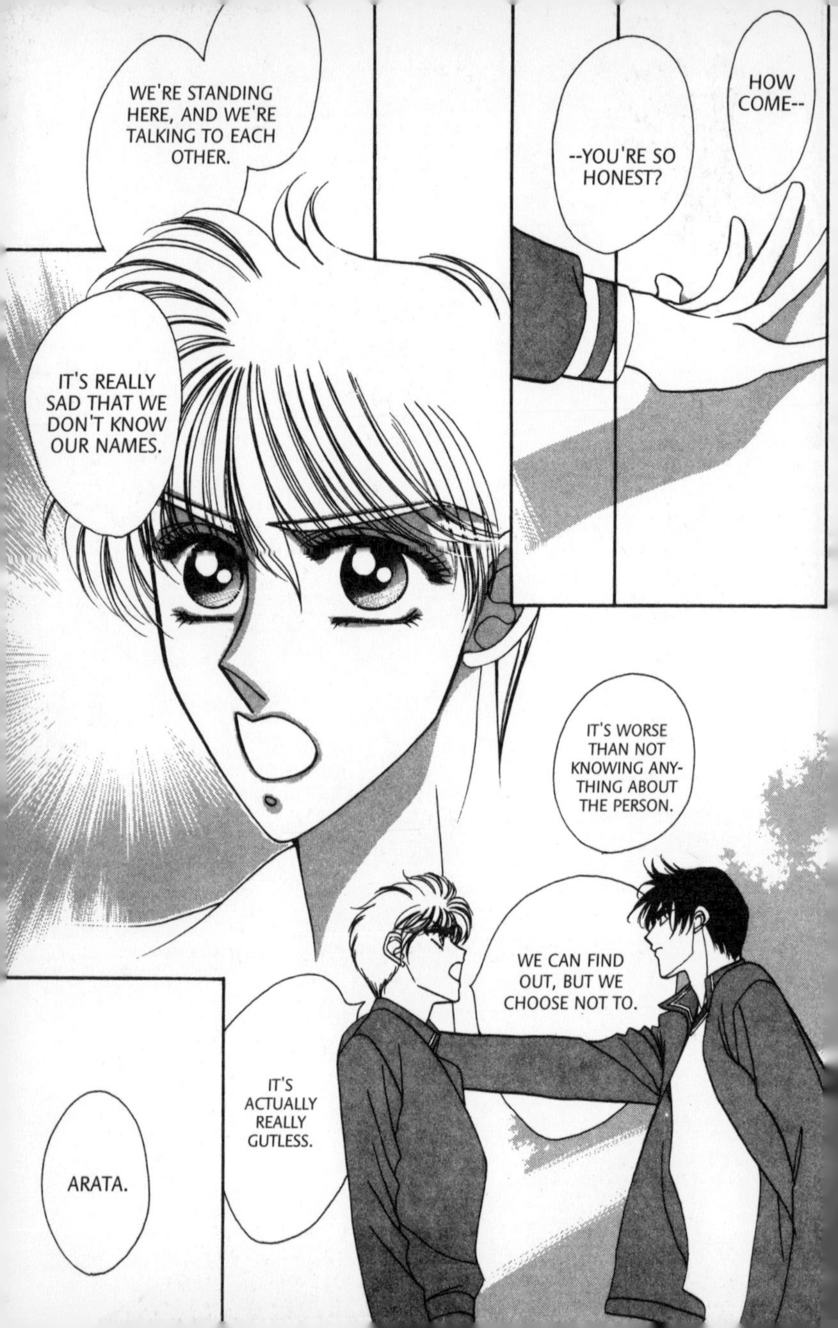
HOW COME--
--YOU'RE SO HONEST?
WE'RE STANDING HERE, AND WE'RE TALKING TO EACH OTHER.
IT'S REALLY SAD THAT WE DON'T KNOW OUR NAMES.
IT'S WORSE THAN NOT KNOWING ANY-THING ABOUT THE PERSON.
WE CAN FIND OUT, BUT WE CHOOSE NOT TO.
IT'S ACTUALLY REALLY GUTLESS.
ARATA.

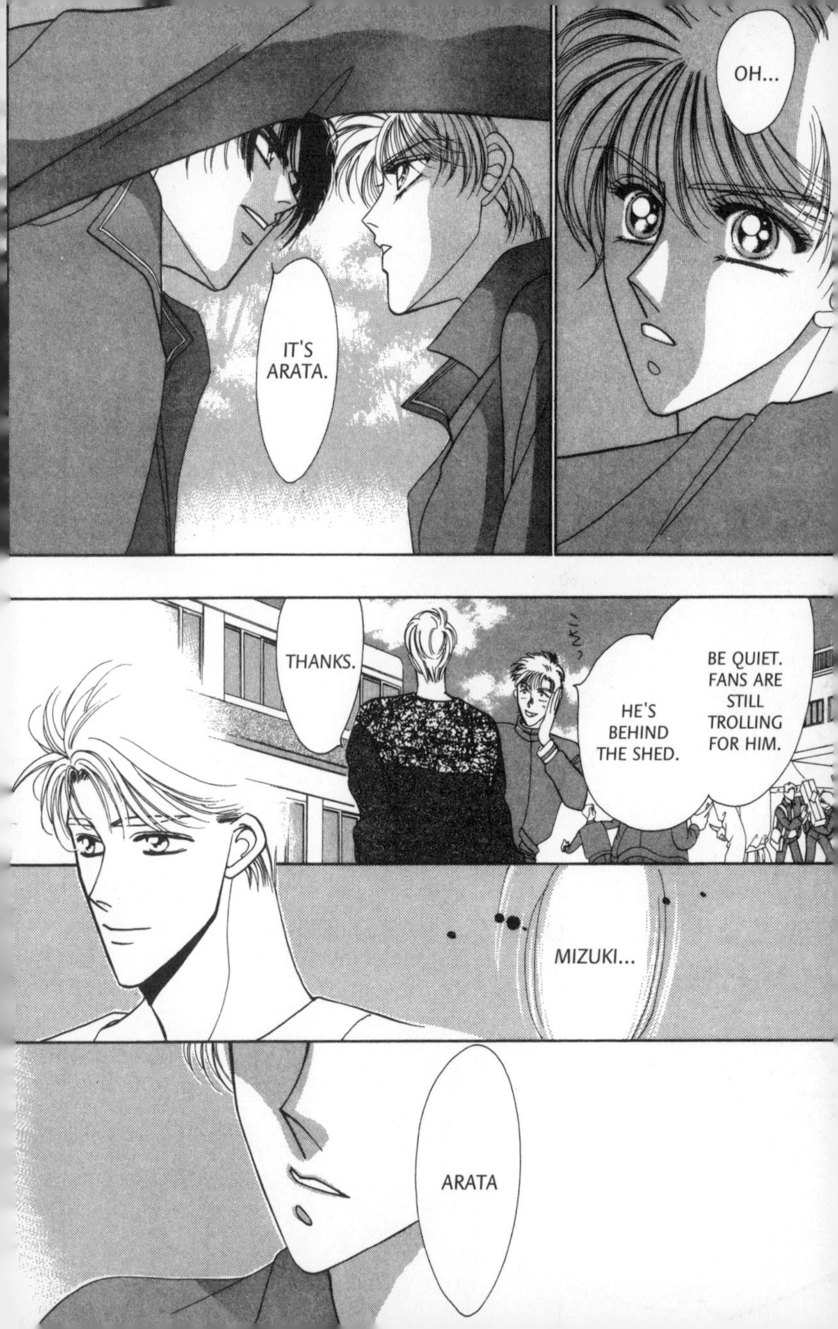
OH...
IT'S ARATA.
BE QUIET. FANS ARE STILL TROLLING FOR HIM.
HE'S BEHIND THE SHED.
THANKS.
MIZUKI...
ARATA

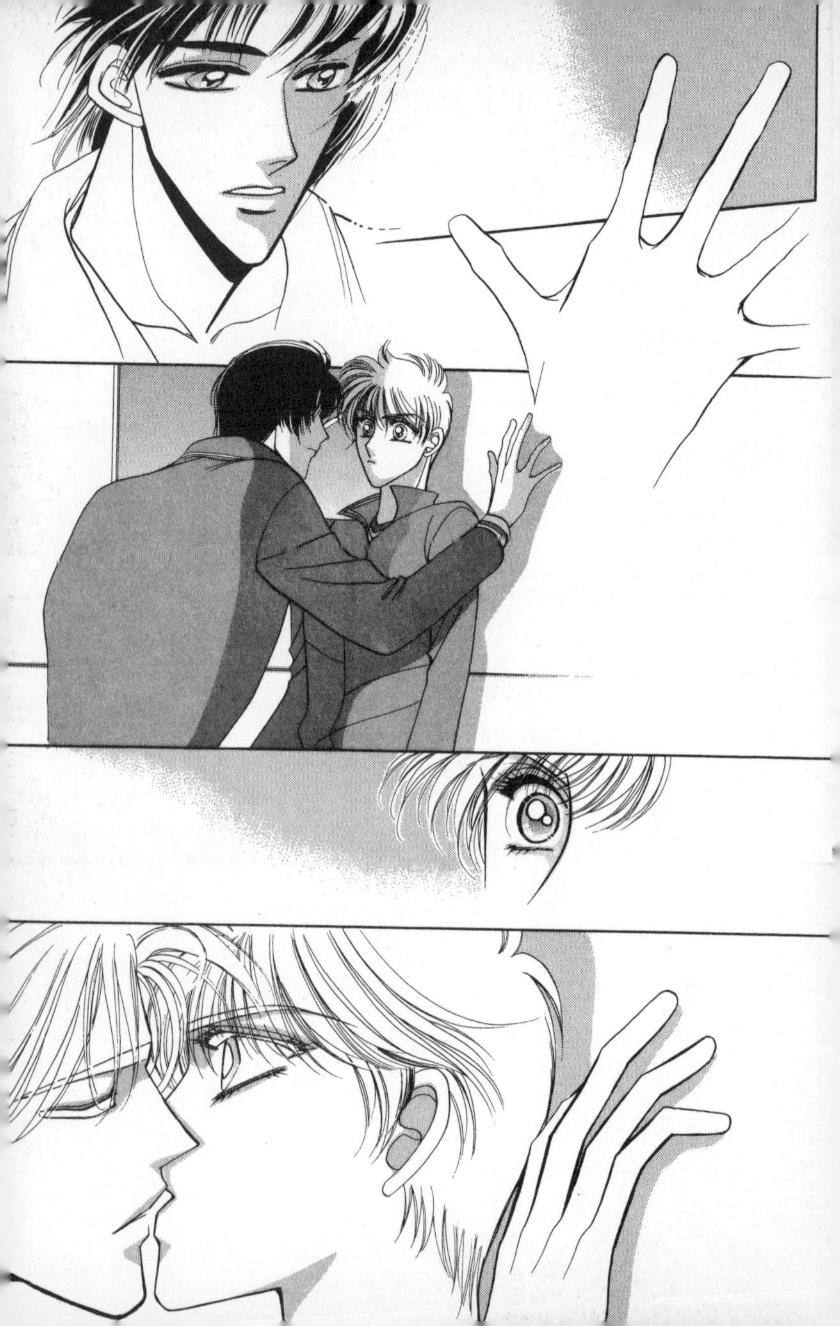

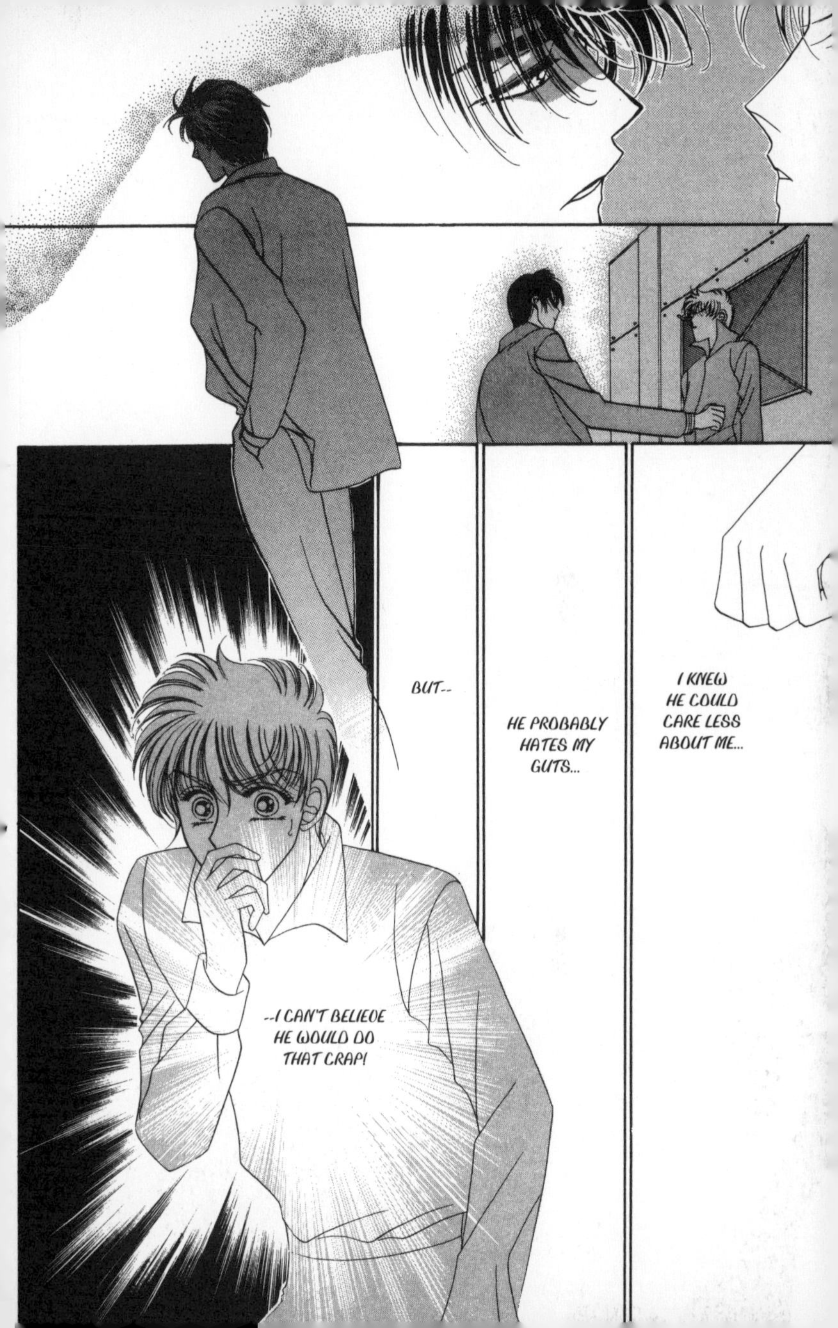
I KNEW HE COULD CARE LESS ABOUT ME...
HE PROBABLY HATES MY GUTS...
BUT--
--I CAN'T BELIEVE HE WOULD DO THAT CRAP!

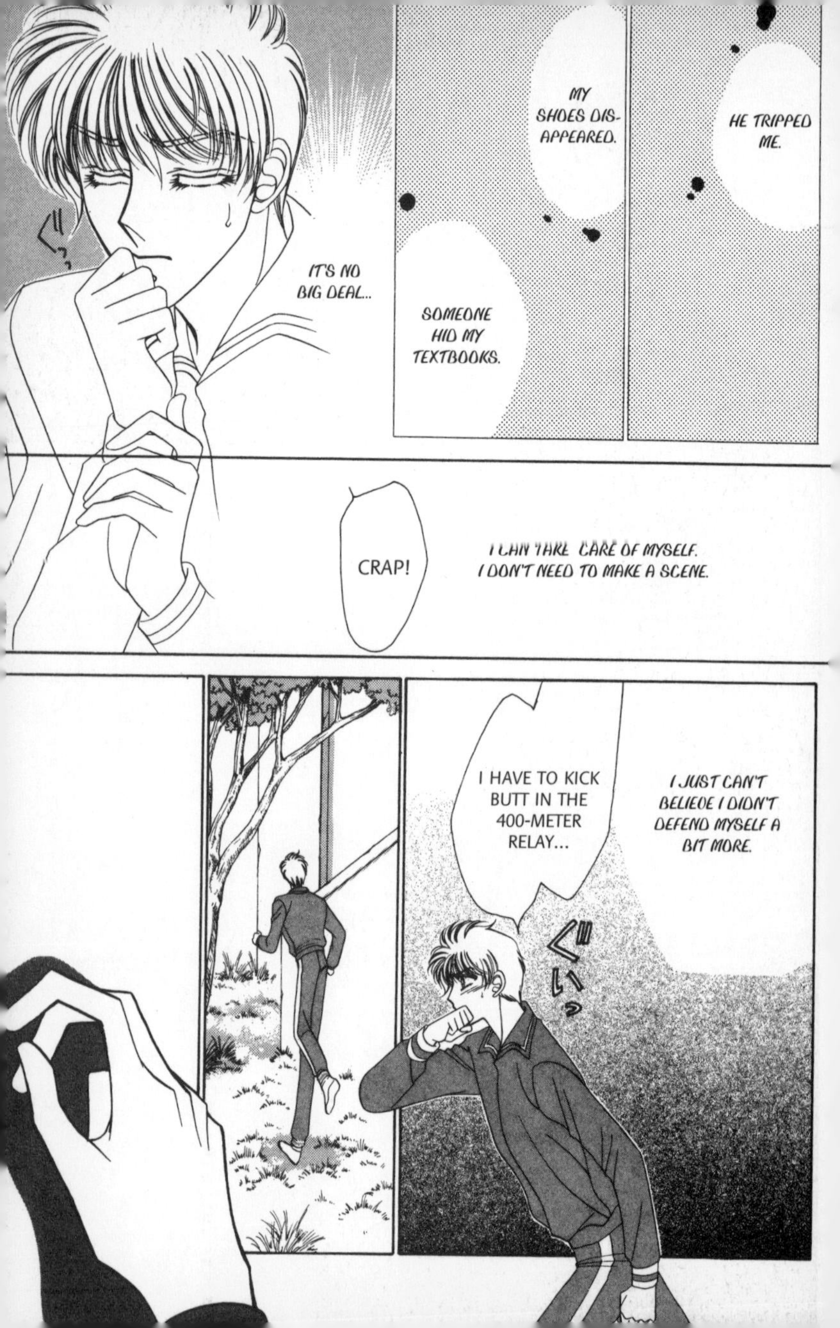
HE TRIPPED ME.
MY SHOES DIS-APPEARED.
SOMEONE HID MY TEXTBOOKS.
IT'S NO BIG DEAL...
I CAN TAKE CARE OF MYSELF. I DON'T NEED TO MAKE A SCENE.
CRAP!
I JUST CAN'T BELIEVE I DIDN'T DEFEND MYSELF A BIT MORE.
I HAVE TO KICK BUTT IN THE 400-METER RELAY...
ぐいっ

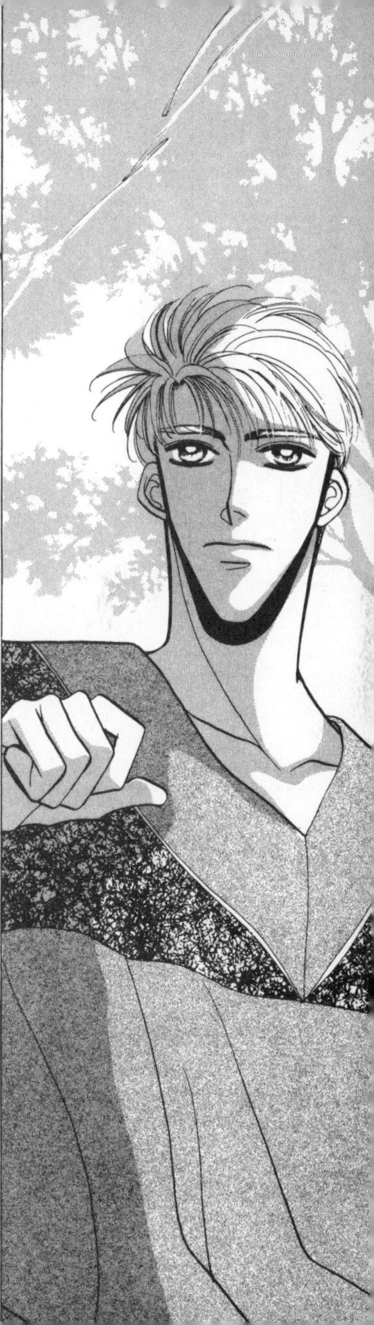

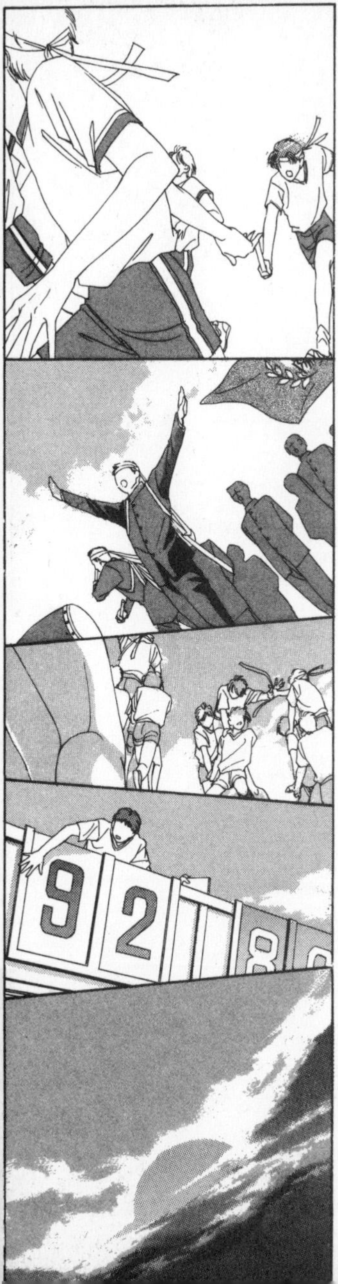
92

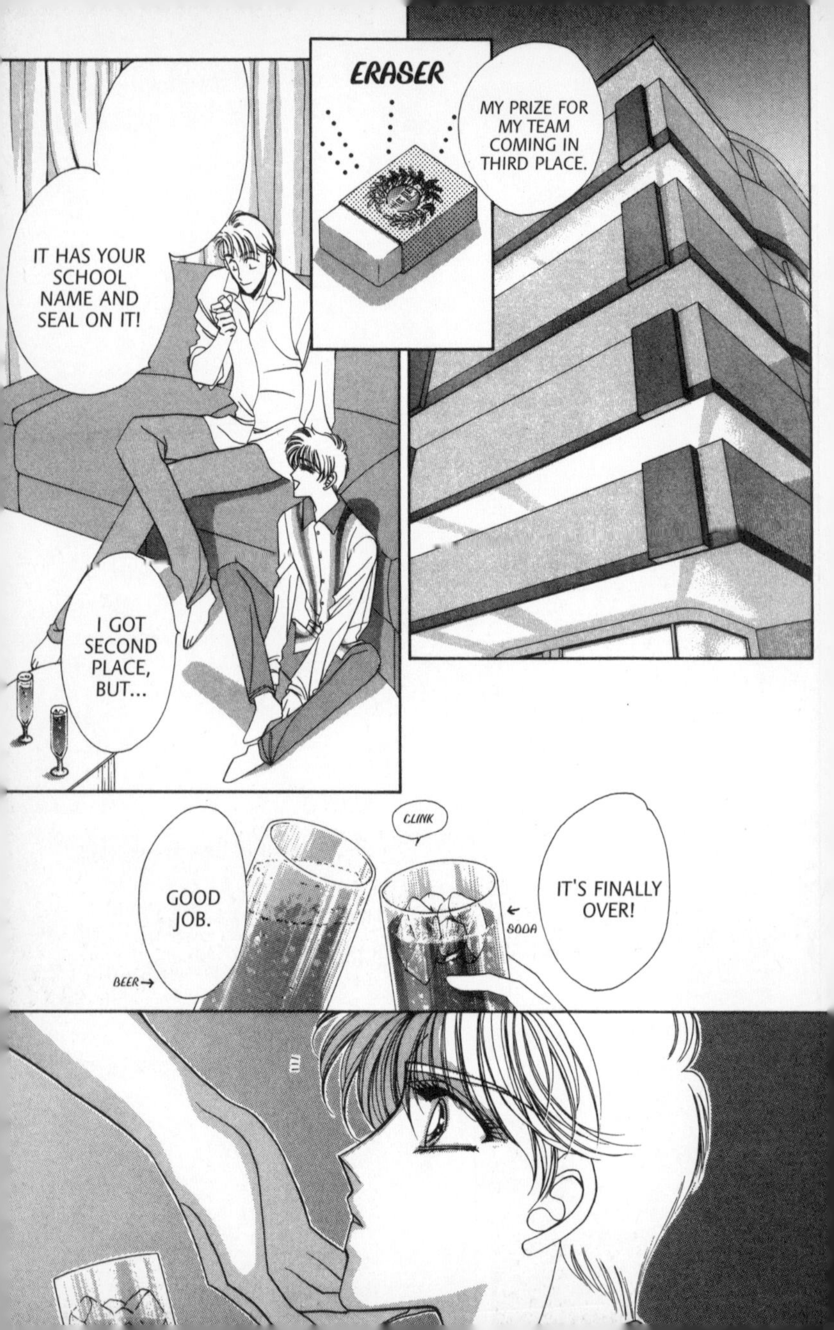
MY PRIZE FOR MY TEAM COMING IN THIRD PLACE.
ERASER
IT HAS YOUR SCHOOL NAME AND SEAL ON IT!
I GOT SECOND PLACE, BUT...
IT'S FINALLY OVER!
SODA
CLINK
GOOD JOB.
BEER

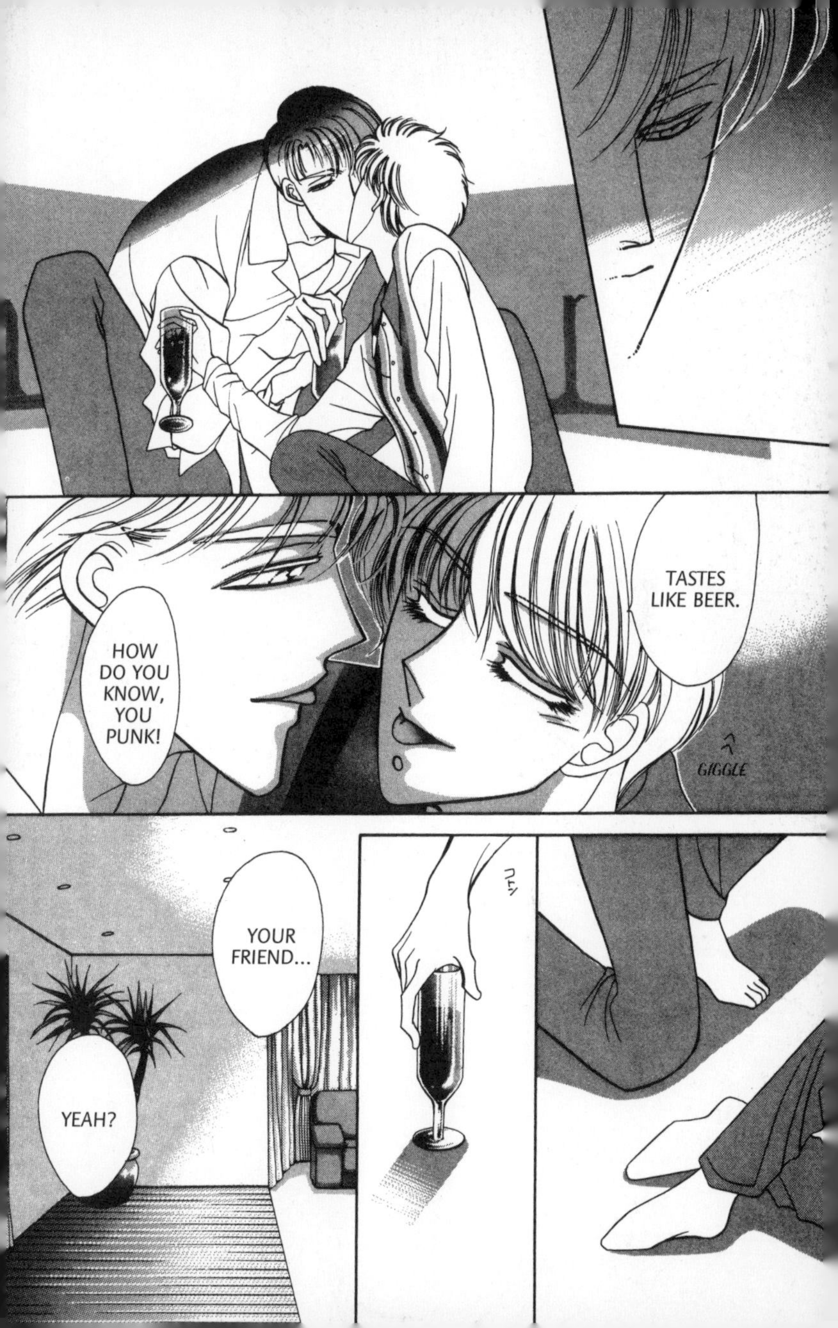
TASTES LIKE BEER.
GIGGLE
HOW DO YOU KNOW, YOU PUNK!
YOUR FRIEND...
YEAH?

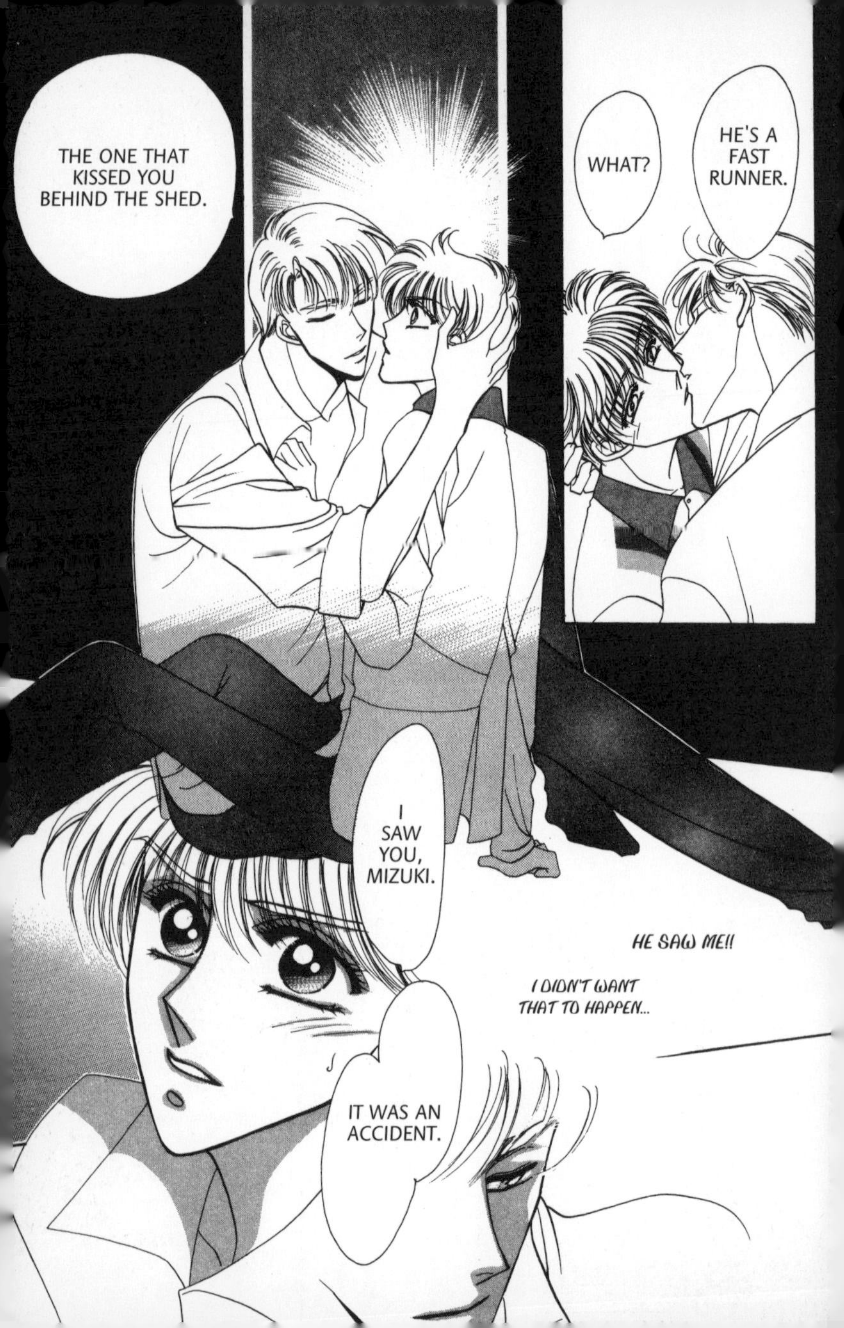
HE'S A FAST RUNNER.
WHAT?
THE ONE THAT KISSED YOU BEHIND THE SHED.
I SAW YOU, MIZUKI.
HE SAW ME!!
I DIDN'T WANT THAT TO HAPPEN...
IT WAS AN ACCIDENT.

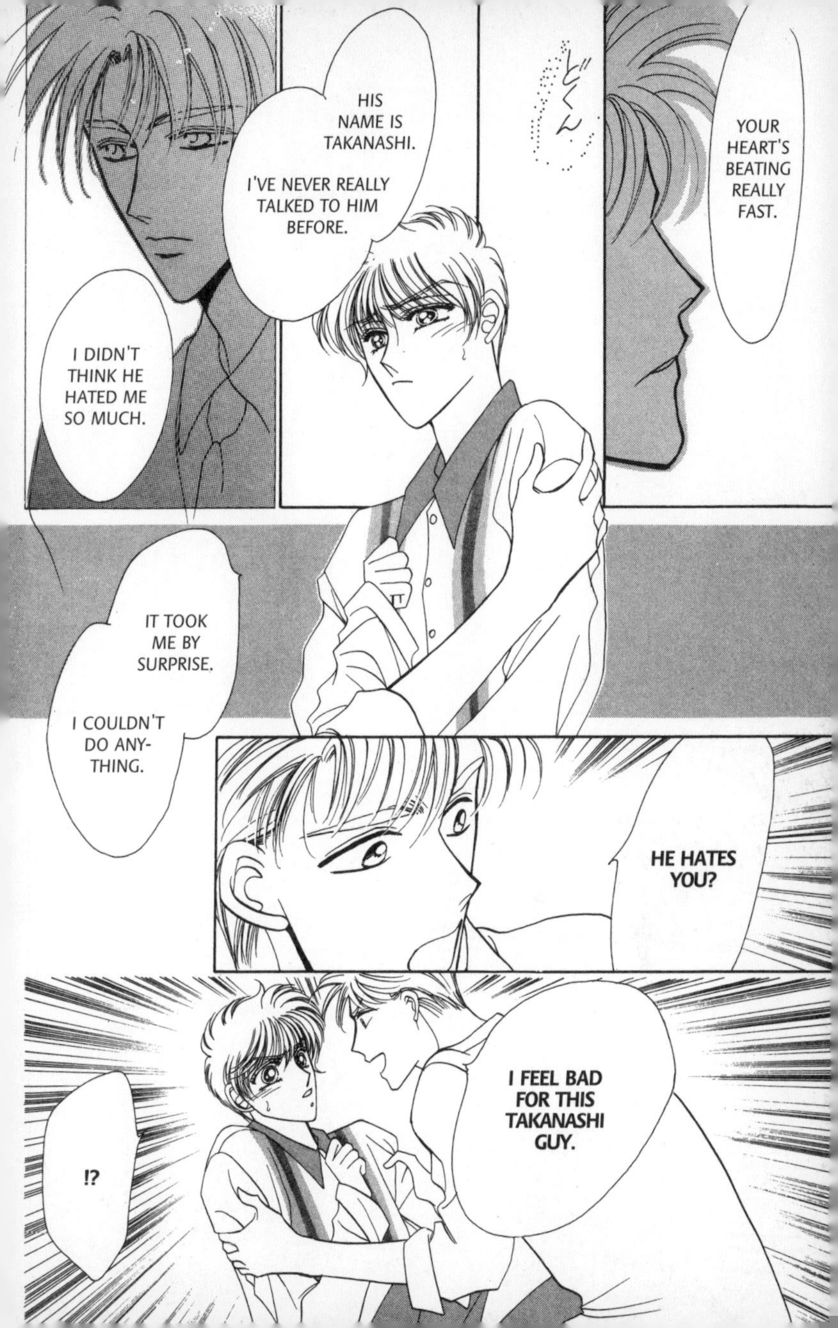
YOUR HEART'S BEATING REALLY FAST.
どくん
HIS NAME IS TAKANASHI.
I'VE NEVER REALLY TALKED TO HIM BEFORE.
I DIDN'T THINK HE HATED ME SO MUCH.
IT TOOK ME BY SURPRISE.
I COULDN'T DO ANY-THING.
HE HATES YOU?
I FEEL BAD FOR THIS TAKANASHI GUY.
!?

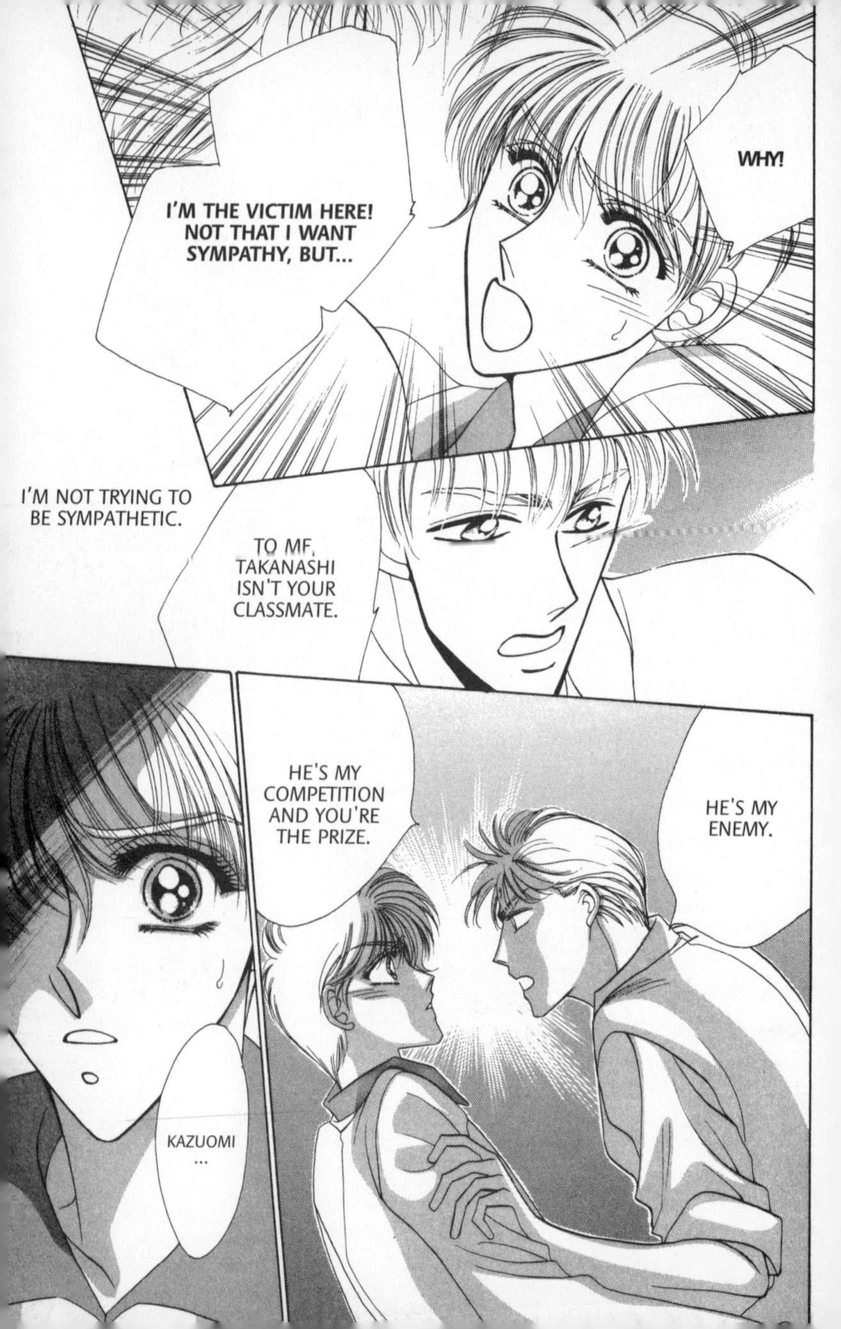
WHY!
I'M THE VICTIM HERE! NOT THAT I WANT SYMPATHY, BUT...
I'M NOT TRYING TO BE SYMPATHETIC.
TO ME, TAKANASHI ISN'T YOUR CLASSMATE.
HE'S MY ENEMY.
HE'S MY COMPETITION AND YOU'RE THE PRIZE.
KAZUOMI ...

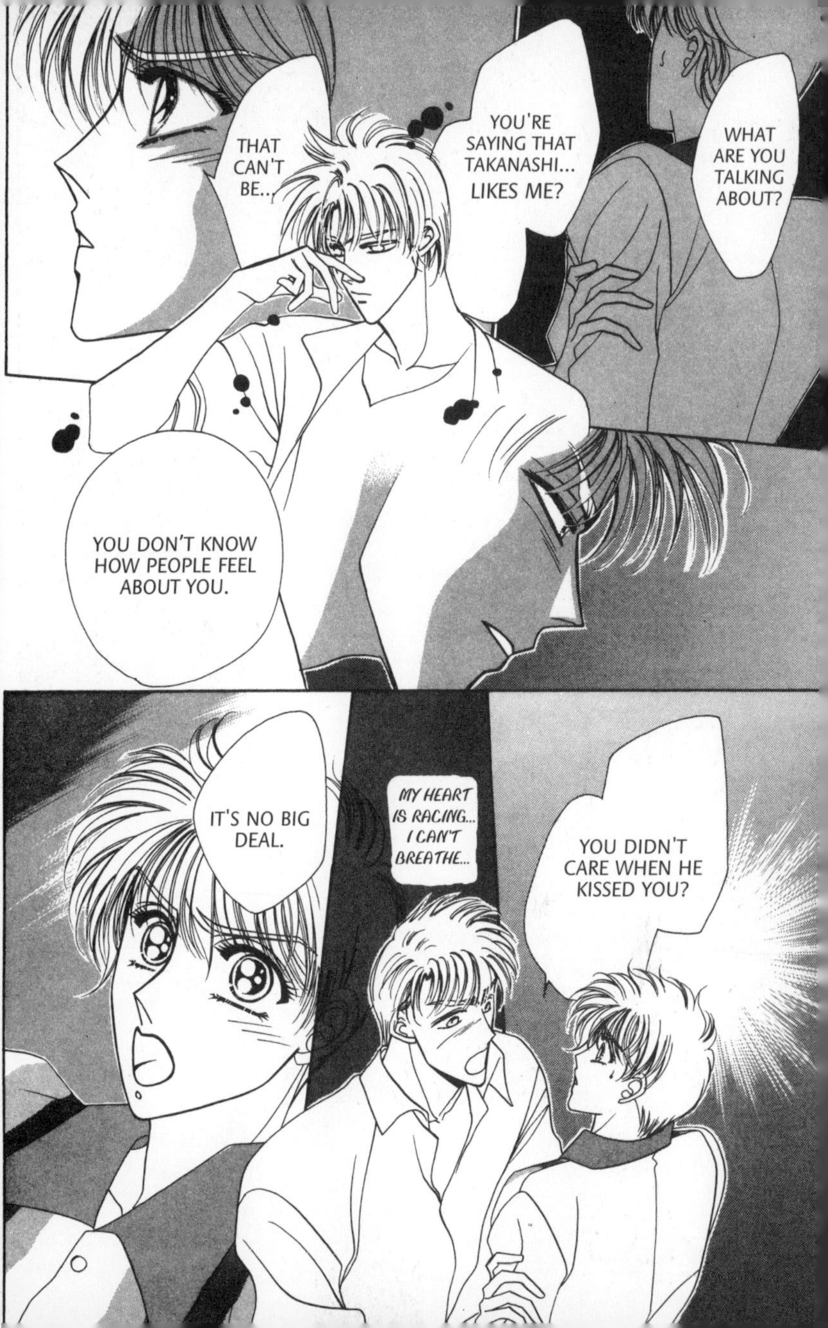
WHAT ARE YOU TALKING ABOUT?
YOU'RE SAYING THAT TAKANASHI... LIKES ME?
THAT CAN'T BE...
YOU DON'T KNOW HOW PEOPLE FEEL ABOUT YOU.
YOU DIDN'T CARE WHEN HE KISSED YOU?
MY HEART IS RACING... I CAN'T BREATHE...
IT'S NO BIG DEAL.

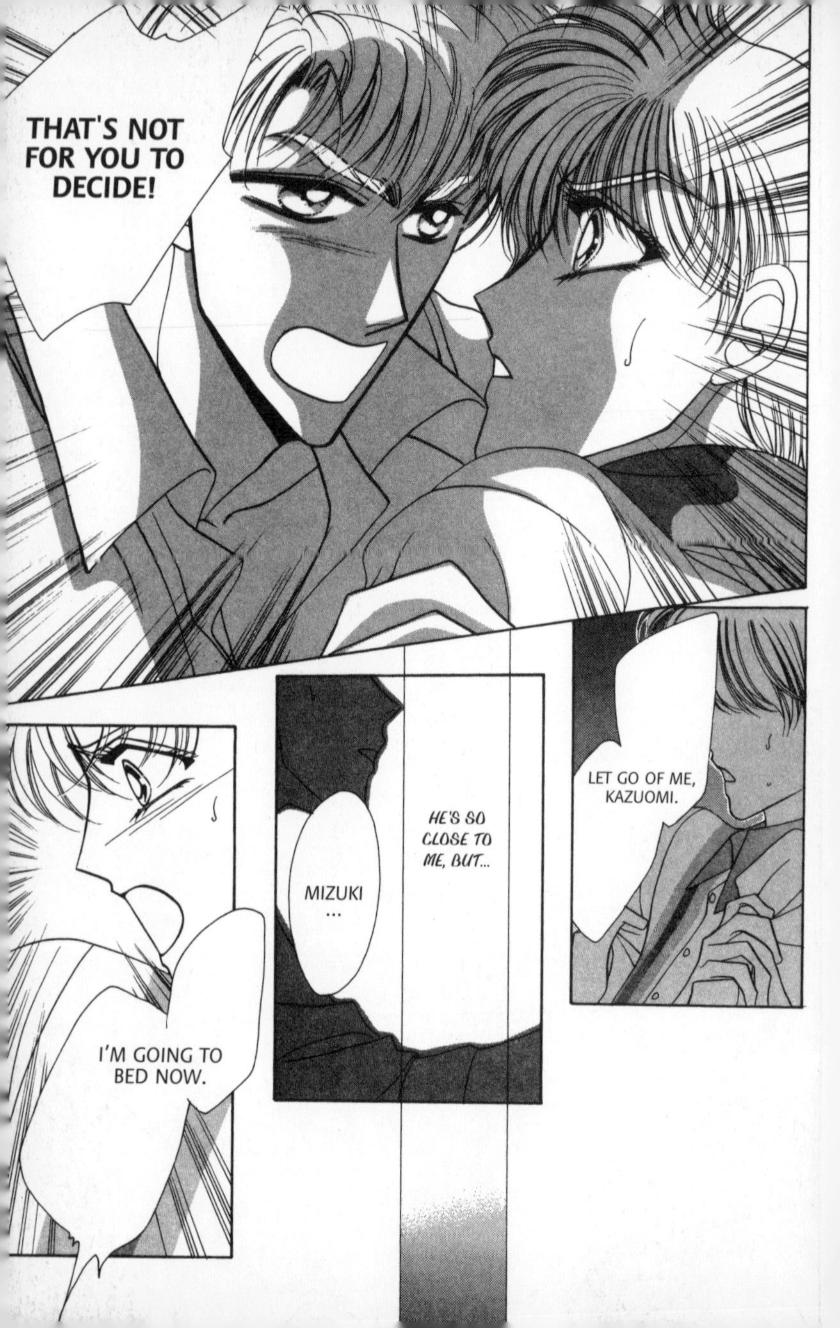
THAT'S NOT FOR YOU TO DECIDE!
LET GO OF ME, KAZUOMI.
HE'S SO CLOSE TO ME, BUT...
MIZUKI ...
I'M GOING TO BED NOW.

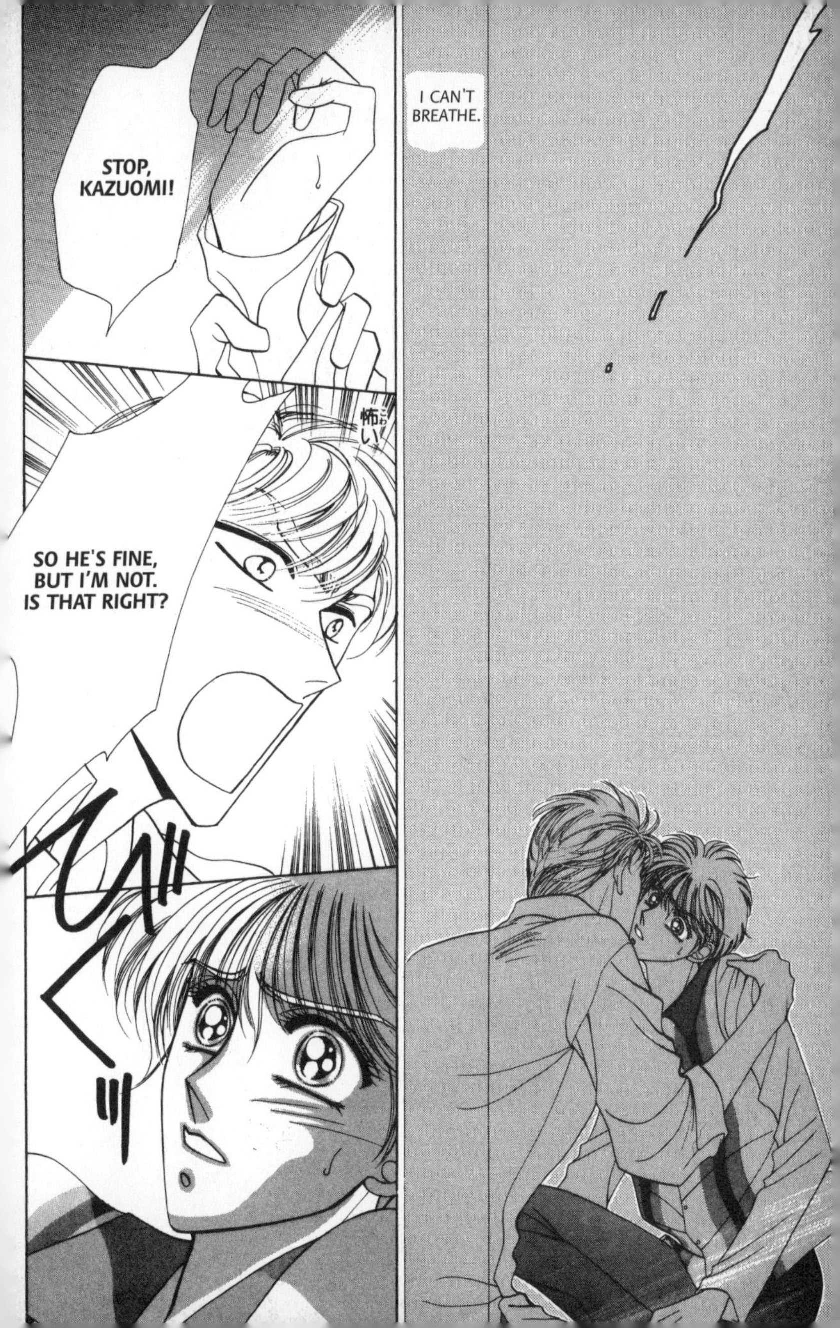
I CAN'T BREATHE.
STOP, KAZUOMI!
怖い
SO HE'S FINE, BUT I'M NOT. IS THAT RIGHT?

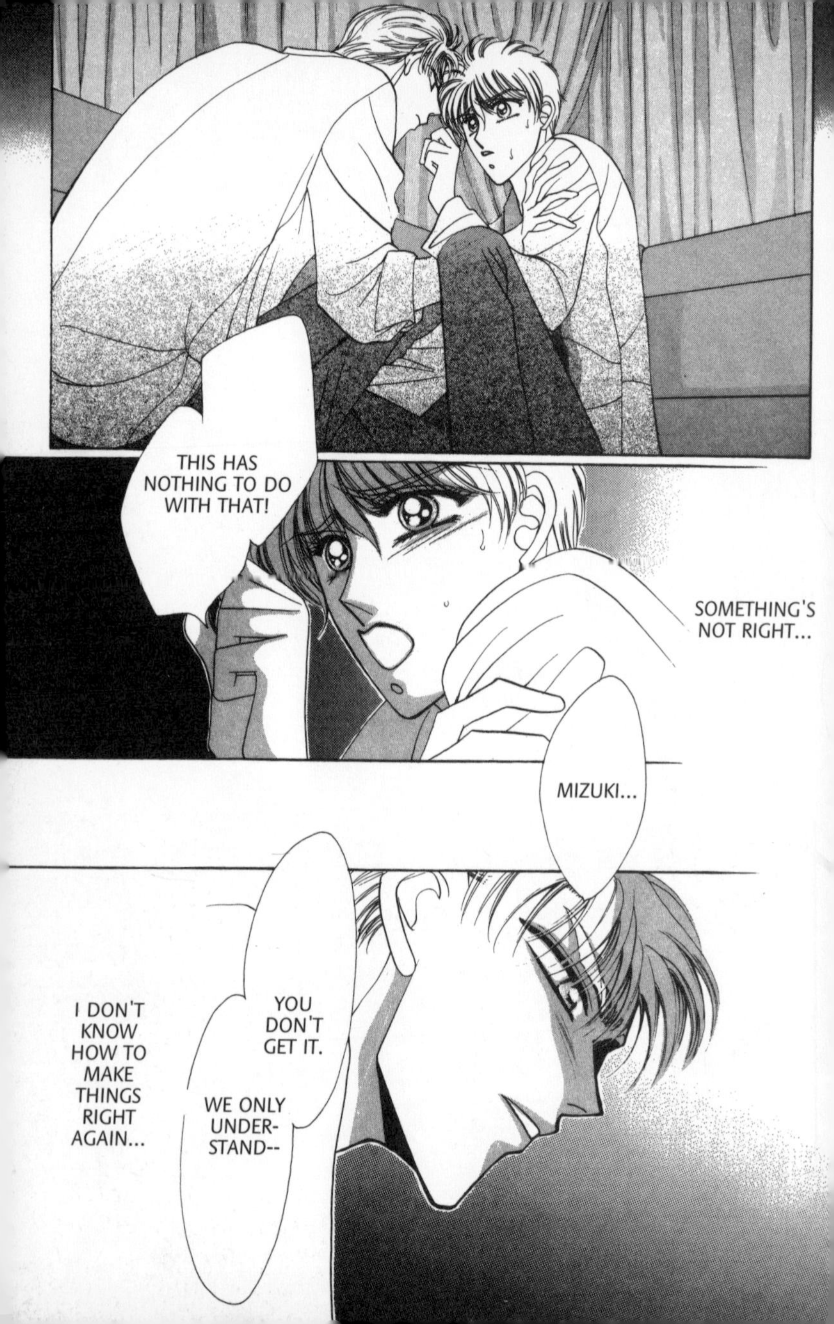
SOMETHING'S NOT RIGHT...
THIS HAS NOTHING TO DO WITH THAT!
MIZUKI...
YOU DON'T GET IT.
WE ONLY UNDER-STAND--
I DON'T KNOW HOW TO MAKE THINGS RIGHT AGAIN...

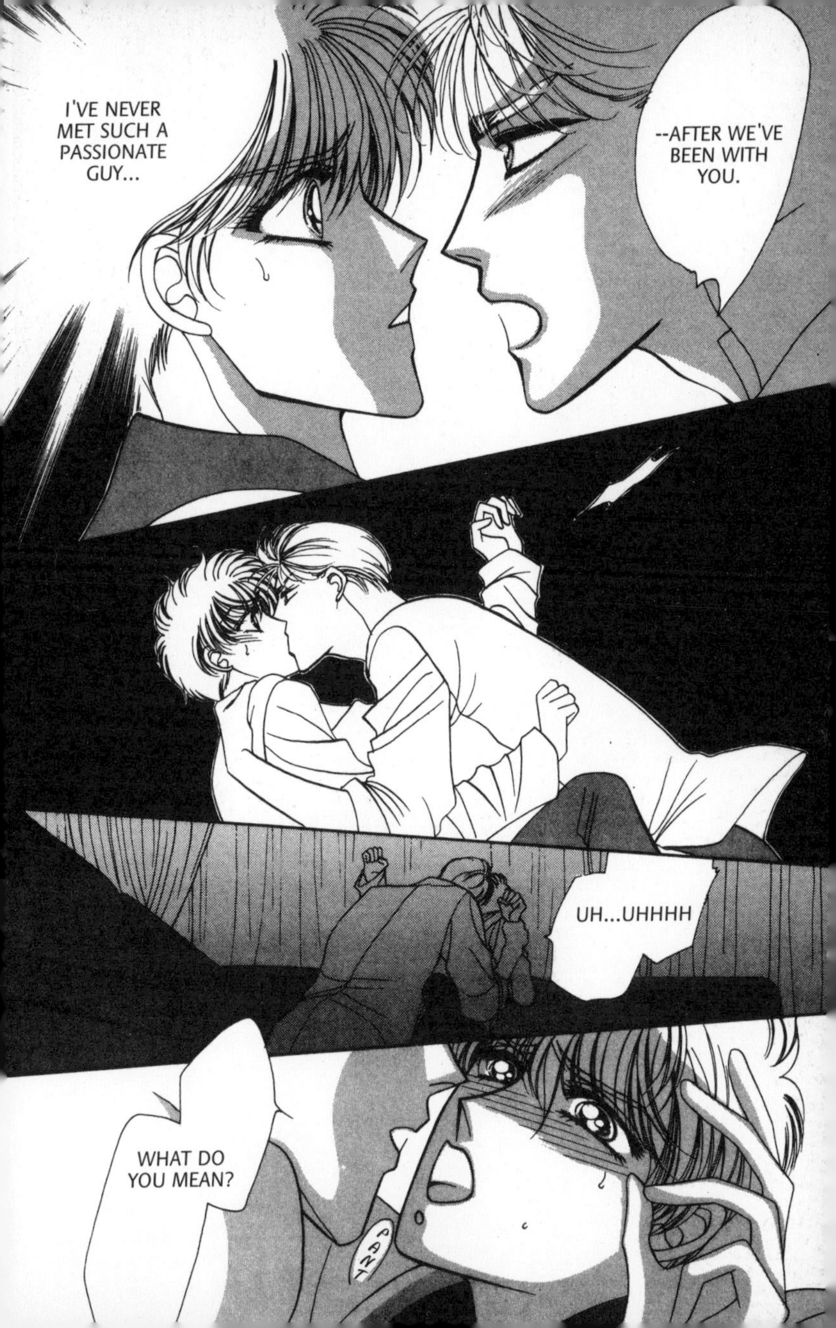
--AFTER WE'VE BEEN WITH YOU.
I'VE NEVER MET SUCH A PASSIONATE GUY...
UH...UHHHH
WHAT DO YOU MEAN?
PANT

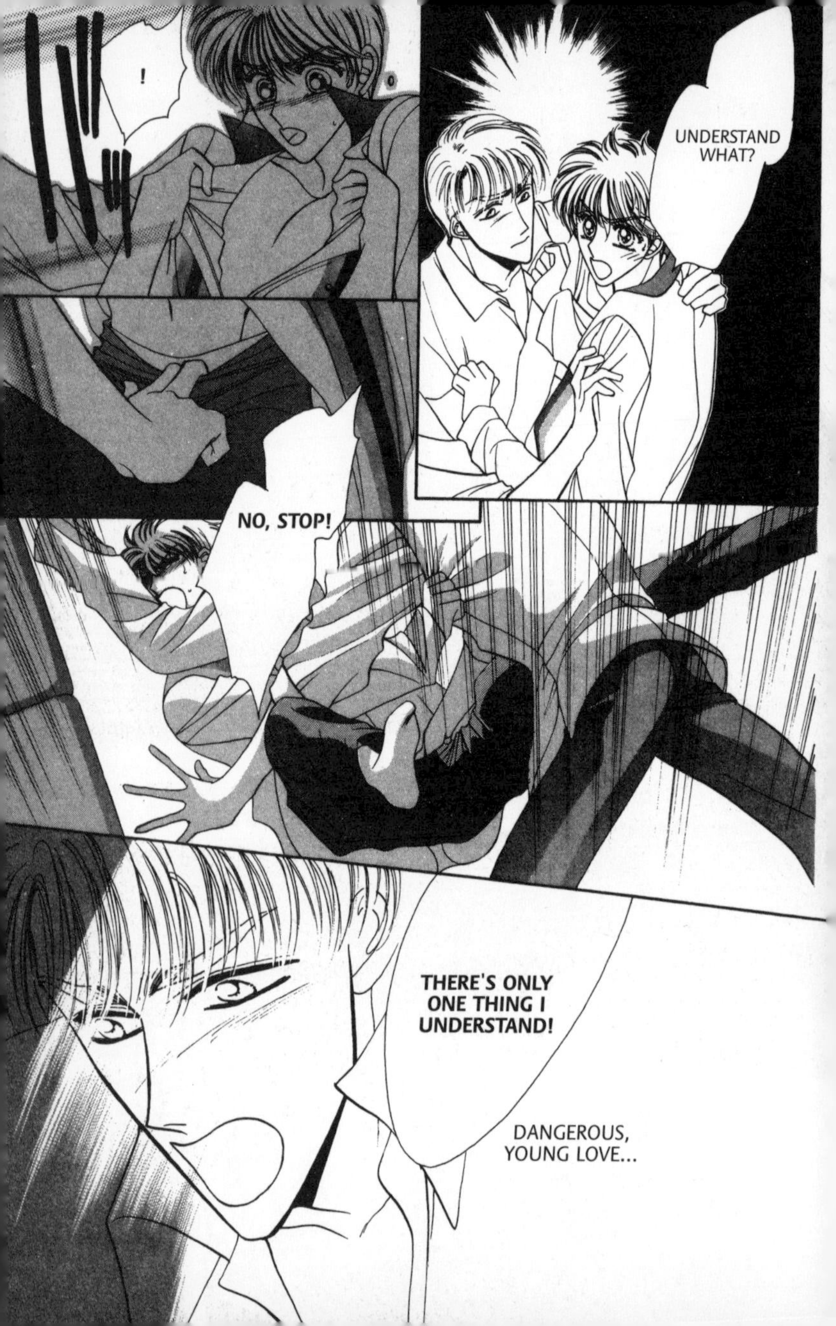
UNDERSTAND WHAT?
!
NO, STOP!
THERE'S ONLY ONE THING I UNDERSTAND!
DANGEROUS, YOUNG LOVE...

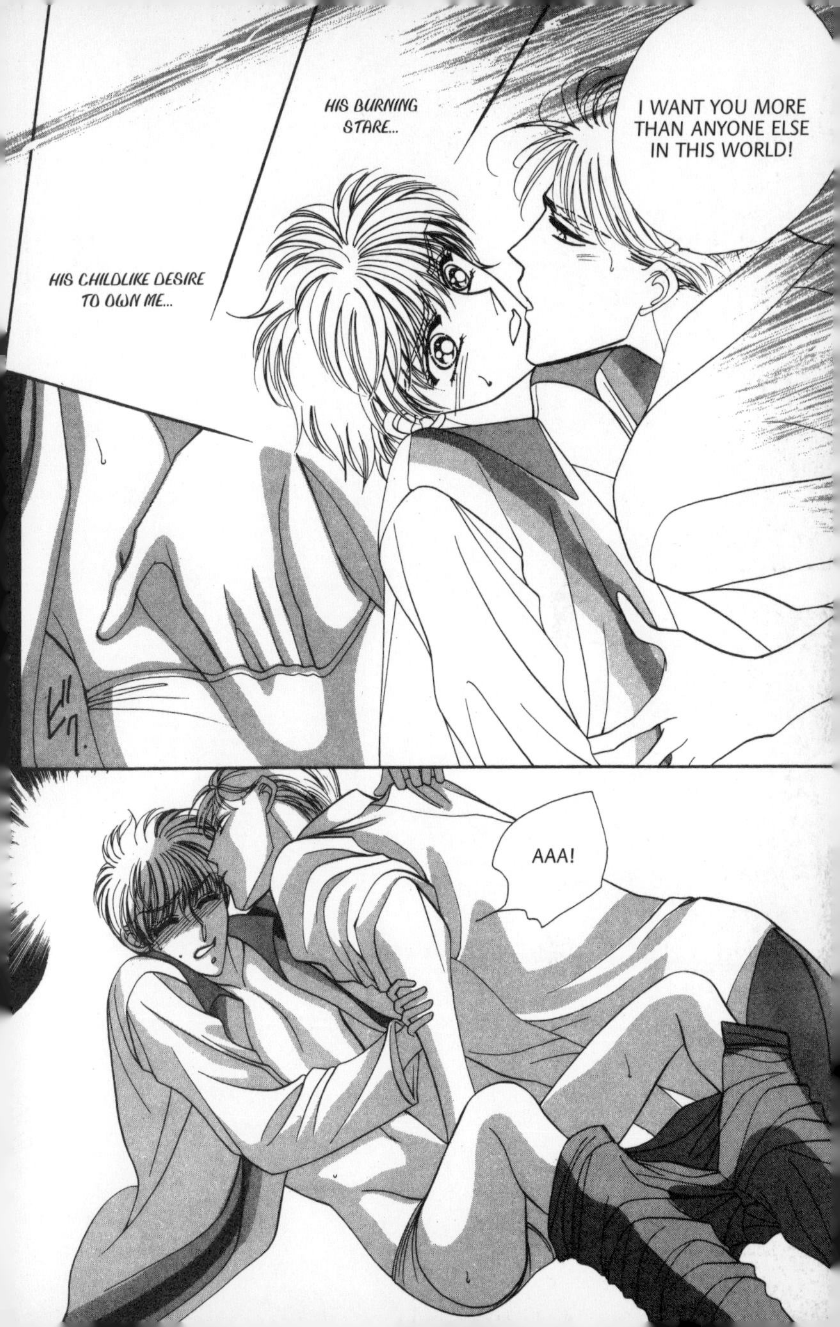
I WANT YOU MORE THAN ANYONE ELSE IN THIS WORLD!
HIS BURNING STARE...
HIS CHILDLIKE DESIRE TO OWN ME...
AAA!

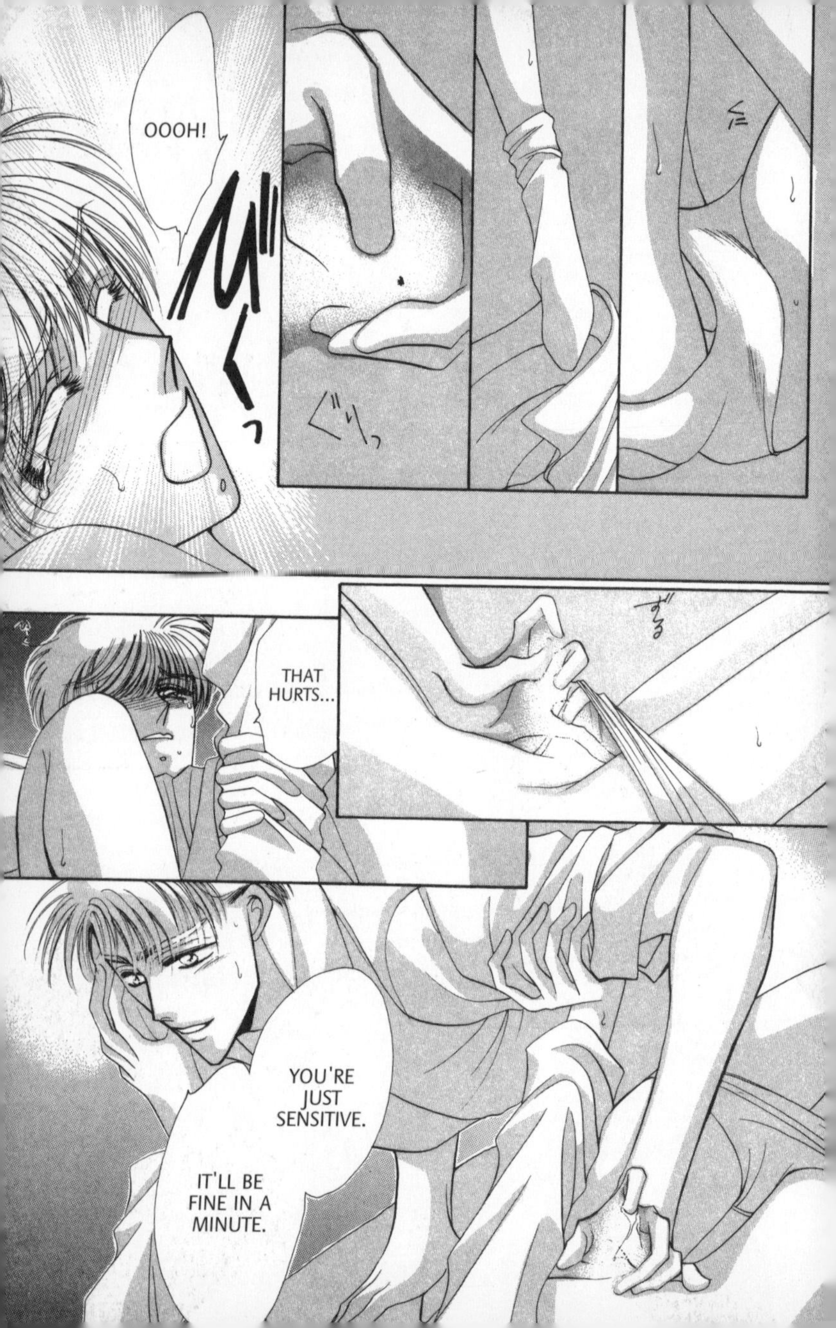
OOOH!
THAT HURTS...
YOU'RE JUST SENSITIVE.
IT'LL BE FINE IN A MINUTE.

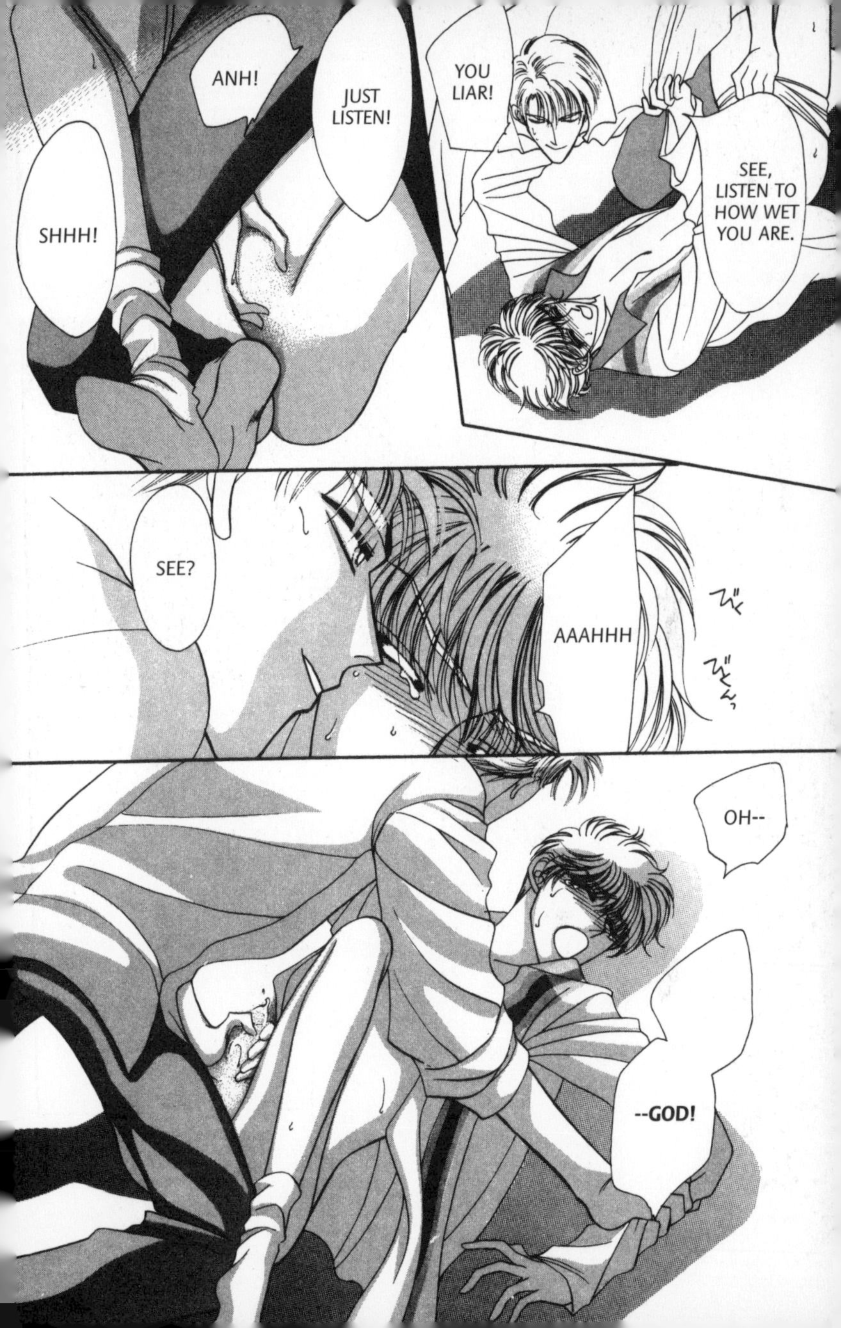
YOU LIAR!
SEE, LISTEN TO HOW WET YOU ARE.
JUST LISTEN!
ANH!
SHHH!
AAAHHH
SEE?
OH--
--GOD!

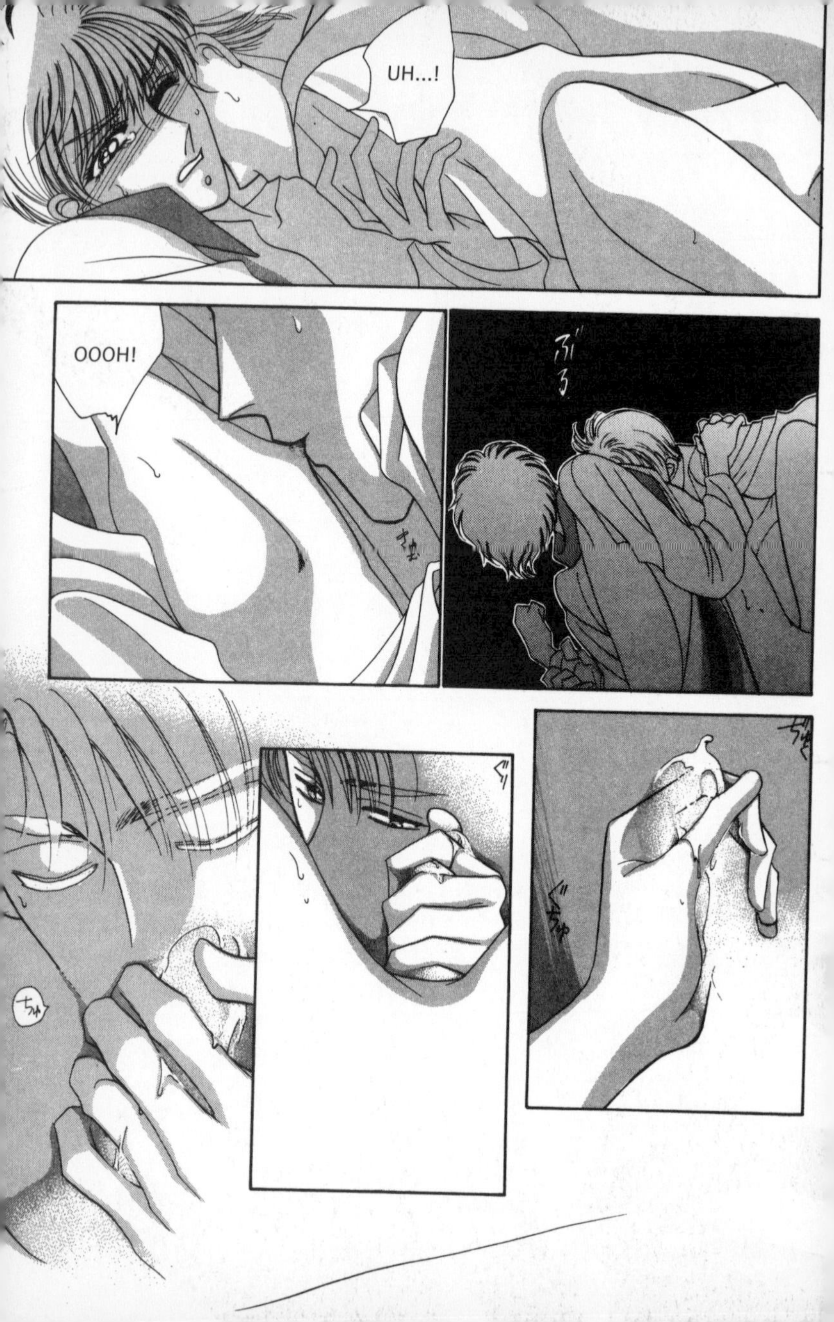
UH...!
OOOH!

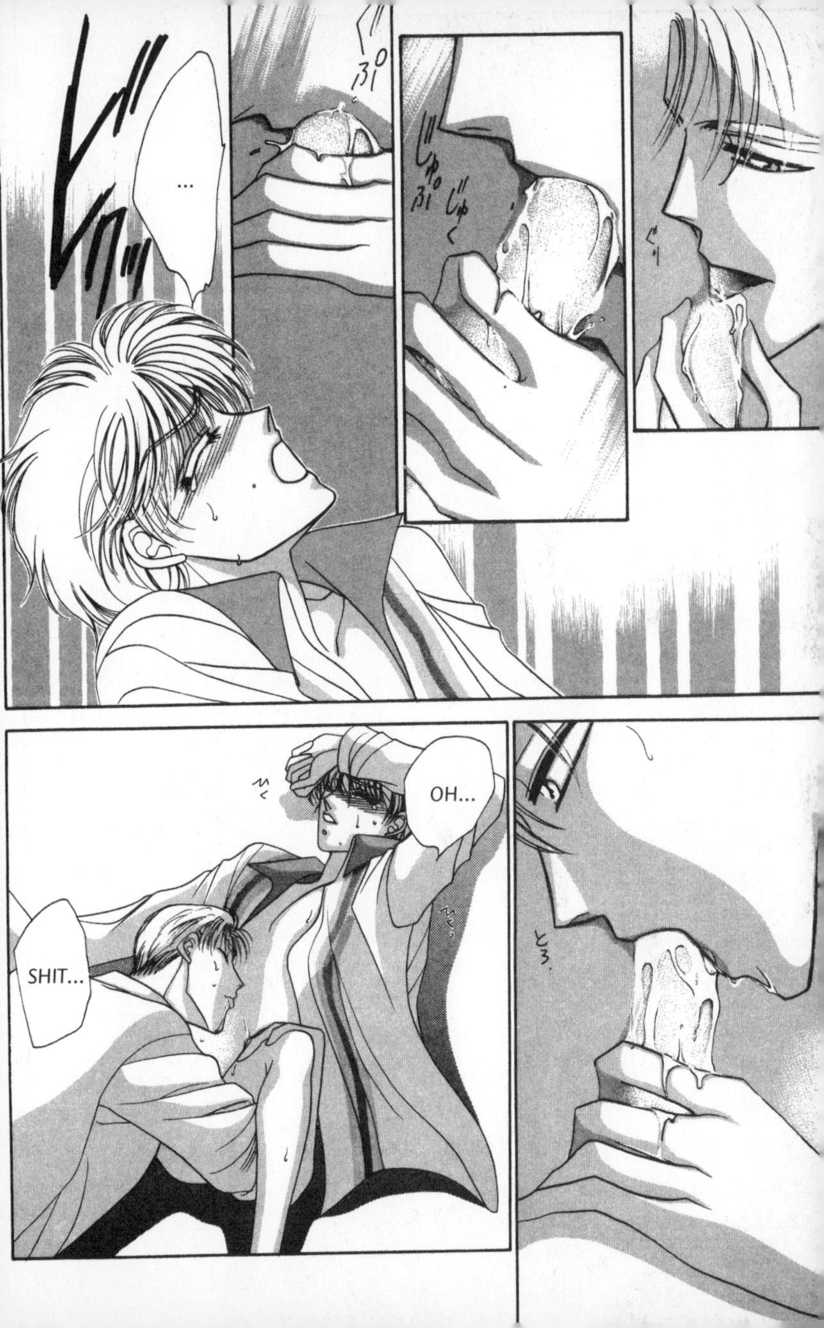
...
OH...
SHIT...

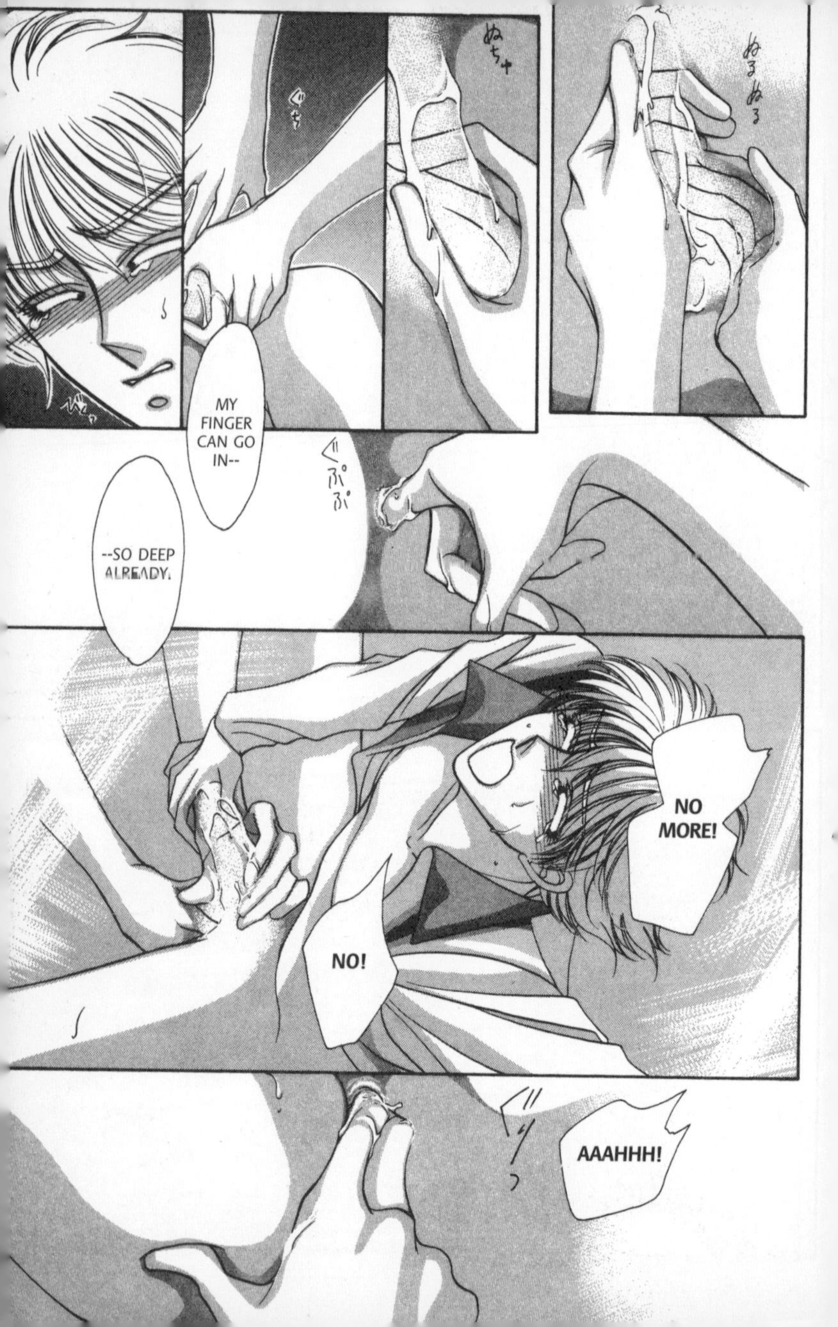
ぬるぬる
ぬちゅ
ぐちゅ
MY FINGER CAN GO IN--
--SO DEEP ALREADY!
ぐぷぷ
NO MORE!
NO!
グリッ
AAAHHH!

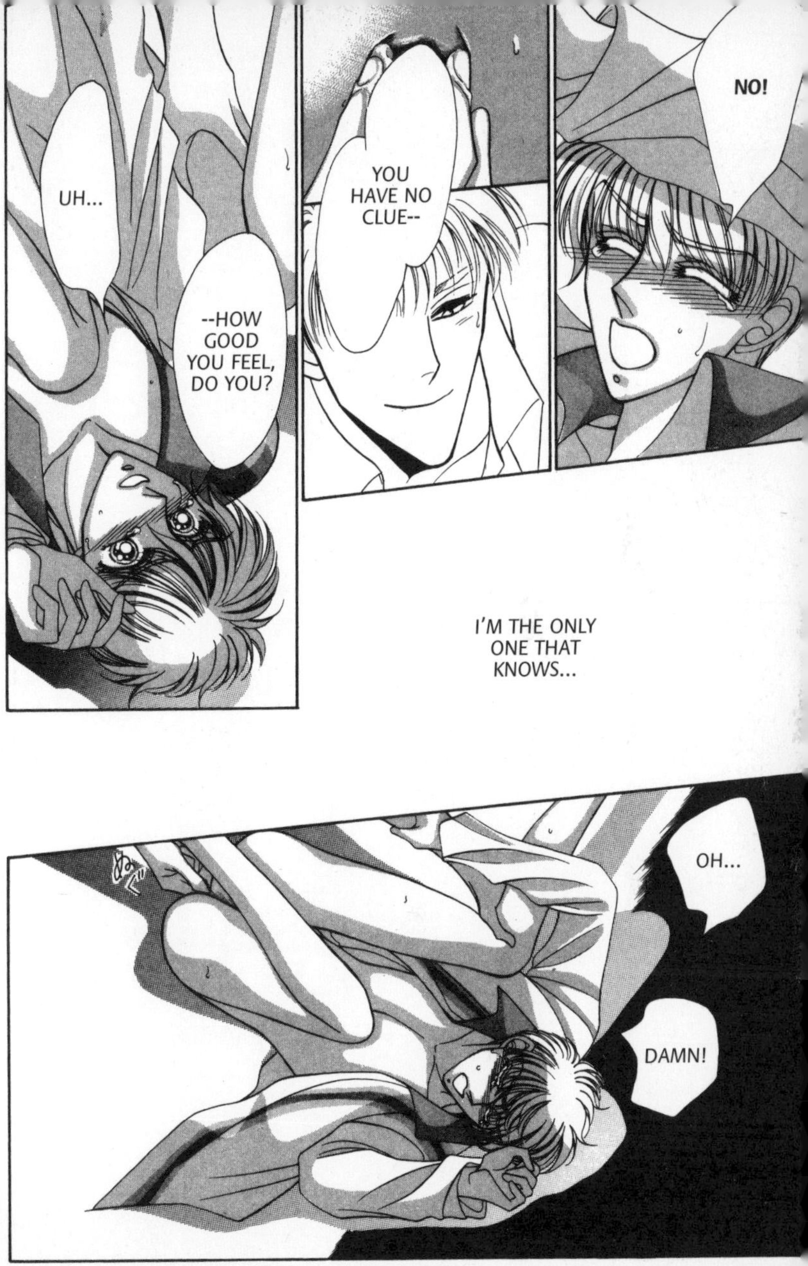
NO!
YOU HAVE NO CLUE--
UH...
--HOW GOOD YOU FEEL, DO YOU?
I'M THE ONLY ONE THAT KNOWS...
OH...
DAMN!

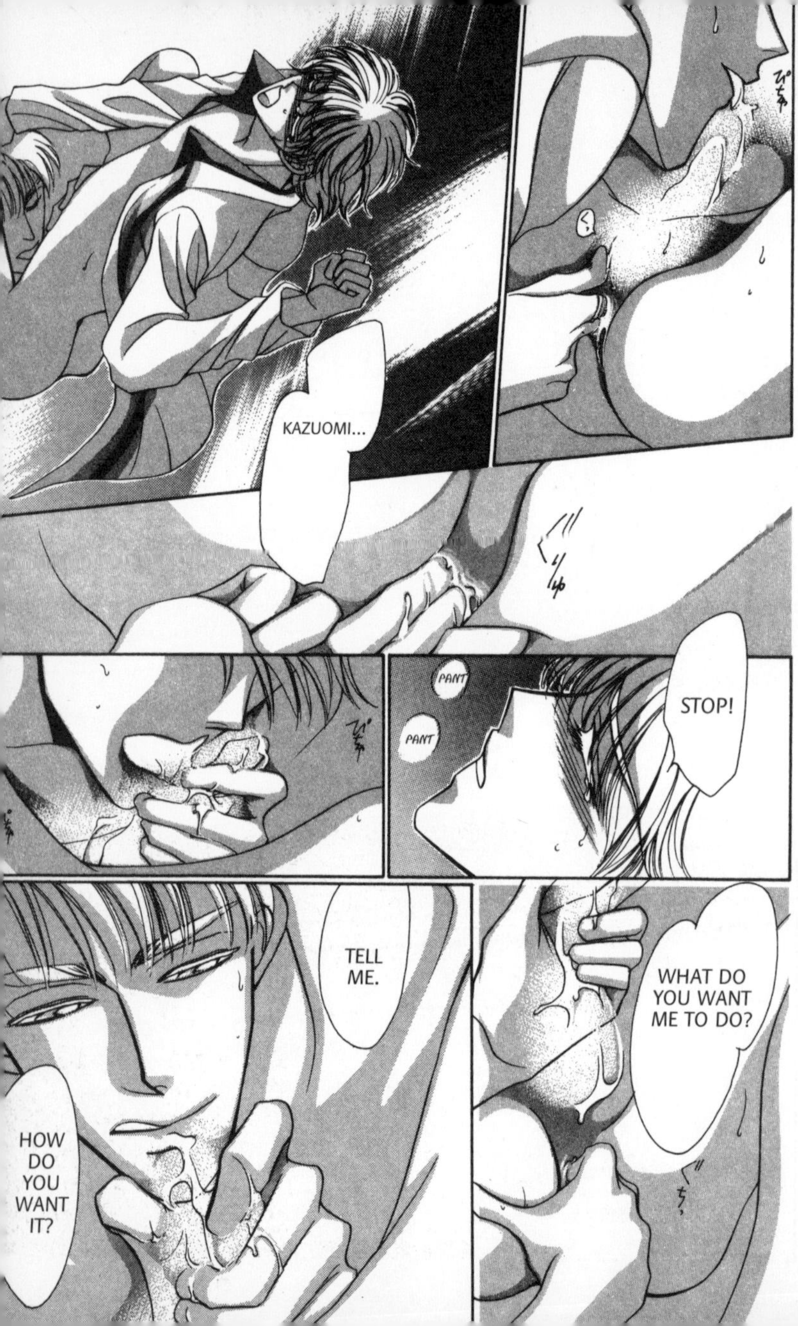
KAZUOMI...
STOP!
PANT
PANT
WHAT DO YOU WANT ME TO DO?
TELL ME.
HOW DO YOU WANT IT?

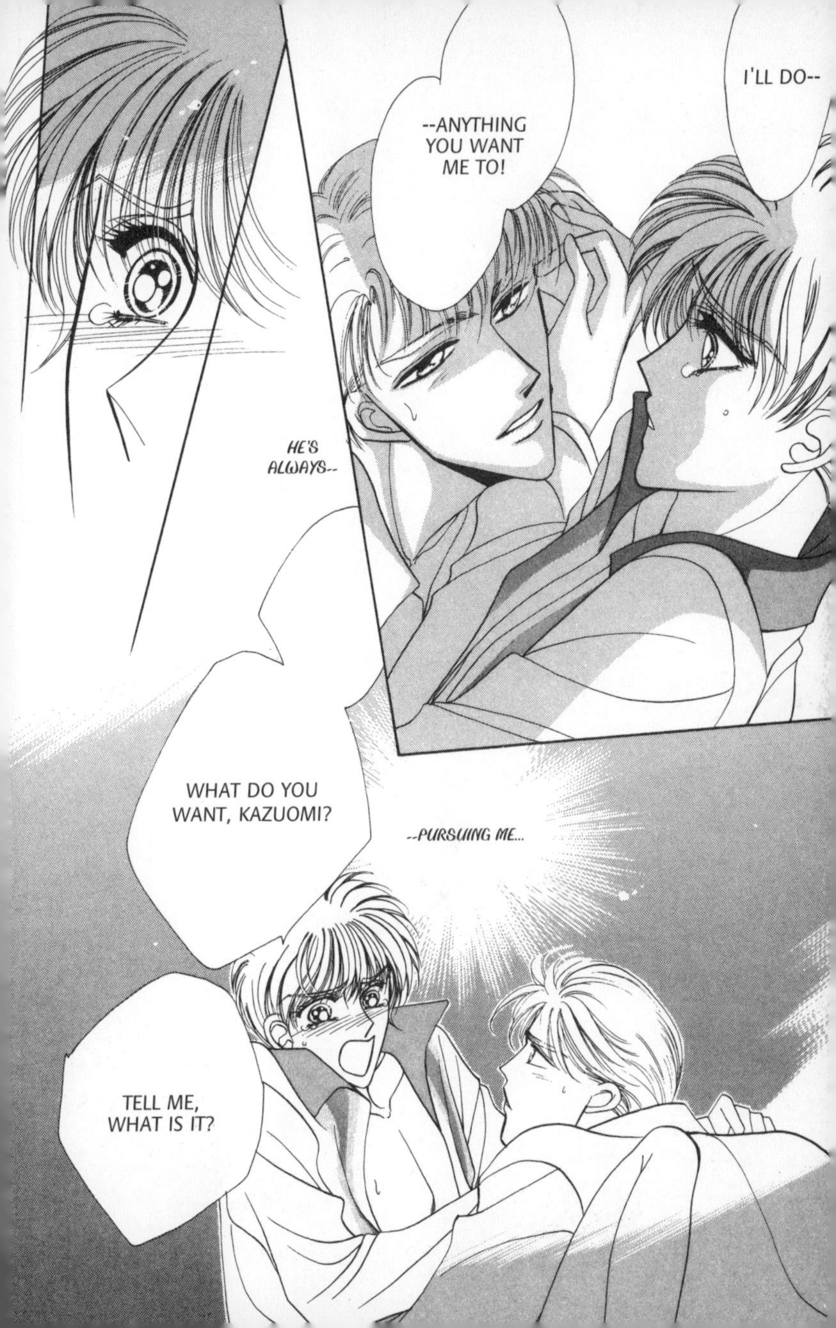

I'LL DO--
--ANYTHING YOU WANT ME TO!
HE'S ALWAYS--
--PURSUING ME...
WHAT DO YOU WANT, KAZUOMI?
TELL ME, WHAT IS IT?

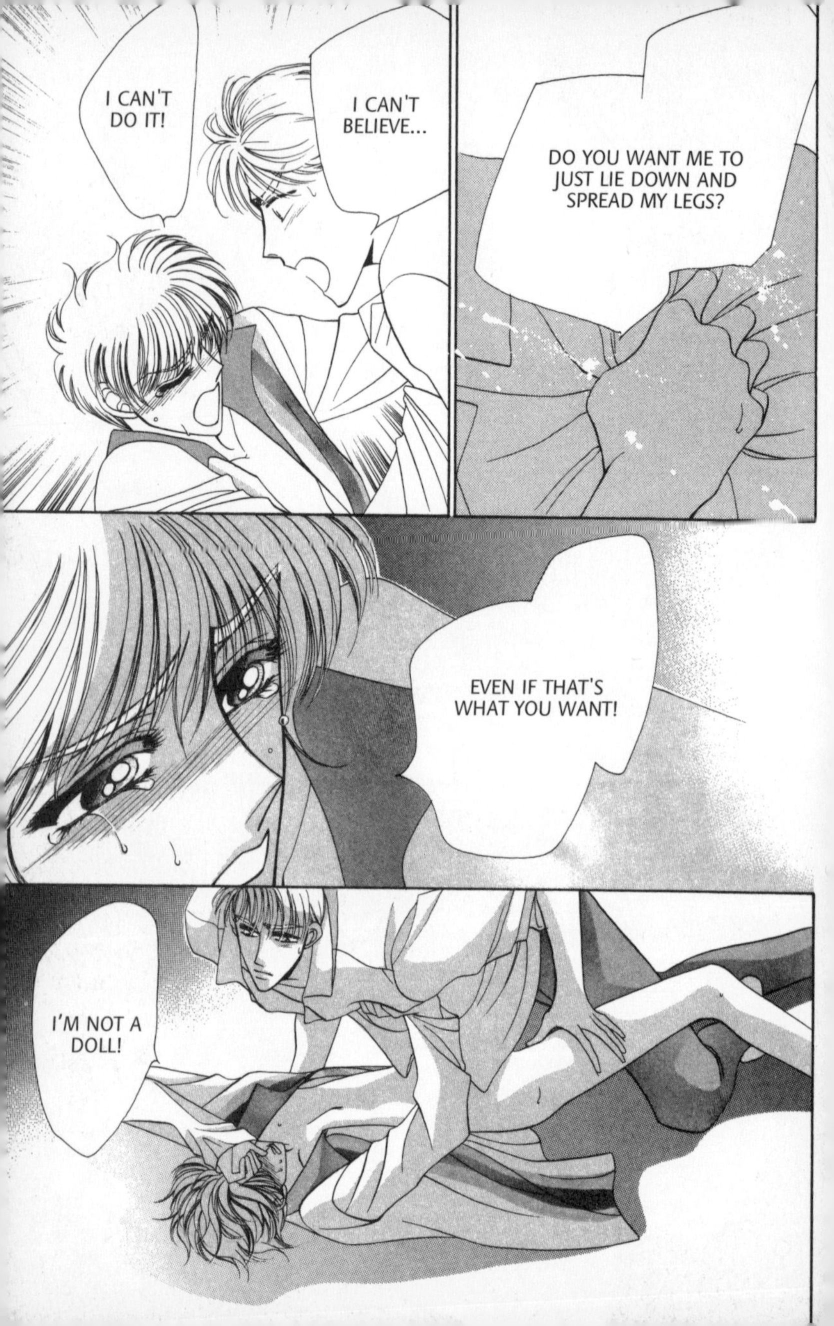
DO YOU WANT ME TO JUST LIE DOWN AND SPREAD MY LEGS?
I CAN'T BELIEVE...
I CAN'T DO IT!
EVEN IF THAT'S WHAT YOU WANT!
I'M NOT A DOLL!

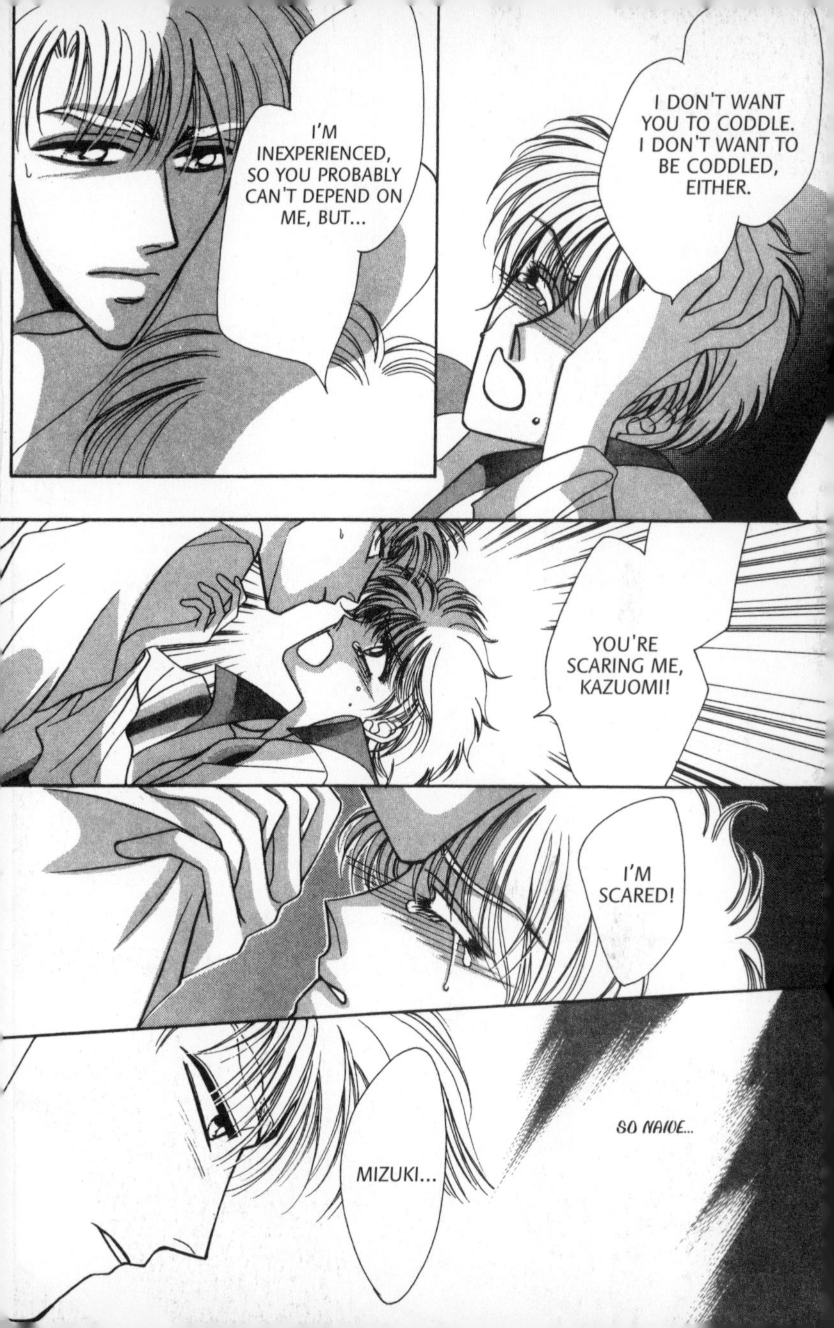
I DON'T WANT YOU TO CODDLE. I DON'T WANT TO BE CODDLED, EITHER.
I'M INEXPERIENCED, SO YOU PROBABLY CAN'T DEPEND ON ME, BUT...
YOU'RE SCARING ME, KAZUOMI!
I'M SCARED!
SO NAIVE...
MIZUKI...

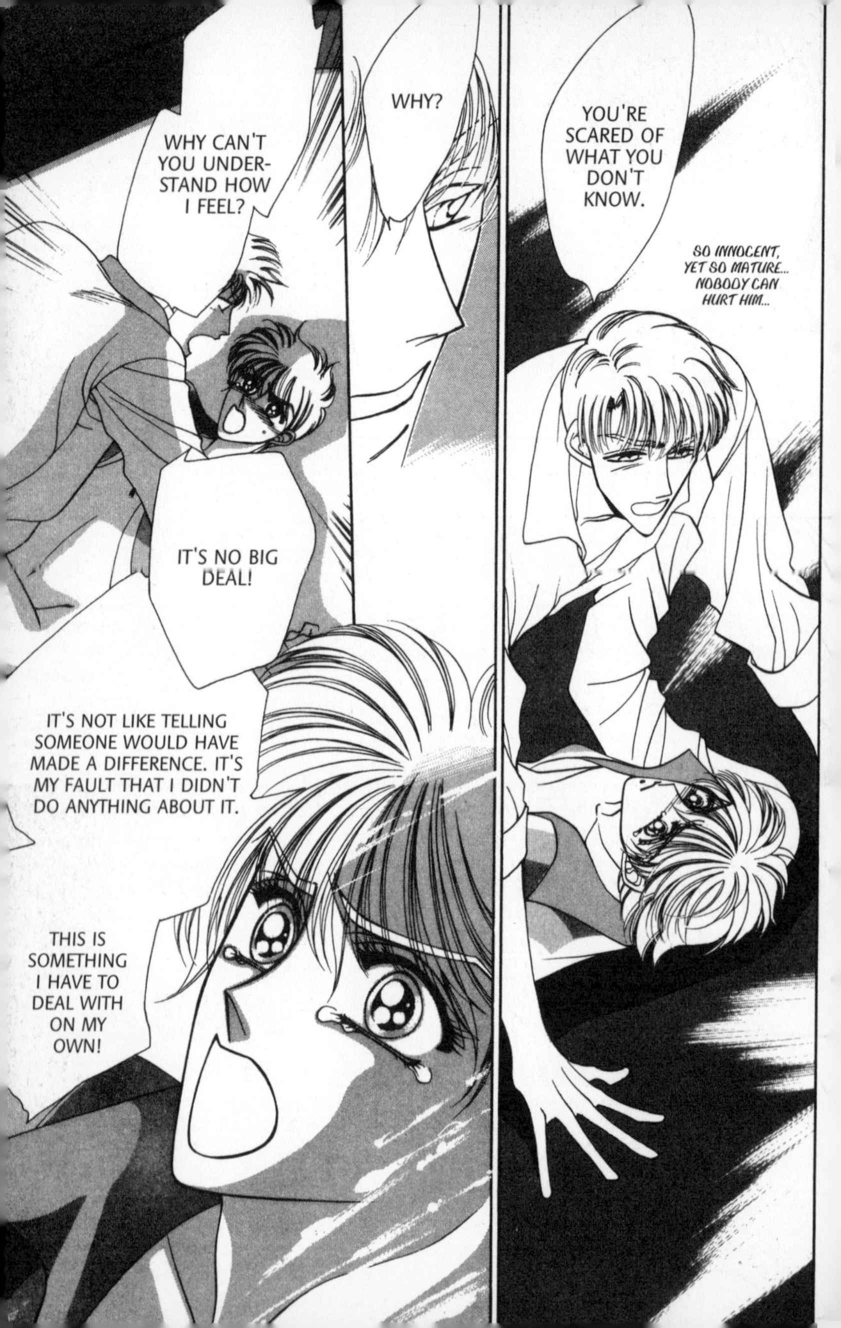
YOU'RE SCARED OF WHAT YOU DON'T KNOW.
SO INNOCENT, YET SO MATURE... NOBODY CAN HURT HIM...
WHY?
WHY CAN'T YOU UNDERSTAND HOW I FEEL?
IT'S NO BIG DEAL!
IT'S NOT LIKE TELLING SOMEONE WOULD HAVE MADE A DIFFERENCE. IT'S MY FAULT THAT I DIDN'T DO ANYTHING ABOUT IT.
THIS IS SOMETHING I HAVE TO DEAL WITH ON MY OWN!

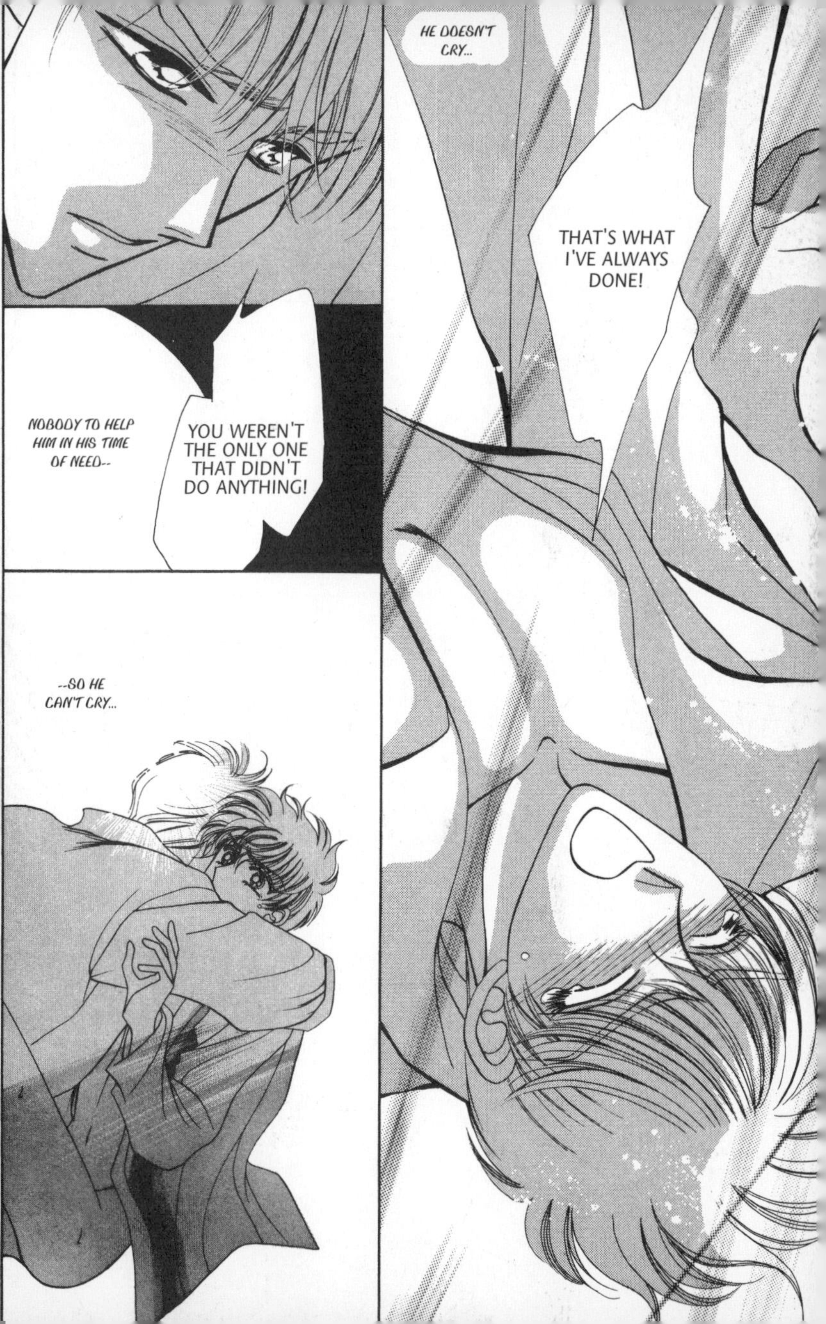
HE DOESN'T CRY...
THAT'S WHAT I'VE ALWAYS DONE!
YOU WEREN'T THE ONLY ONE THAT DIDN'T DO ANYTHING!
NOBODY TO HELP HIM IN HIS TIME OF NEED--
--SO HE CAN'T CRY...

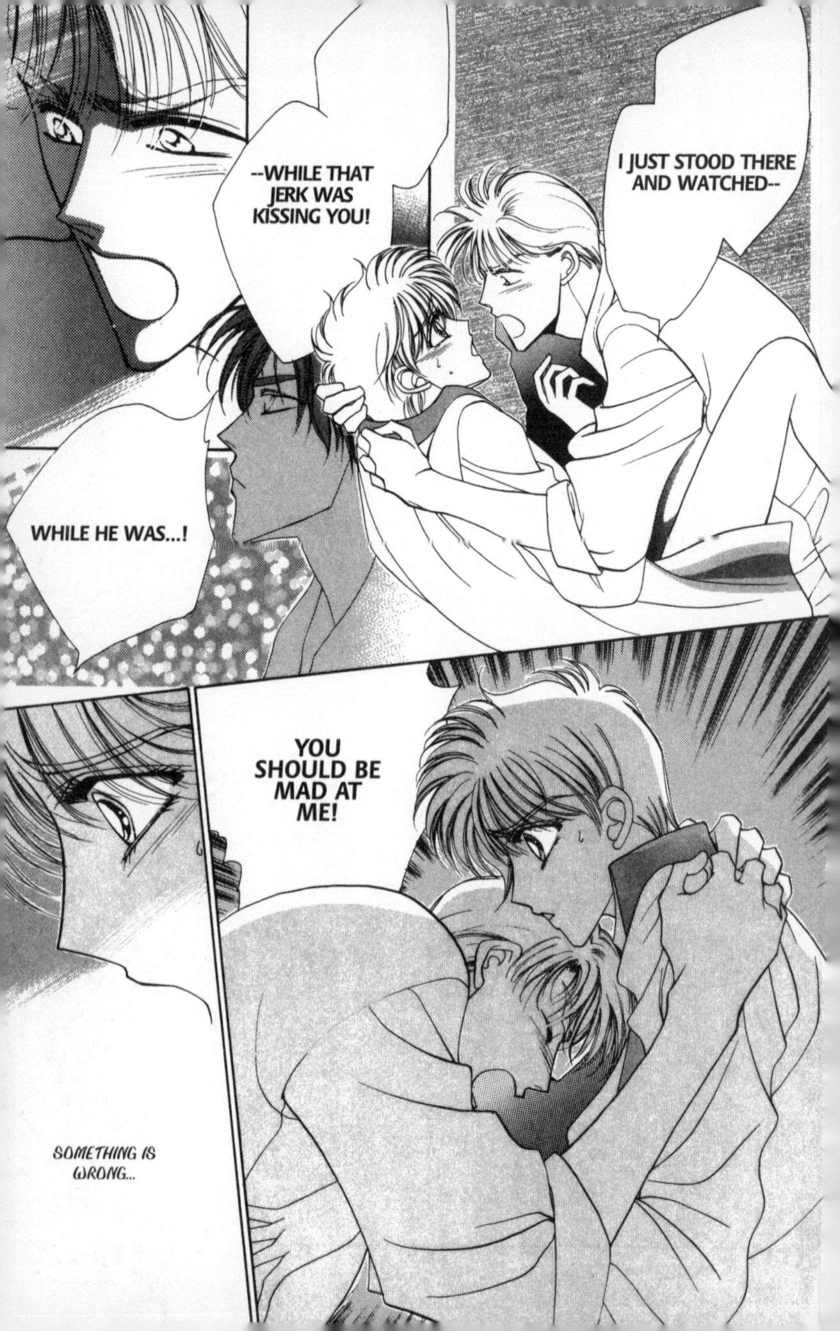
I JUST STOOD THERE AND WATCHED--
--WHILE THAT JERK WAS KISSING YOU!
WHILE HE WAS...!
YOU SHOULD BE MAD AT ME!
SOMETHING IS WRONG...

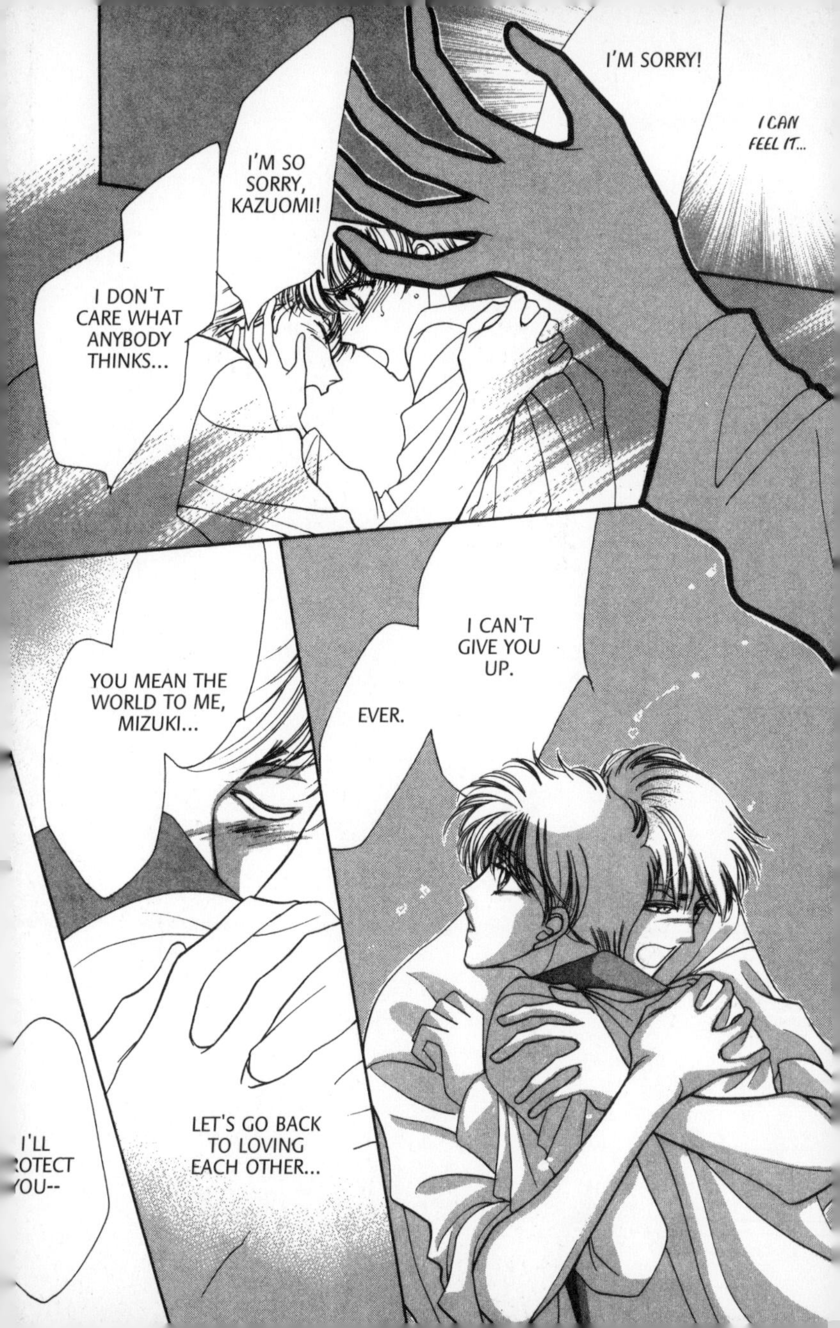
I'M SORRY!
I CAN FEEL IT...
I'M SO SORRY, KAZUOMI!
I DON'T CARE WHAT ANYBODY THINKS...
I CAN'T GIVE YOU UP.
EVER.
YOU MEAN THE WORLD TO ME, MIZUKI...
LET'S GO BACK TO LOVING EACH OTHER...
I'LL OTECT YOU--

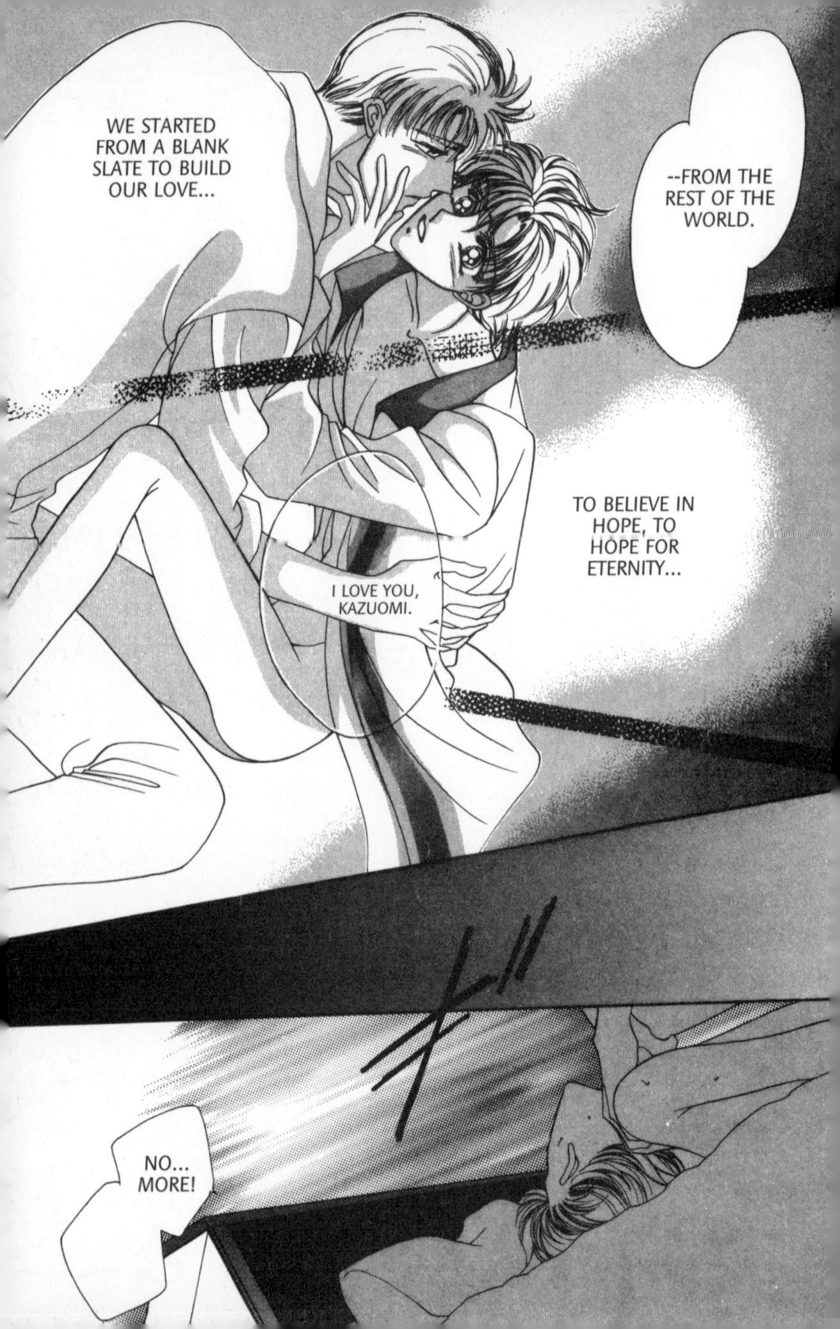
--FROM THE REST OF THE WORLD.
WE STARTED FROM A BLANK SLATE TO BUILD OUR LOVE...
TO BELIEVE IN HOPE, TO HOPE FOR ETERNITY...
I LOVE YOU, KAZUOMI.
NO... MORE!

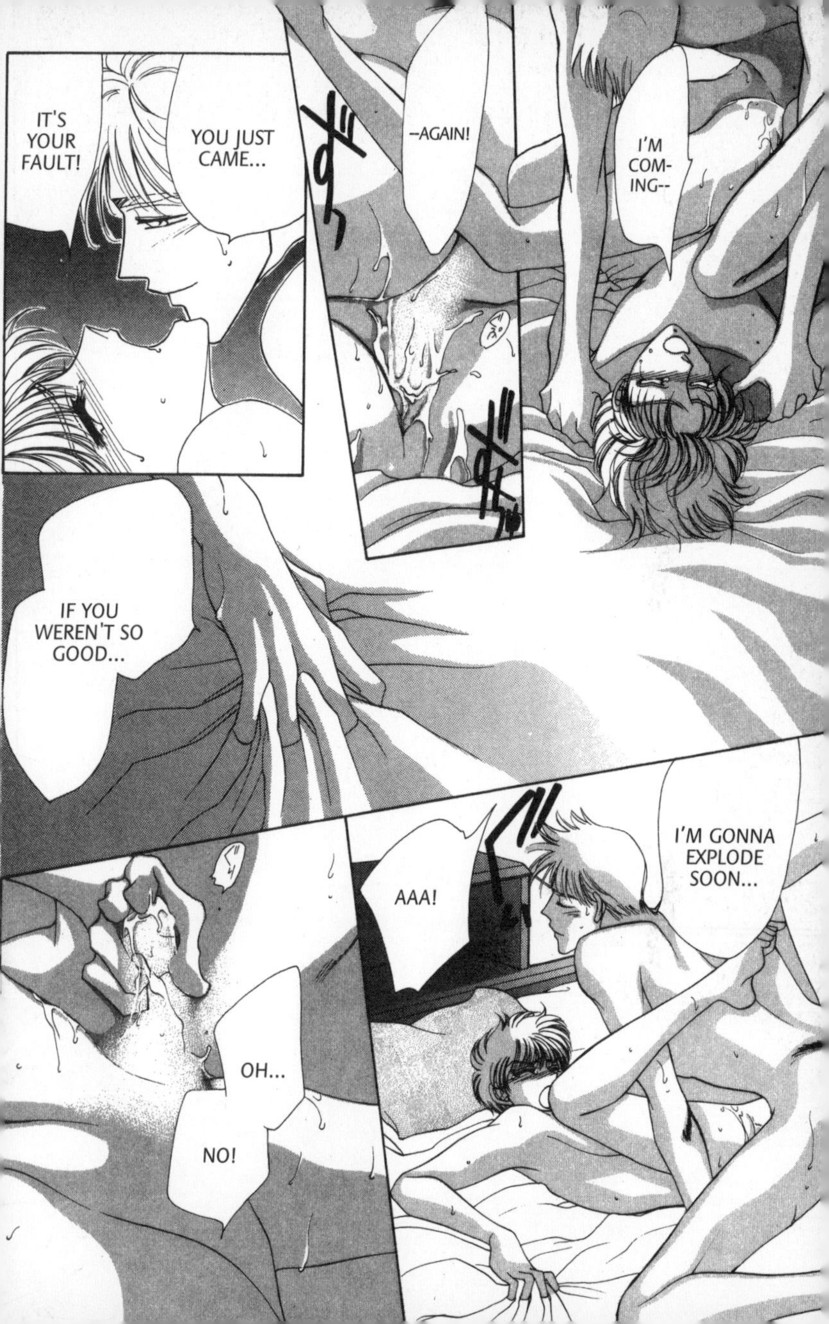
I'M COMING--
—AGAIN!
YOU JUST CAME...
IT'S YOUR FAULT!
IF YOU WEREN'T SO GOOD...
I'M GONNA EXPLODE SOON...
AAA!
OH...
NO!

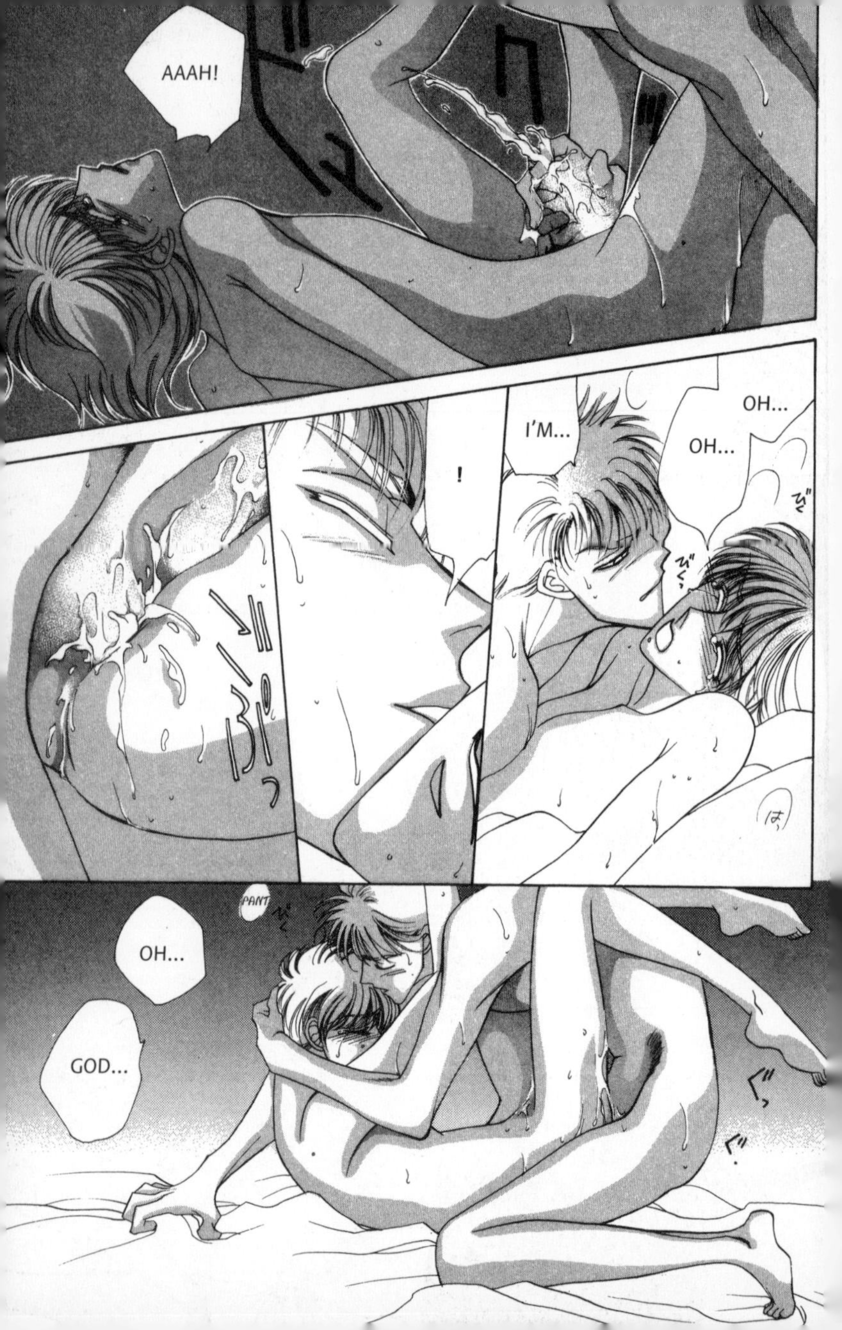
AAAH!
OH...
OH...
I'M...
!
PANT
OH...
GOD...

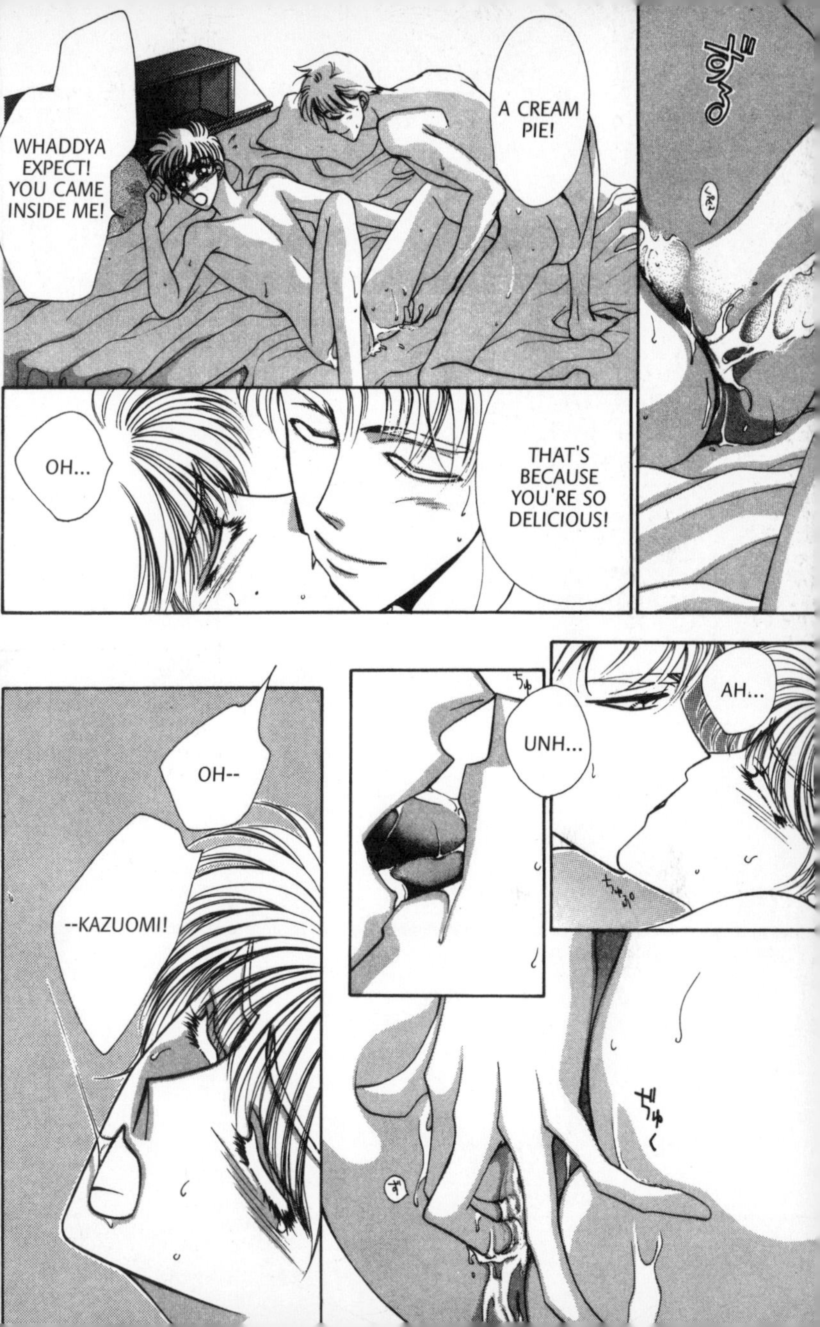
A CREAM PIE!
WHADDYA EXPECT! YOU CAME INSIDE ME!
THAT'S BECAUSE YOU'RE SO DELICIOUS!
OH...
AH...
UNH...
OH--
--KAZUOMI!

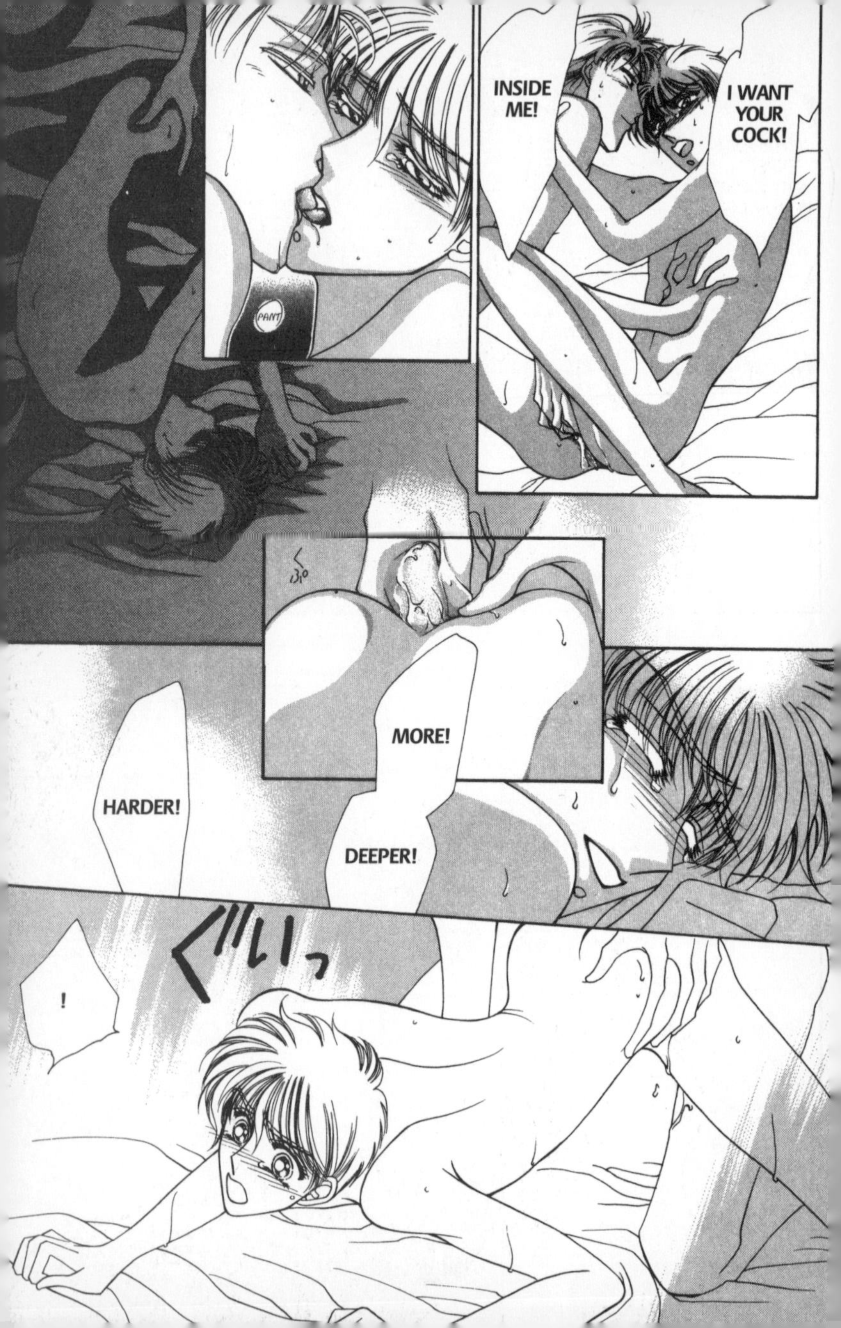
I WANT YOUR COCK!
INSIDE ME!
PANT
MORE!
DEEPER!
HARDER!
ぐいっ
!

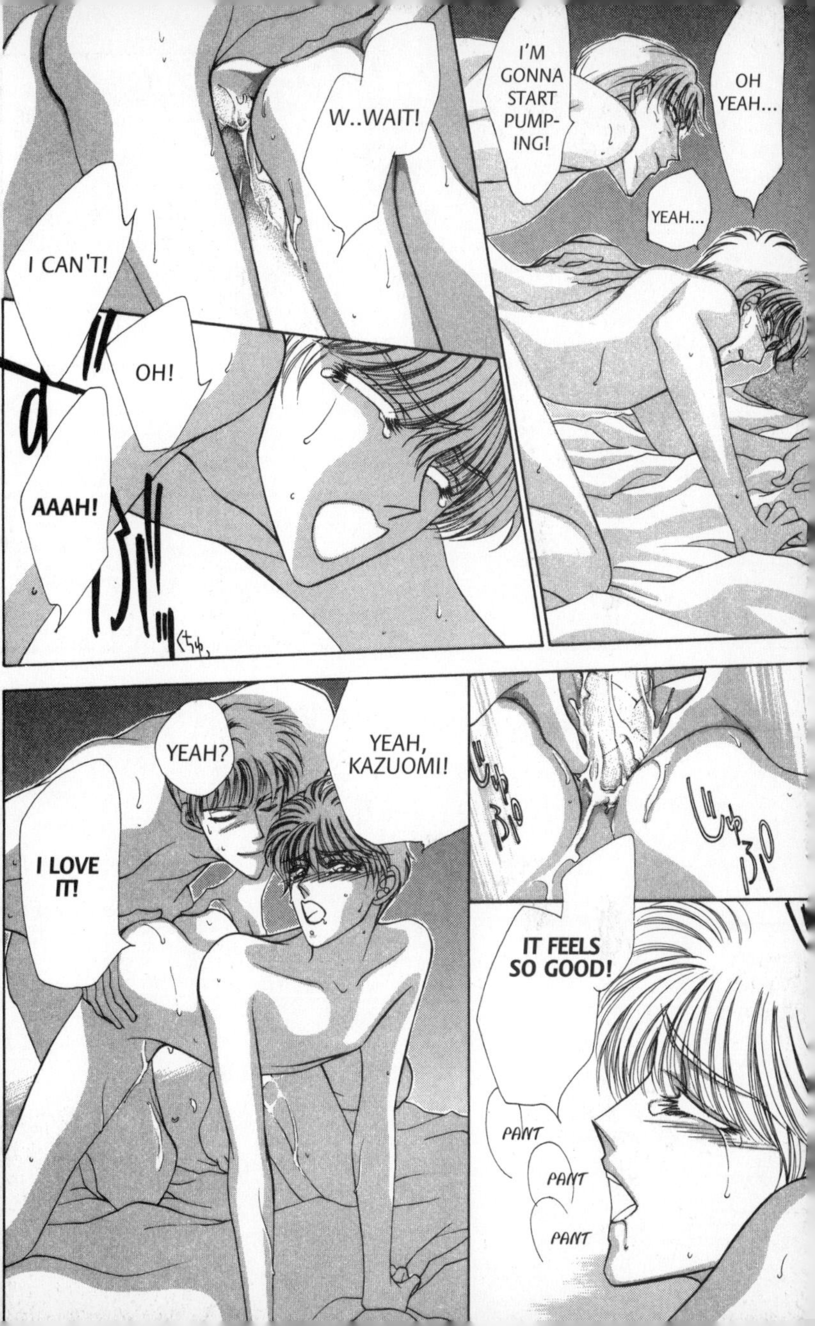
OH YEAH...
I'M GONNA START PUMPING!
YEAH...
W..WAIT!
I CAN'T!
OH!
AAAH!
くちゅ,
IT FEELS SO GOOD!
PANT
PANT
PANT
YEAH, KAZUOMI!
YEAH?
I LOVE IT!

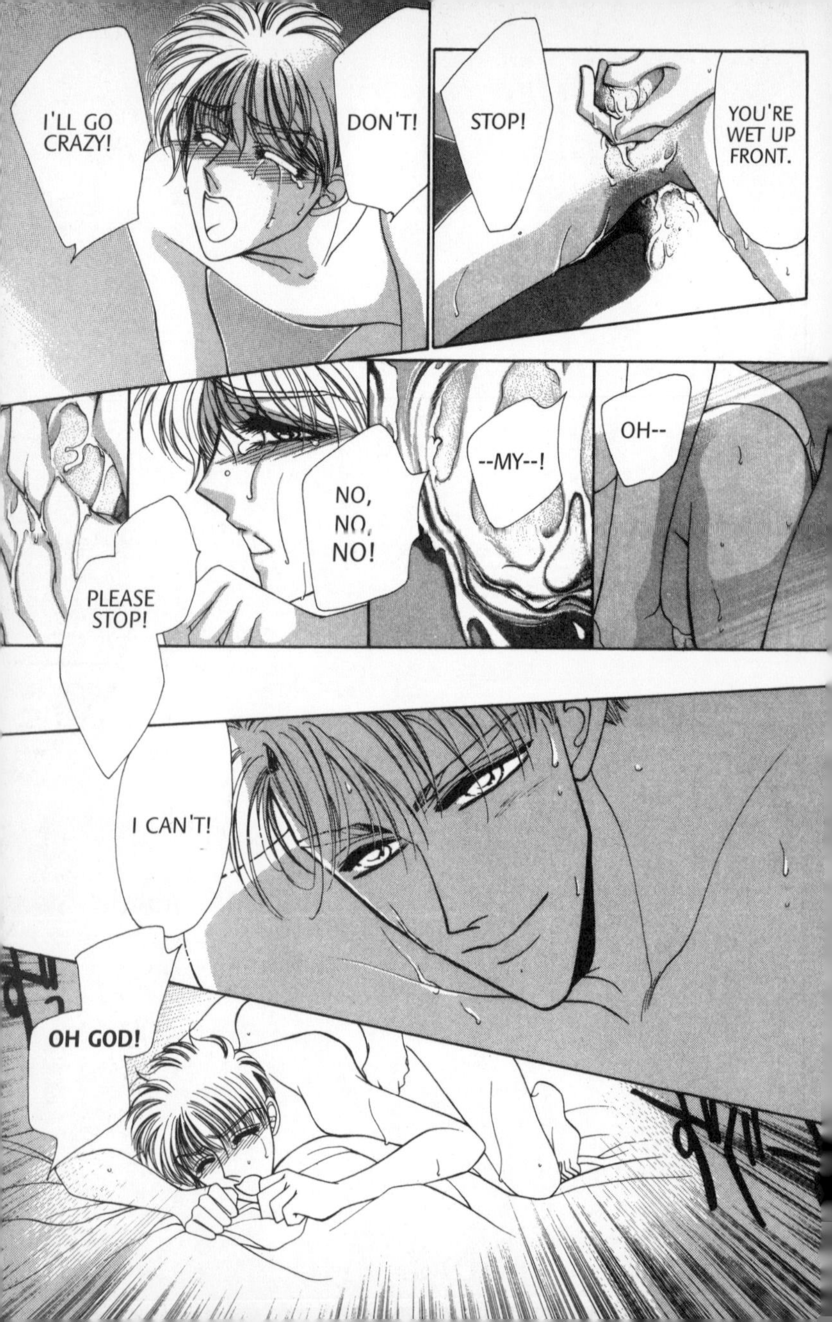
YOU'RE WET UP FRONT.
STOP!
DON'T!
I'LL GO CRAZY!
OH--
--MY--!
NO, NO, NO!
PLEASE STOP!
I CAN'T!
OH GOD!

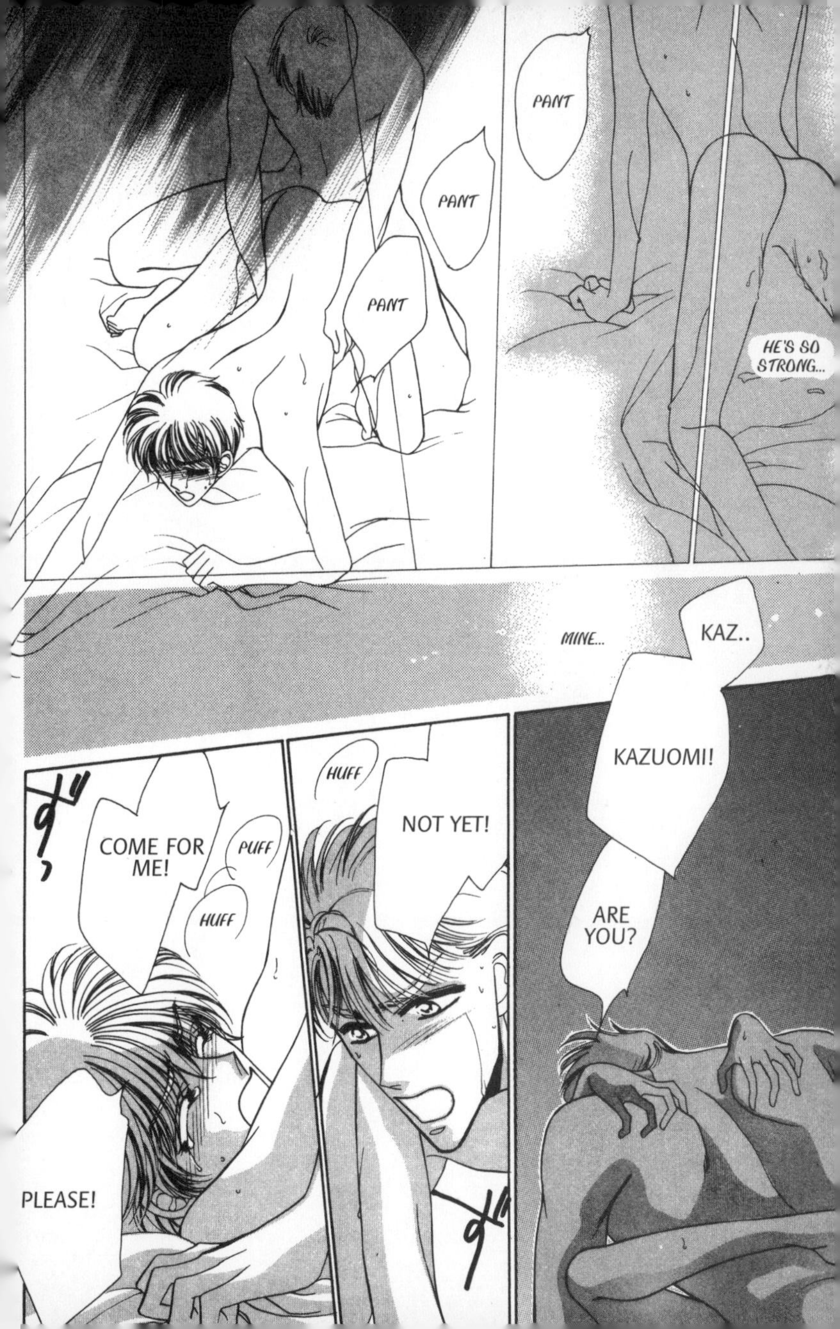
PANT
HE'S SO STRONG...
PANT
PANT
KAZ..
MINE...
KAZUOMI!
ARE YOU?
HUFF
NOT YET!
COME FOR ME!
PUFF
HUFF
PLEASE!

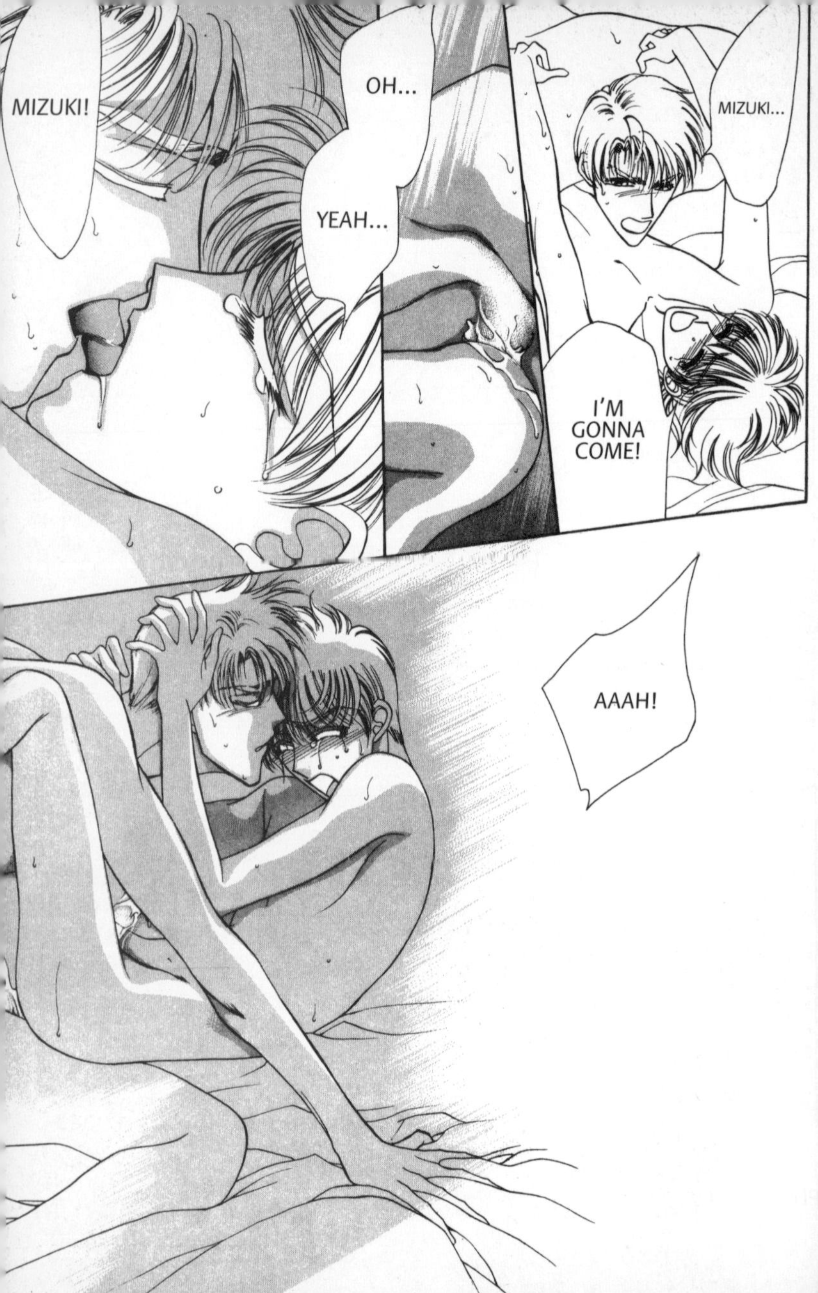
MIZUKI...
I'M GONNA COME!
OH...
YEAH...
MIZUKI!
AAAH!

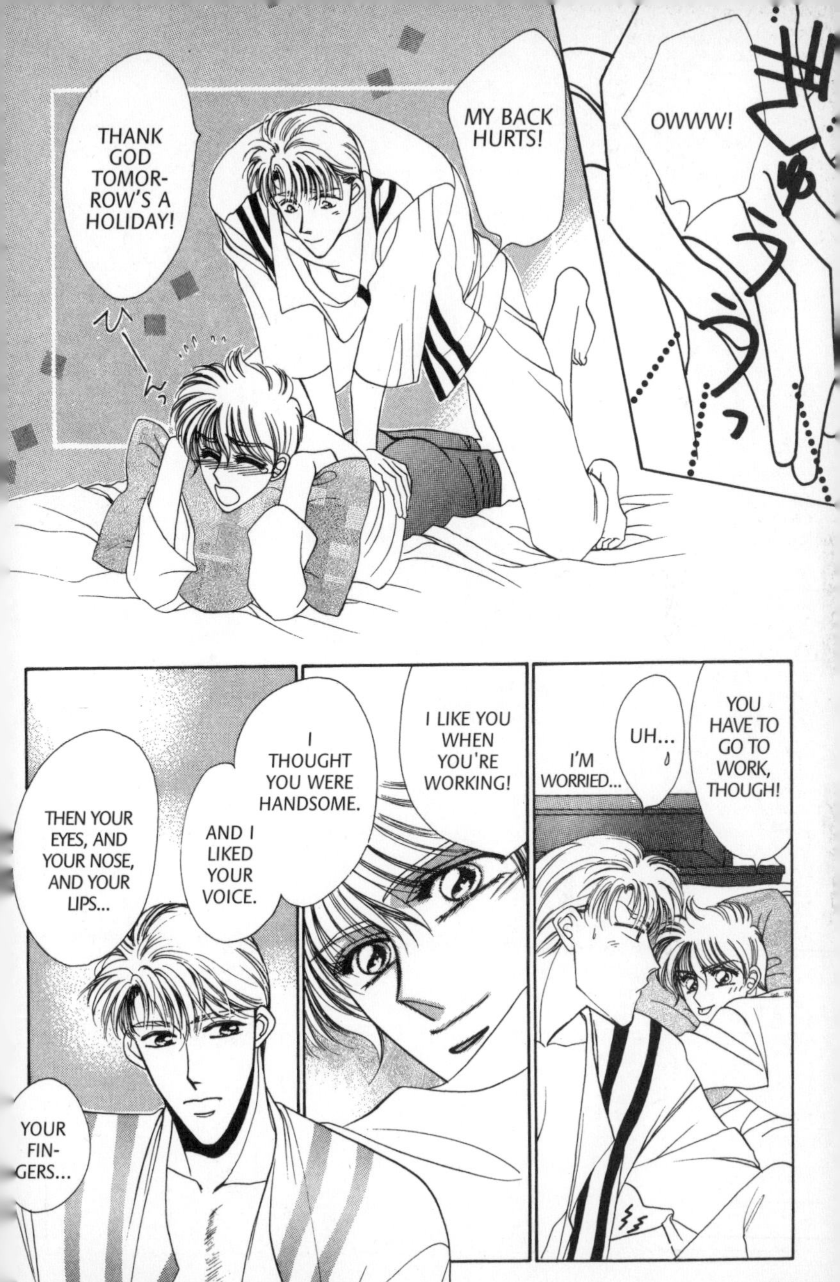
OWWW!
MY BACK HURTS!
THANK GOD TOMOR-ROW'S A HOLIDAY!
YOU HAVE TO GO TO WORK, THOUGH!
UH...
I'M WORRIED...
I LIKE YOU WHEN YOU'RE WORKING!
I THOUGHT YOU WERE HANDSOME.
AND I LIKED YOUR VOICE.
THEN YOUR EYES, AND YOUR NOSE, AND YOUR LIPS...
YOUR FIN-GERS...

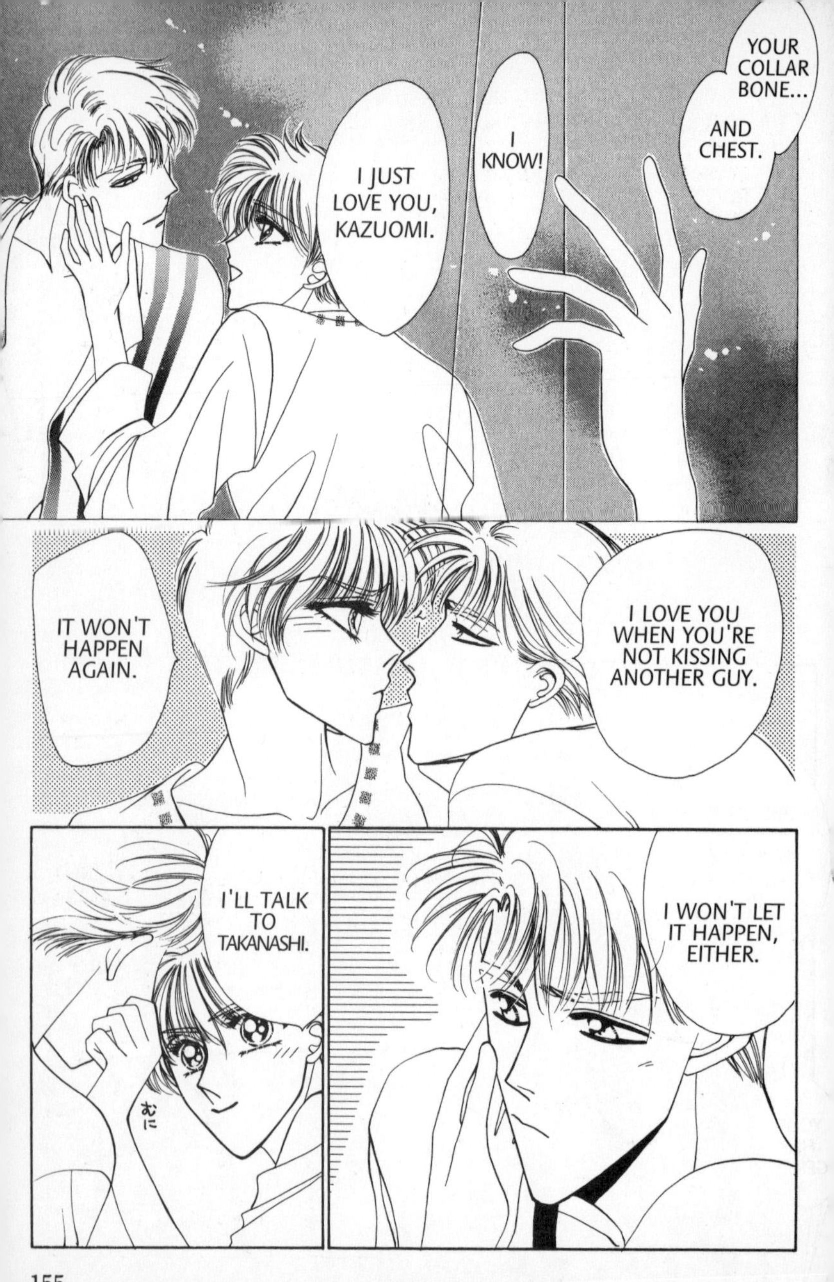
YOUR COLLAR BONE... AND CHEST.
I KNOW!
I JUST LOVE YOU, KAZUOMI.
I LOVE YOU WHEN YOU'RE NOT KISSING ANOTHER GUY.
IT WON'T HAPPEN AGAIN.
I WON'T LET IT HAPPEN, EITHER.
I'LL TALK TO TAKANASHI.
むに

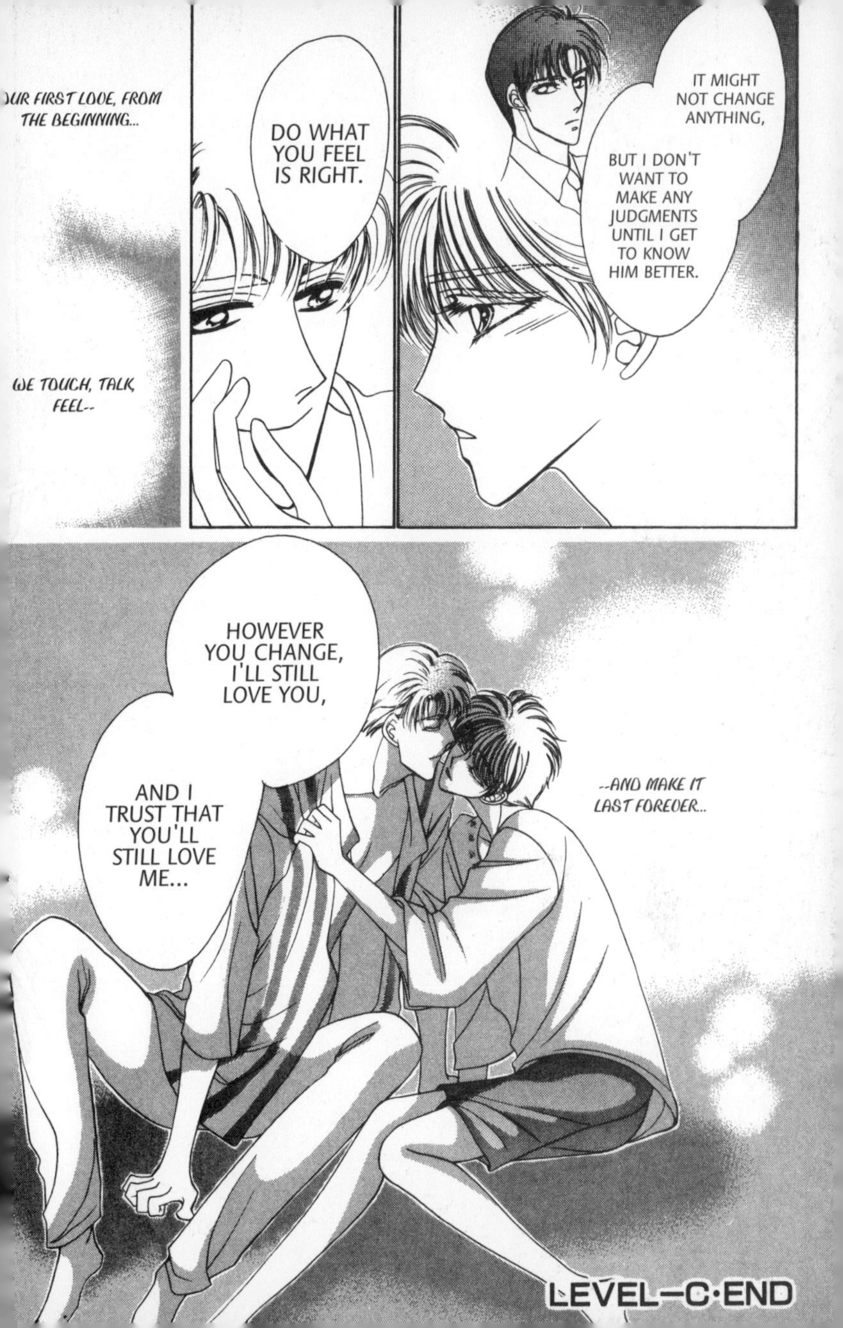
IT MIGHT NOT CHANGE ANYTHING,
BUT I DON'T WANT TO MAKE ANY JUDGMENTS UNTIL I GET TO KNOW HIM BETTER.
DO WHAT YOU FEEL IS RIGHT.
UR FIRST LOVE, FROM THE BEGINNING...
WE TOUCH, TALK, FEEL--
--AND MAKE IT LAST FOREVER...
HOWEVER YOU CHANGE, I'LL STILL LOVE YOU,
AND I TRUST THAT YOU'LL STILL LOVE ME...
LEVEL—C•END

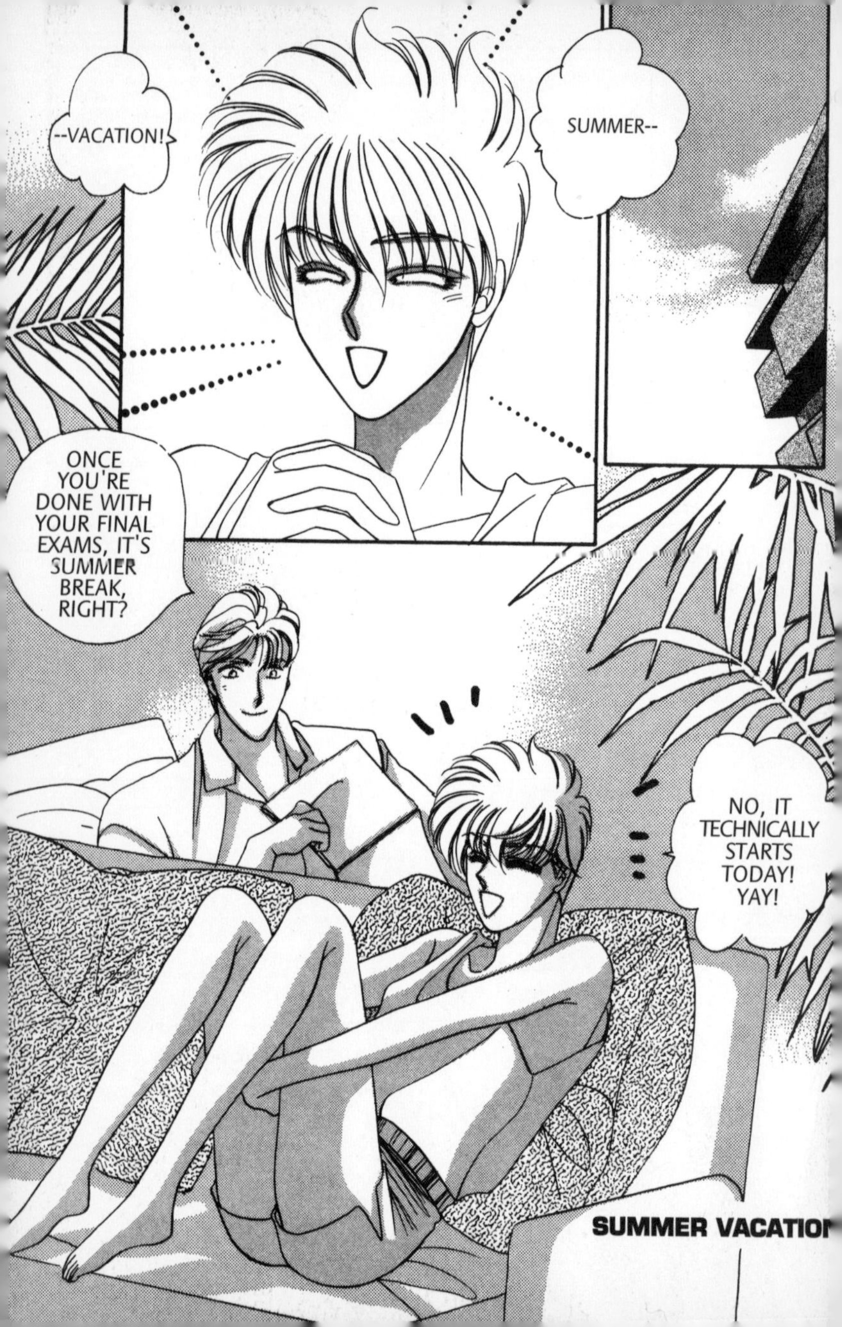

SUMMER--
--VACATION!
ONCE YOU'RE DONE WITH YOUR FINAL EXAMS, IT'S SUMMER BREAK, RIGHT?
NO, IT TECHNICALLY STARTS TODAY! YAY!
SUMMER VACATIO

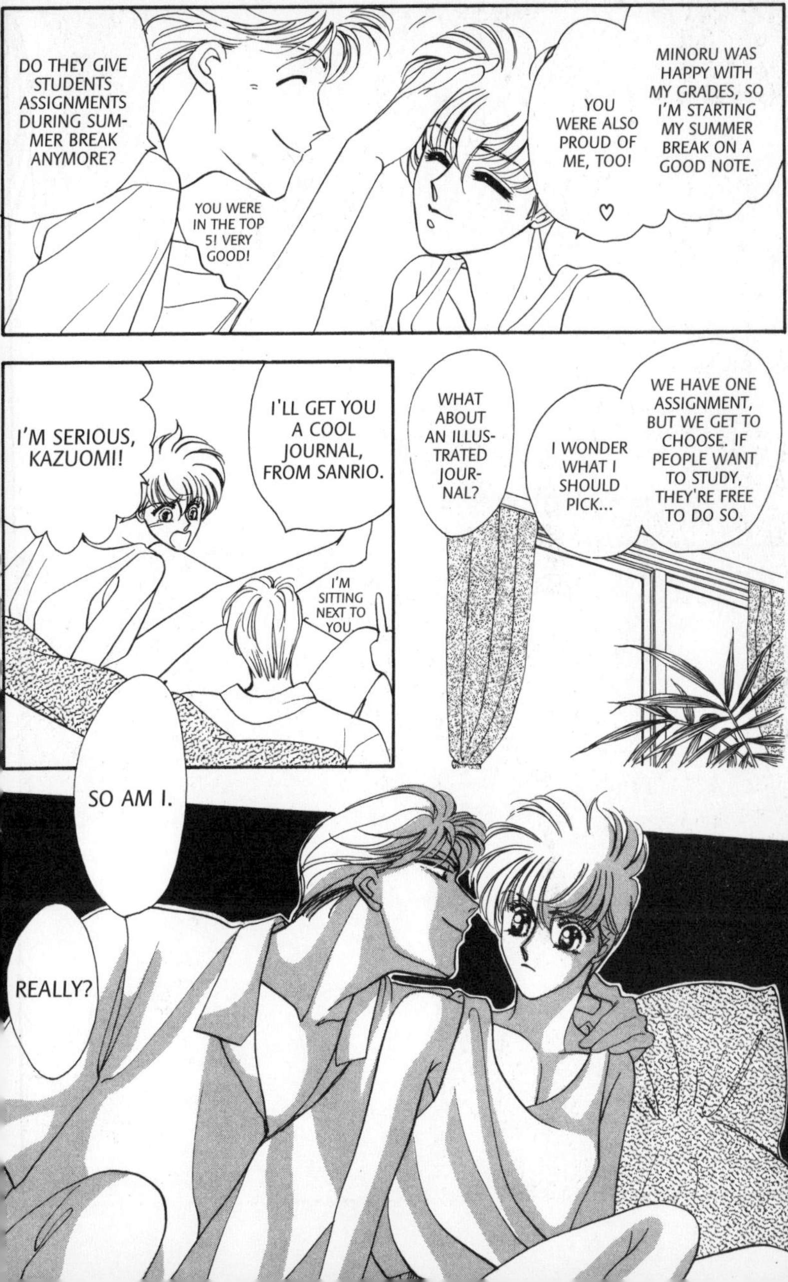
MINORU WAS HAPPY WITH MY GRADES, SO I'M STARTING MY SUMMER BREAK ON A GOOD NOTE.
YOU WERE ALSO PROUD OF ME, TOO! ♡
YOU WERE IN THE TOP 5! VERY GOOD!
DO THEY GIVE STUDENTS ASSIGNMENTS DURING SUMMER BREAK ANYMORE?
WE HAVE ONE ASSIGNMENT, BUT WE GET TO CHOOSE. IF PEOPLE WANT TO STUDY, THEY'RE FREE TO DO SO.
I WONDER WHAT I SHOULD PICK...
WHAT ABOUT AN ILLUSTRATED JOURNAL?
I'LL GET YOU A COOL JOURNAL, FROM SANRIO.
I'M SERIOUS, KAZUOMI!
I'M SITTING NEXT TO YOU
SO AM I.
REALLY?

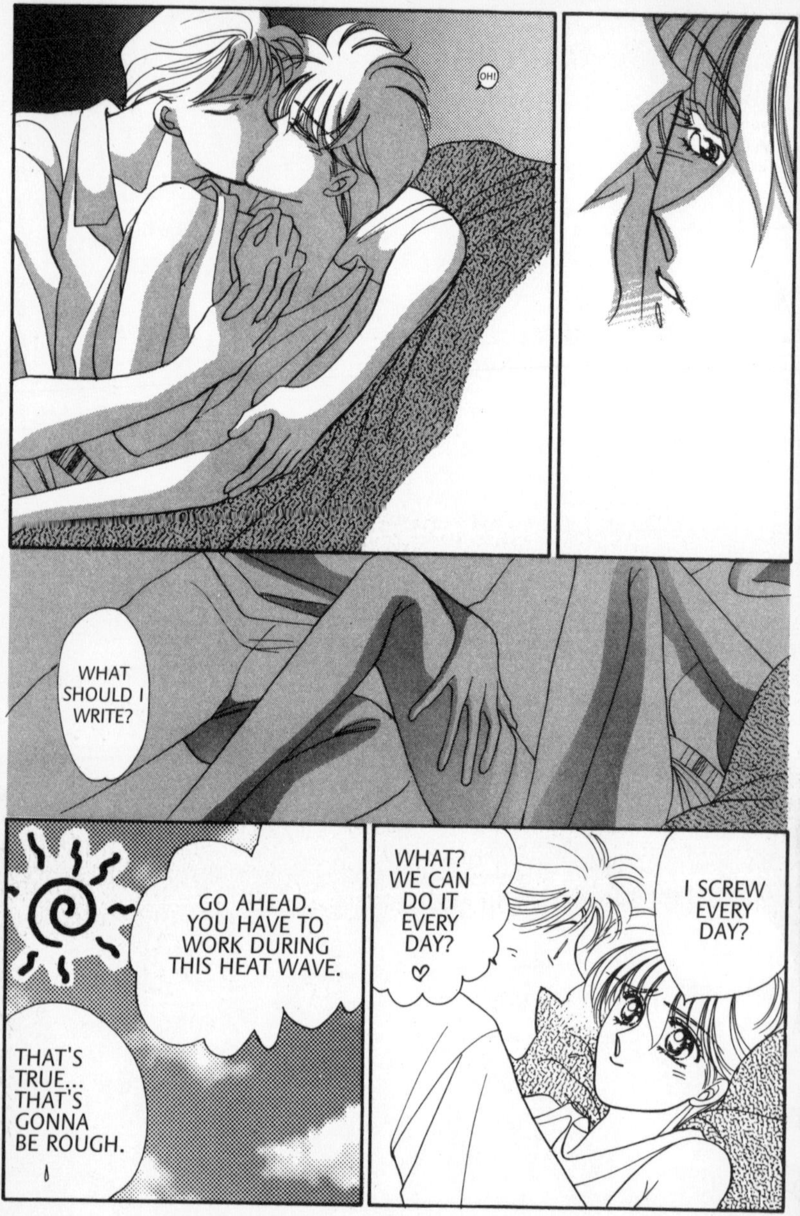
OH!
WHAT SHOULD I WRITE?
I SCREW EVERY DAY?
WHAT? WE CAN DO IT EVERY DAY? ♡
GO AHEAD. YOU HAVE TO WORK DURING THIS HEAT WAVE.
THAT'S TRUE... THAT'S GONNA BE ROUGH.

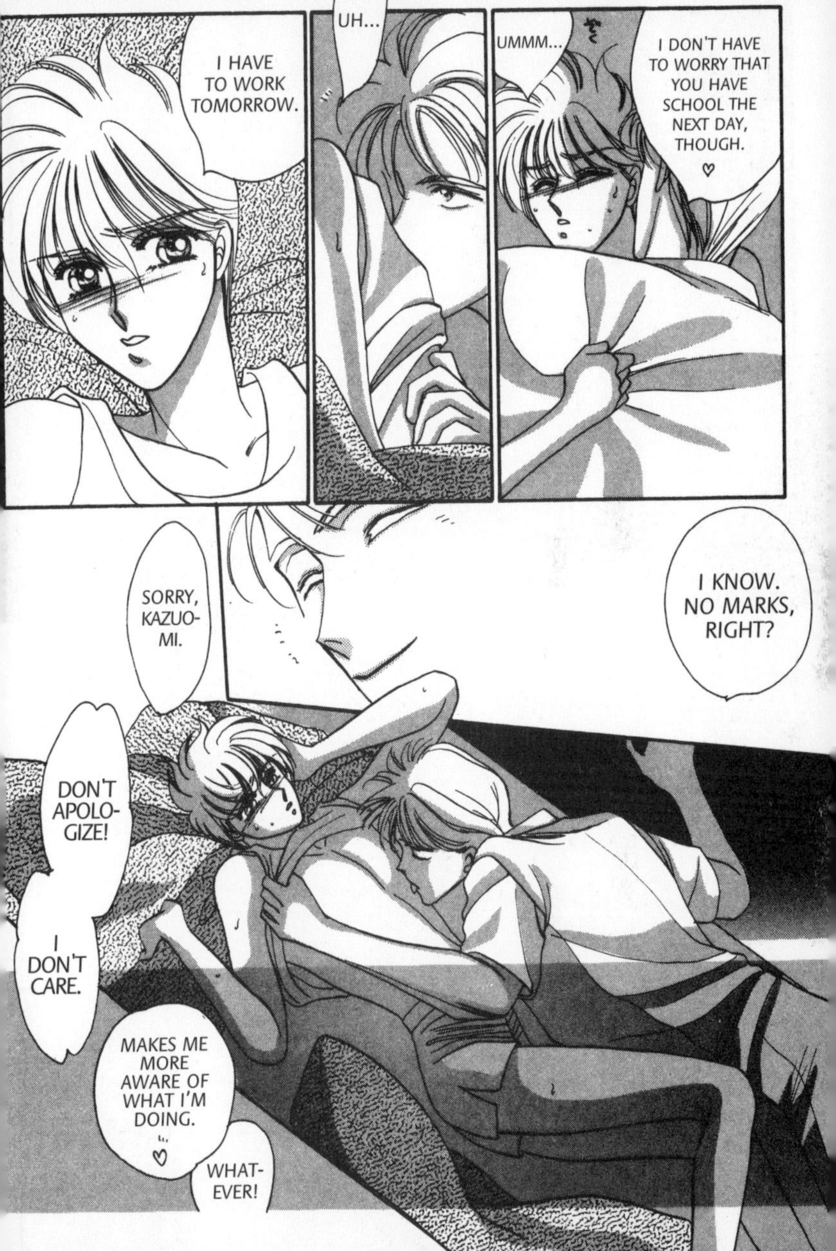
I DON'T HAVE TO WORRY THAT YOU HAVE SCHOOL THE NEXT DAY, THOUGH. ♡
UMMM...
UH...
I HAVE TO WORK TOMORROW.
I KNOW. NO MARKS, RIGHT?
SORRY, KAZUO-MI.
DON'T APOLOGIZE!
I DON'T CARE.
MAKES ME MORE AWARE OF WHAT I'M DOING.
♡
WHAT-EVER!

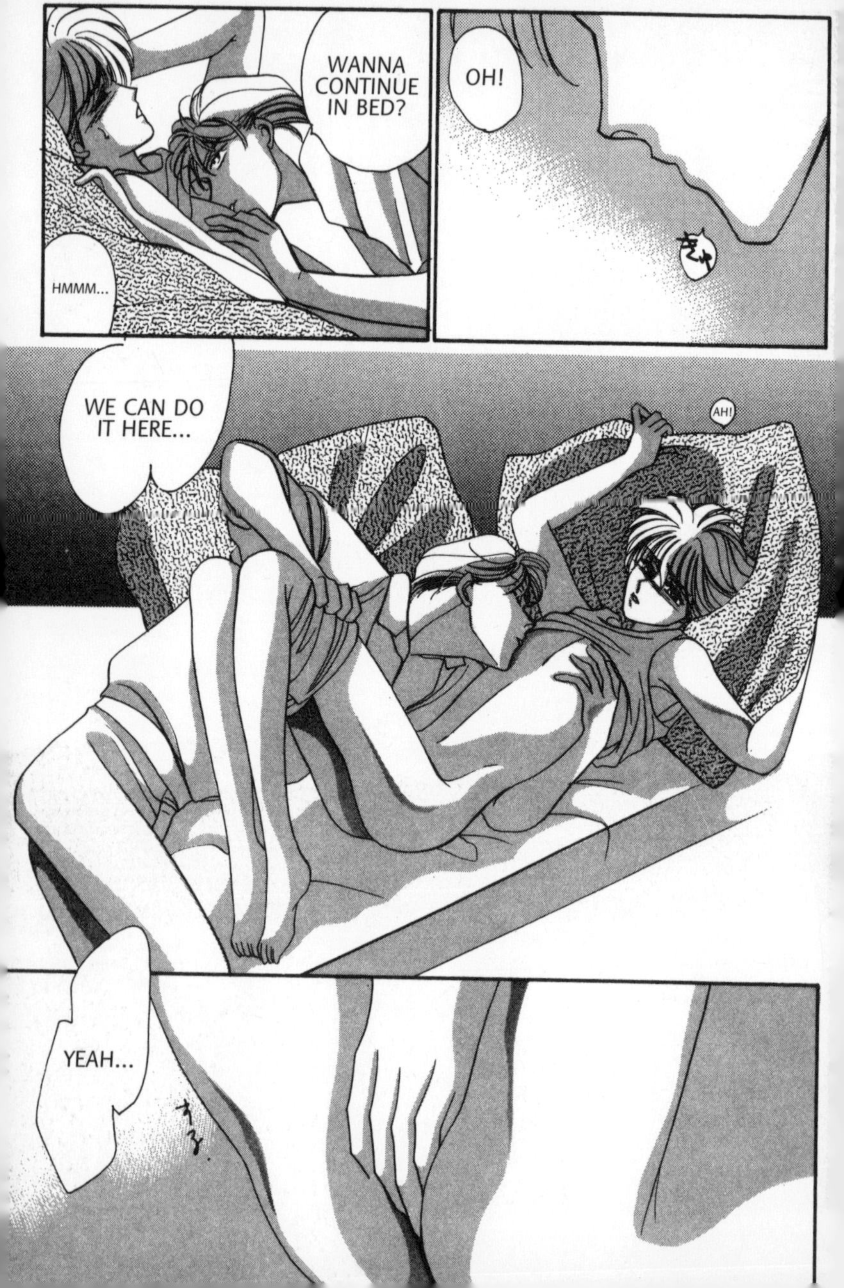
OH!
WANNA CONTINUE IN BED?
HMMM...
WE CAN DO IT HERE...
AH!
YEAH...

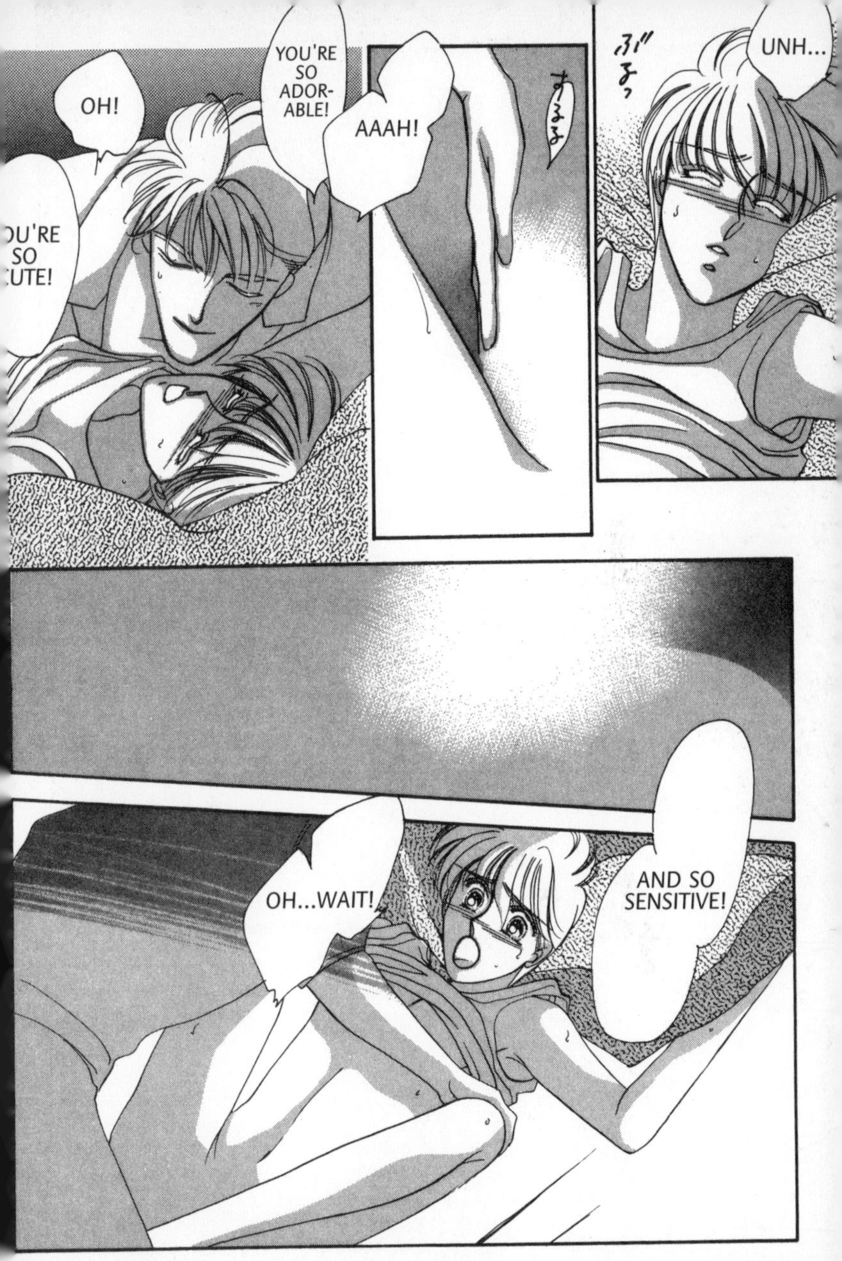

UNH...
AAAH!
YOU'RE SO ADORABLE!
OH!
OU'RE SO UTE!
AND SO SENSITIVE!
OH...WAIT!

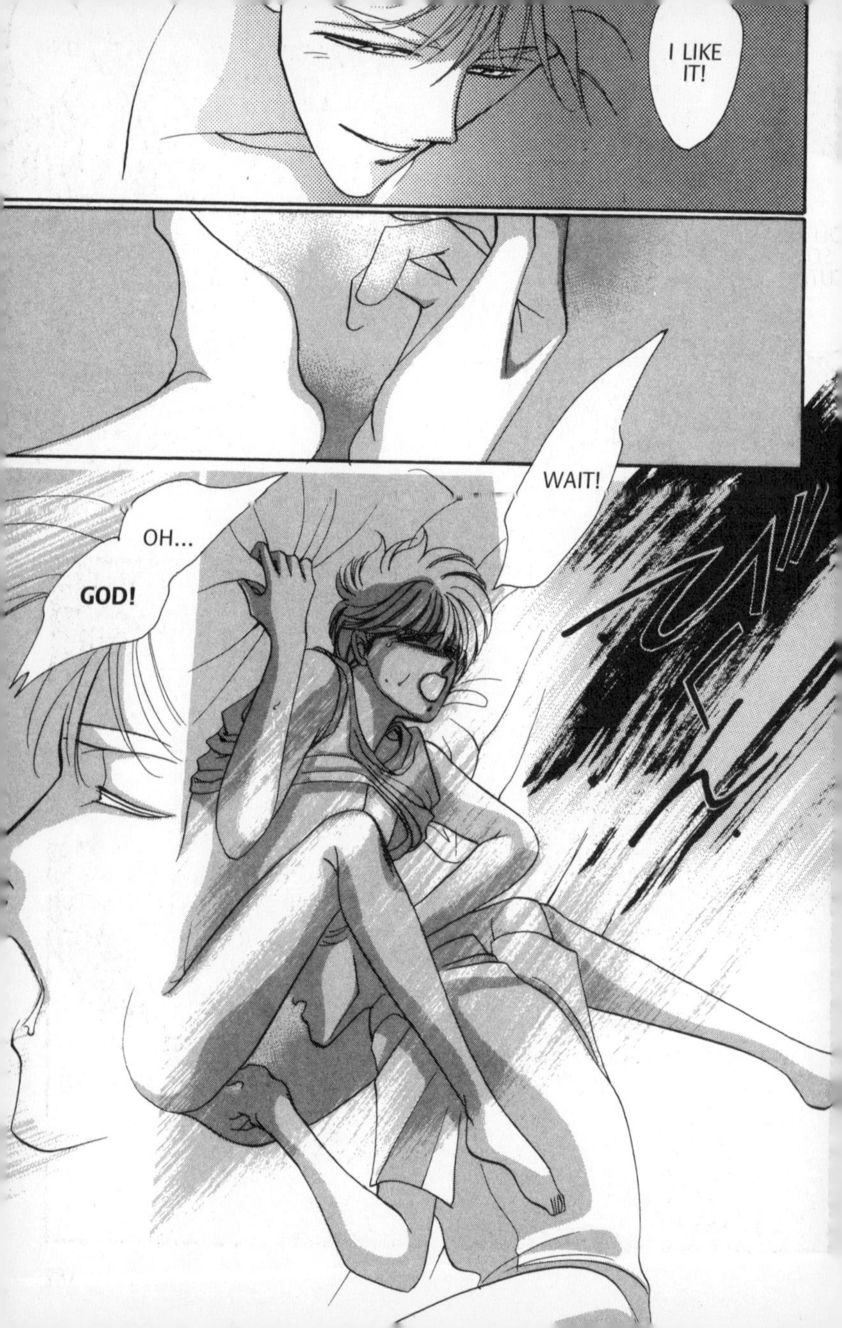
I LIKE IT!
WAIT!
OH...
GOD!

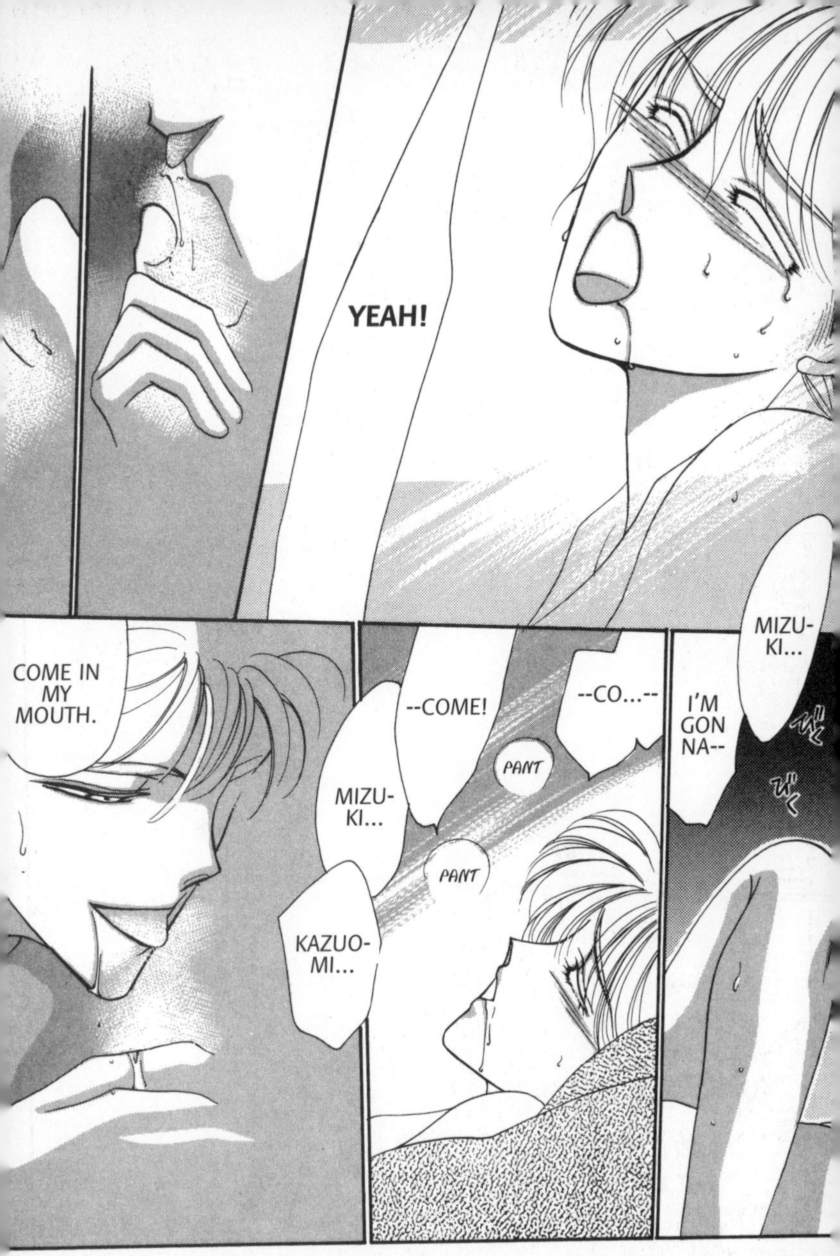
YEAH!
MIZU-KI...
I'M GONNA--
--CO...--
PANT
--COME!
MIZU-KI...
PANT
KAZUO-MI...
COME IN MY MOUTH.

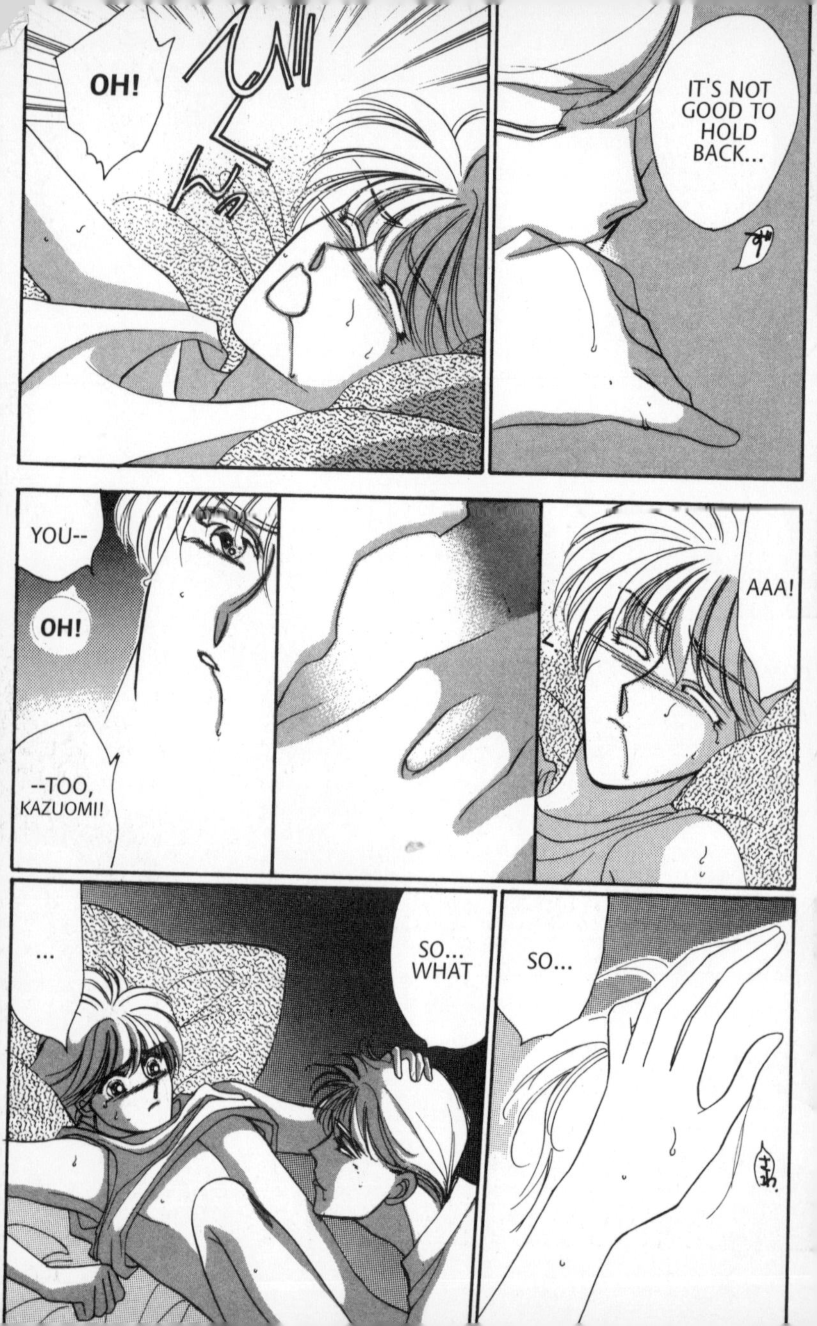
IT'S NOT GOOD TO HOLD BACK...
OH!
AAA!
YOU--
OH!
--TOO, KAZUOMI!
SO...
SO... WHAT
...

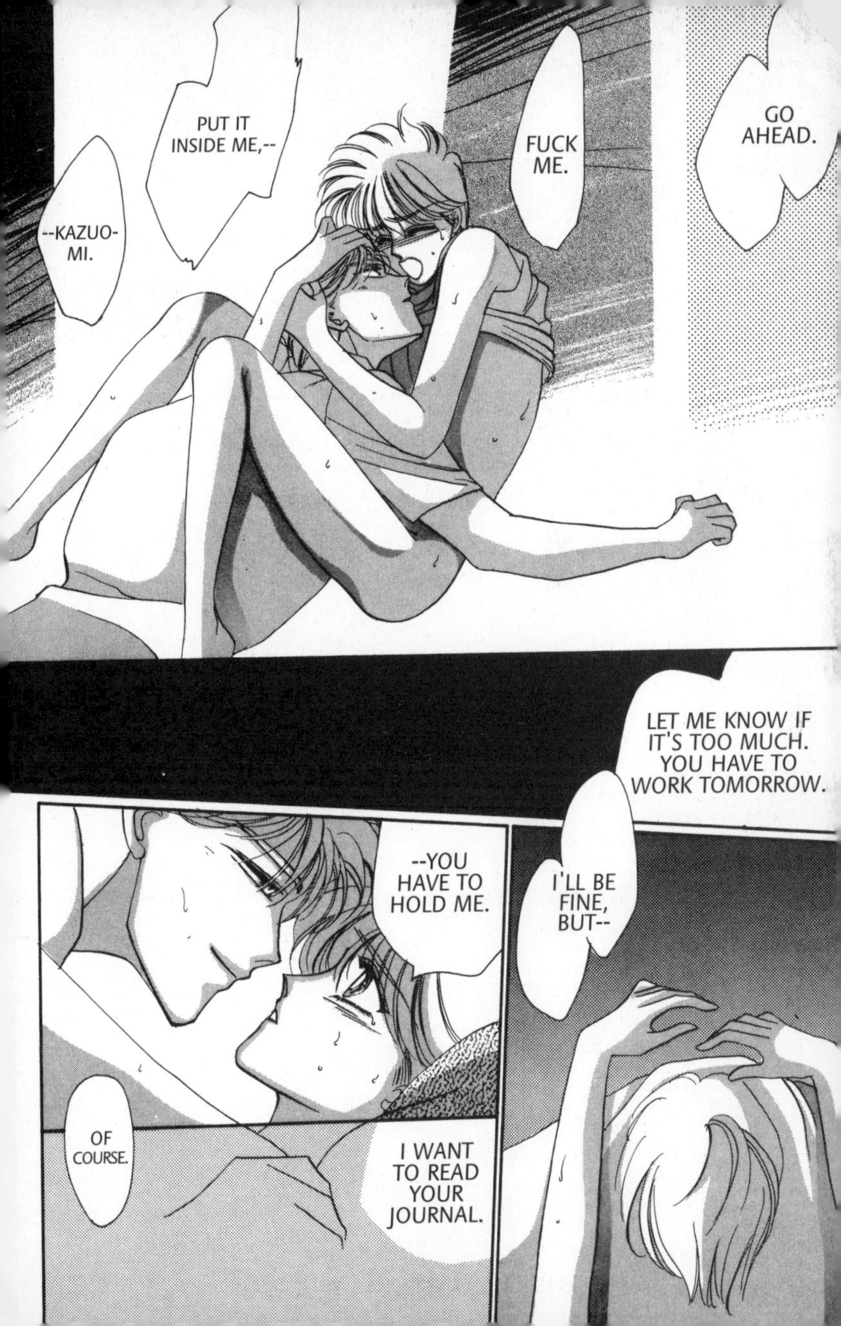
GO AHEAD.
FUCK ME.
PUT IT INSIDE ME,--
--KAZUO-MI.
LET ME KNOW IF IT'S TOO MUCH. YOU HAVE TO WORK TOMORROW.
I'LL BE FINE, BUT--
--YOU HAVE TO HOLD ME.
I WANT TO READ YOUR JOURNAL.
OF COURSE.

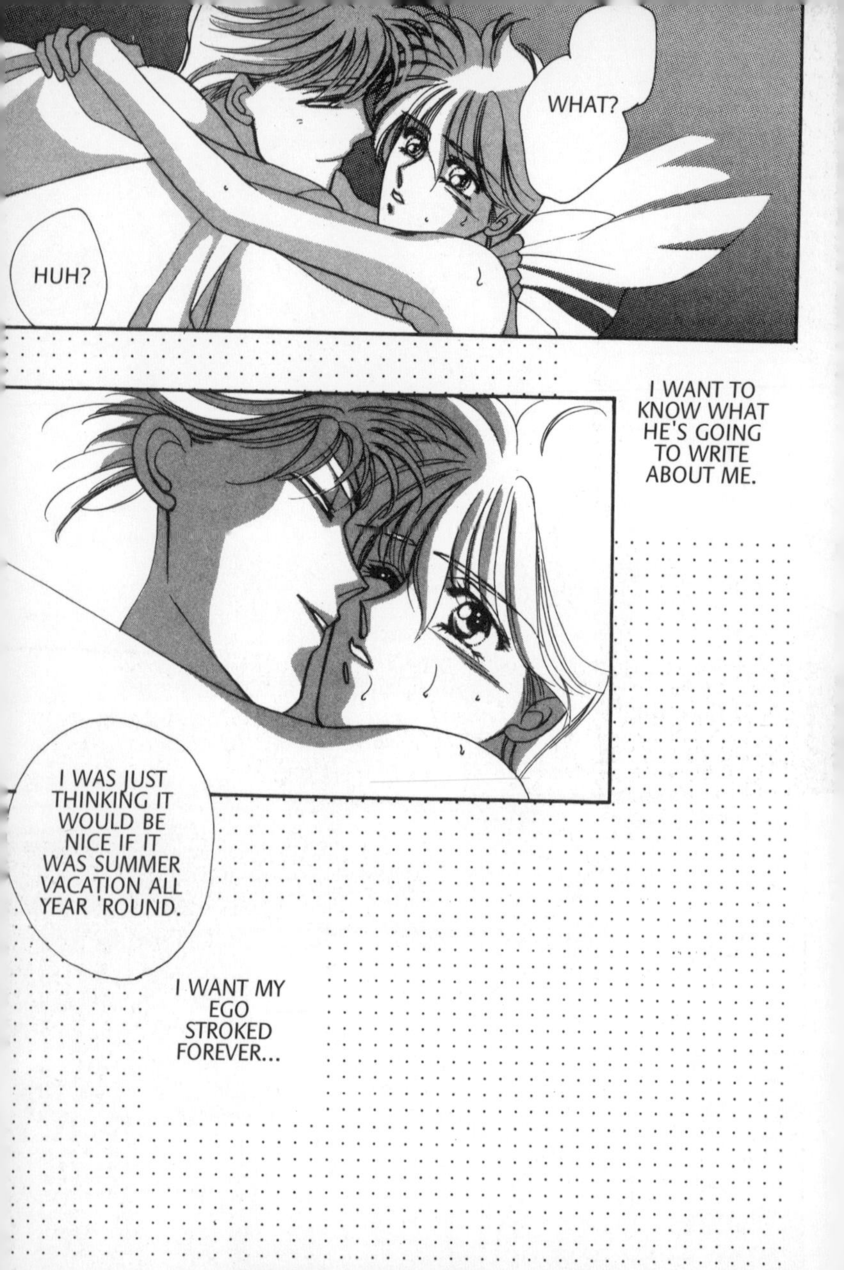
WHAT?
HUH?
I WANT TO KNOW WHAT HE'S GOING TO WRITE ABOUT ME.
I WAS JUST THINKING IT WOULD BE NICE IF IT WAS SUMMER VACATION ALL YEAR 'ROUND.
I WANT MY EGO STROKED FOREVER...

SUMMER VACATION - THE END

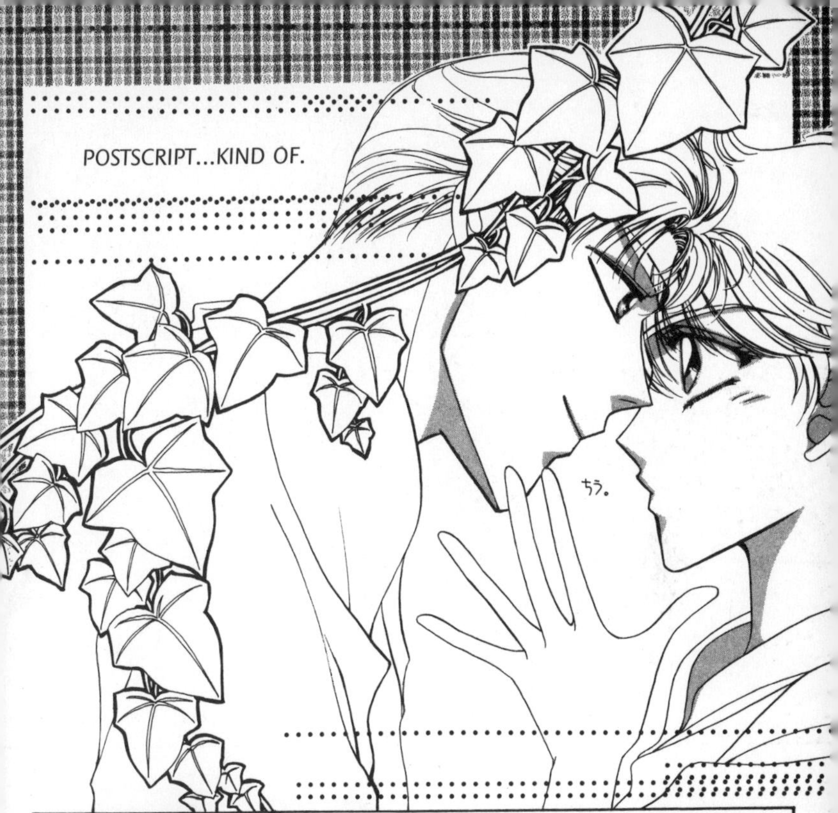
POSTSCRIPT...KIND OF.
ちう。

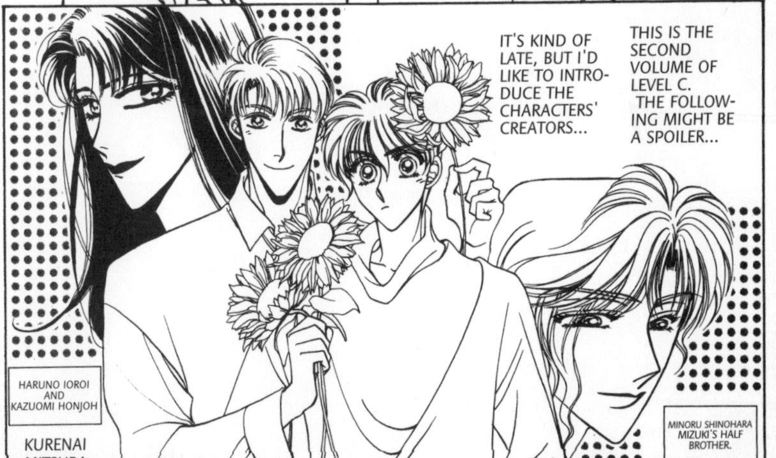
THIS IS THE SECOND VOLUME OF LEVEL C. THE FOLLOWING MIGHT BE A SPOILER...
IT'S KIND OF LATE, BUT I'D LIKE TO INTRODUCE THE CHARACTERS' CREATORS...
MINORU SHINOHARA MIZUKI'S HALF BROTHER.
AOI FUTABA
HARUNO IOROI AND KAZUOMI HONJOH
KURENAI MITSUBA

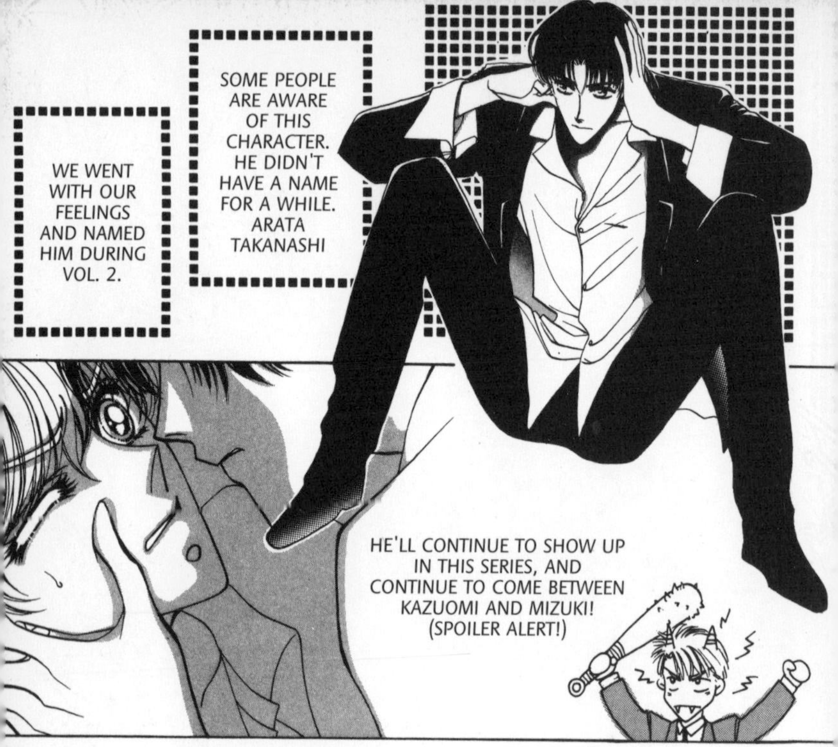
SOME PEOPLE ARE AWARE OF THIS CHARACTER. HE DIDN'T HAVE A NAME FOR A WHILE. ARATA TAKANASHI
WE WENT WITH OUR FEELINGS AND NAMED HIM DURING VOL. 2.
HE'LL CONTINUE TO SHOW UP IN THIS SERIES, AND CONTINUE TO COME BETWEEN KAZUOMI AND MIZUKI! (SPOILER ALERT!)

LEVEL-C END

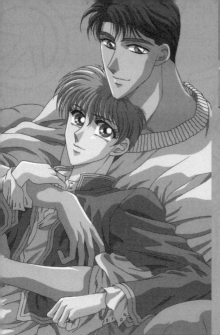

LEVEL-C

Mizuki is a popular male fashion model with a promising future. CEO Haruno wants to make him the centerpiece for her latest promotion. To lure Mizuki in, she calls on her twin brother, Kazo. He is quick to seduce the young supermodel, but things soon escalate beyond business as usual. As Kazo's feelings run wild, it looks like true love for him and Mizuki.

DVD • 30 Minutes • 18 & UP
Japanese w. English Subtitles
Cat# KVDVD-0227 • UPC 6-31595-02276-6
SRP $24.95

My SEXUAL HARASSMENT

Mochizuchi is a young office worker with a knack for falling into bed with his coworkers, clients and bosses. Kept under the thumb of his supervisor, Honma, Mochizuchi does his best to keep the office running smoothly. Will he ever get to be alone with Fujita, the one man who wants him for something other than his body? Or, will he remain as Honma's slave forever?

DVD • 130 Minutes • 18 & UP
Japanese w. English Subtitles
Cat# KVDVD-0309 • UPC 6-31595-03096-9
SRP $29.95

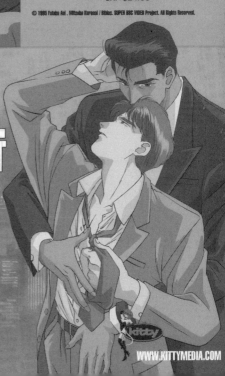

WWW.KITTYMEDIA.COM

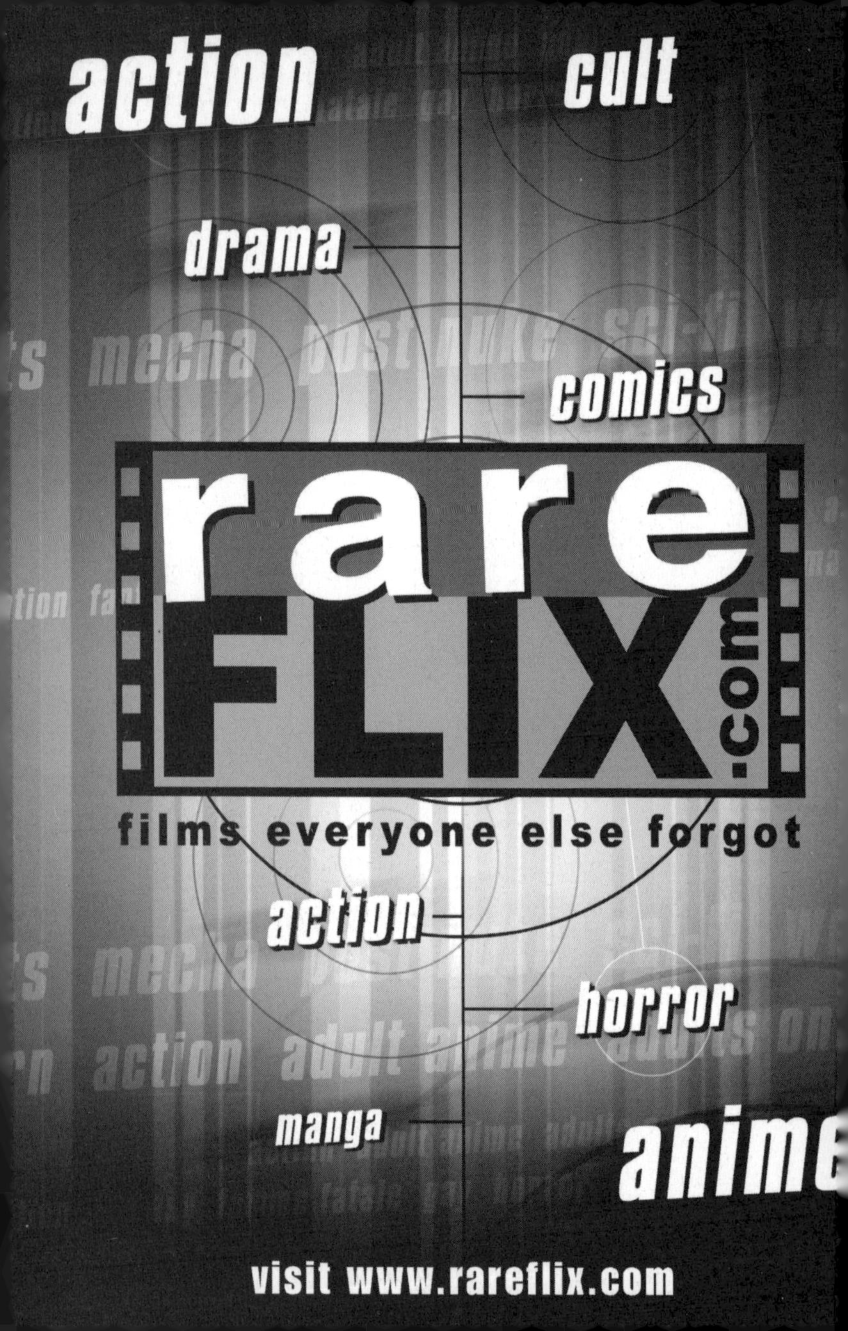
action
cult
drama
comics
rare FLIX .com
films everyone else forgot
action
horror
manga
anime
visit www.rareflix.com

FAKE

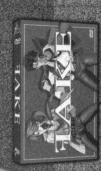

DVD • 60 Minutes • 13 & up
English /Japanese w. English Subtitles
Cat# AWDVD-0093 • UPC 6-31595-00932-3
SRP $24.95

©1997 SANAMI MATOU/BIBLOS • PLACET

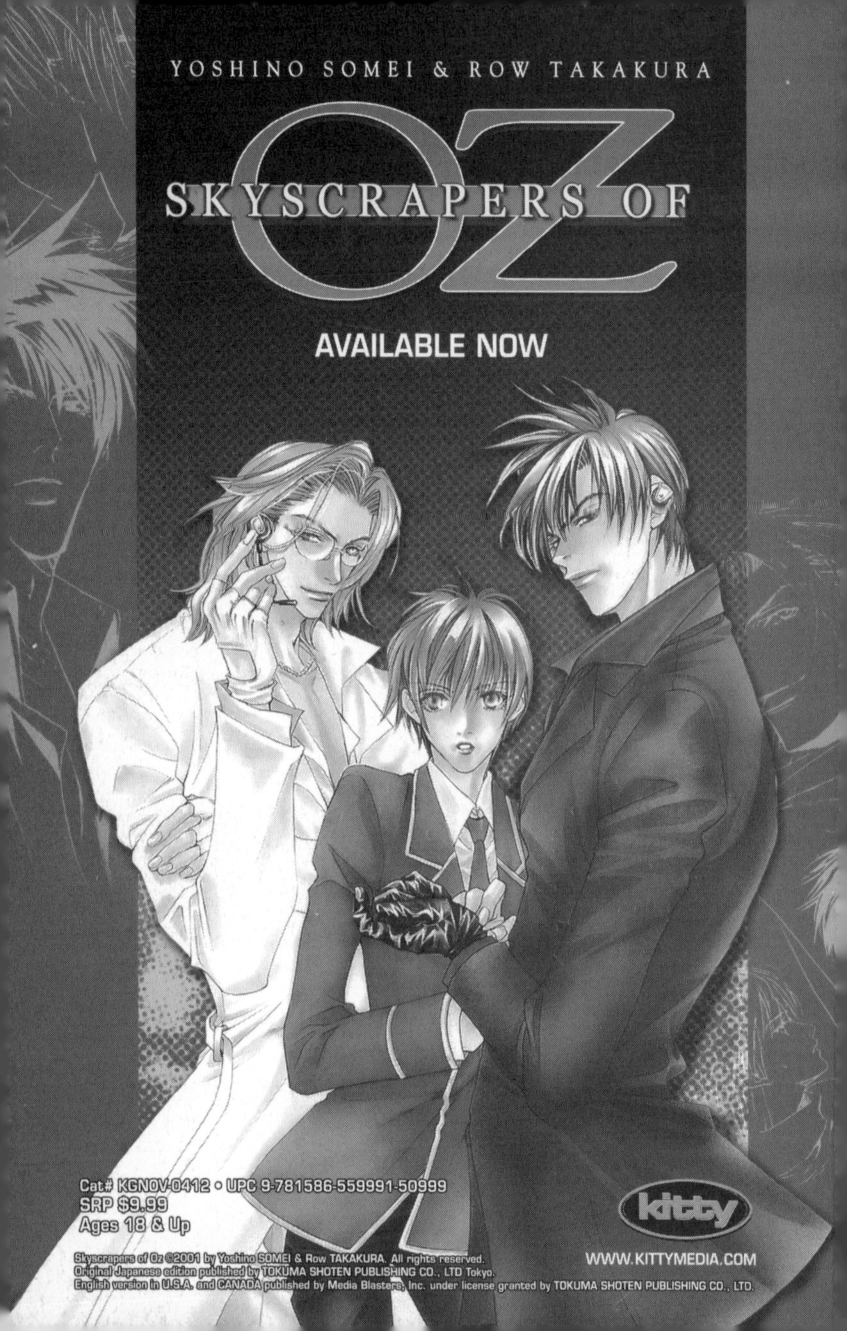
YOSHINO SOMEI & ROW TAKAKURA
SKYSCRAPERS OF OZ
AVAILABLE NOW
Cat# KGNOV-0412 • UPC 9-781586-559991-50999
SRP $9.99
Ages 18 & Up
kitty
Skyscrapers of Oz ©2001 by Yoshino SOMEI & Row TAKAKURA. All rights reserved.
Original Japanese edition published by TOKUMA SHOTEN PUBLISHING CO., LTD Tokyo.
English version in U.S.A. and CANADA published by Media Blasters, Inc. under license granted by TOKUMA SHOTEN PUBLISHING CO., LTD.
WWW.KITTYMEDIA.COM

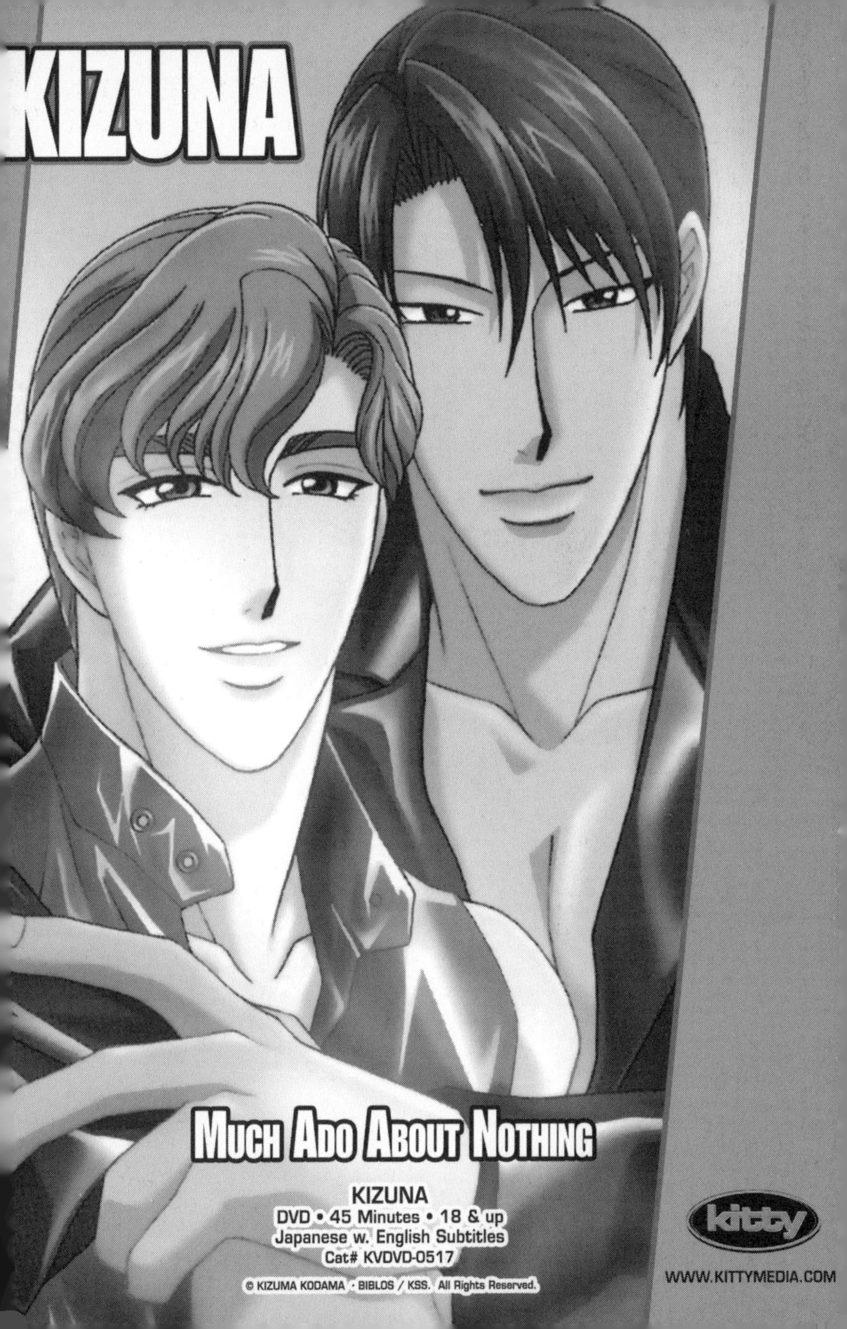
KIZUNA
MUCH ADO ABOUT NOTHING
KIZUNA
DVD • 45 Minutes • 18 & up
Japanese w. English Subtitles
Cat# KVDVD-0517
© KIZUMA KODAMA · BIBLOS / KSS. All Rights Reserved.
kitty
WWW.KITTYMEDIA.COM

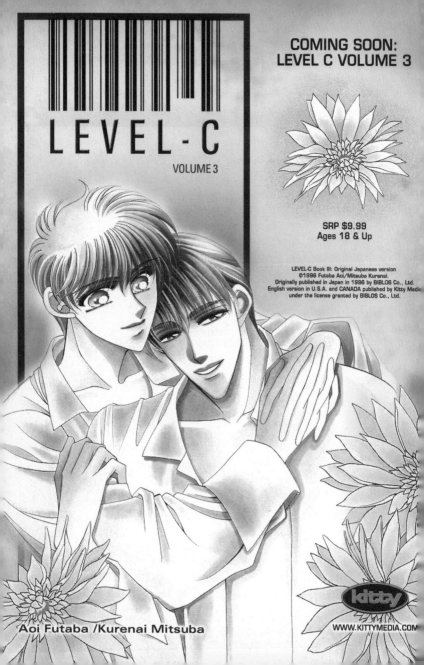

LEVEL-C
VOLUME 3

**COMING SOON:
LEVEL C VOLUME 3**

SRP $9.99
Ages 18 & Up

LEVEL-C Book III: Original Japanese version
©1996 Futaba Aoi/Mitsuba Kurenai.
Originally published in Japan in 1996 by BIBLOS Co., Ltd.
English version in U.S.A. and CANADA published by Kitty Media
under the license granted by BIBLOS Co., Ltd.

Aoi Futaba /Kurenai Mitsuba

kitty
WWW.KITTYMEDIA.COM

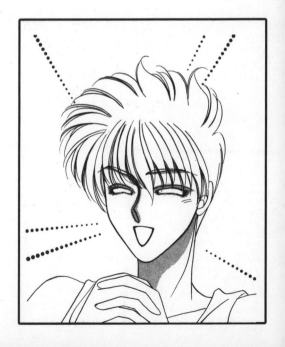